HISTORIC FRASERBURGH

HISTORIC
FRASERBURGH

Archaeology and development

R D Oram
P F Martin
C A McKean
T Neighbour
A Cathcart

THE SCOTTISH BURGH SURVEY

 UNIVERSITY OF STIRLING

Published by the Council for British Archaeology and Historic Scotland

First published in 2010

Copyright © 2010 Historic Scotland

The moral right of the authors has been asserted.

British Library Cataloguing in Publication Data

A catalogue for this book is available from the British Library

Edited by Catrina Appleby, CBA, and Mark Watson, Historic Scotland

Page design and typesetting by Carnegie Publishing Ltd

Printing and binding: Information Press, Oxford

ISBN: 978-1-902771-79-3

Council for British Archaeology

St Mary's House,

66 Bootham,

York YO30 7BZ

www.britarch.ac.uk

Historic Scotland

Longmore House

Salisbury Place

Edinburgh

EH9 1SH

Tel. 0131 668 8600

Fax. 0131 668 8669

www.historic-scotland.gov.uk

Front cover: Fraserburgh from the air looking north, 1946
(Crown copyright: RCAHMS)

Insets: Kinnaird Head by William Daniell, 1822;
detail of the Mercat Cross (courtesy of RIAS)

Half title page: Gill Lodging (courtesy of University of St Andrews Library)

Contents

List of illustrations

Maps

Figures

Abbreviations

Aberdeen Council Register	*Extracts from the Council Register of the Burgh of Aberdeen*, 2 vols (Spalding Club, 1844–48)
Antiquities of Aberdeen and Banff	*Illustrations of the Topography and Antiquities of the Shires of Aberdeen and Banff*, 4 vols (Spalding Club, 1847–69)
Christian Watt Papers	Fraser, Sir D, *The Christian Watt Papers* (Collieston, 1983)
Fasti Academiae	Anderson, P J (ed), *Fasti Academiae Mariscallanae Aberdonensis*, (Spalding Club, 1889)
Frasers of Philorth	Fraser, A (ed), *The Frasers of Philorth*, 3 vols (Edinburgh, 1879)
KC	King's College, Aberdeen
Macfarlane	Mitchell, Sir A (ed), *Geographical Collections Relating to Scotland made by Walter Macfarlane*, 3 vols (SHS, 1906–08)
NAS	National Archives of Scotland
NLS	National Library of Scotland
NMRS	National Monuments Record of Scotland
NSA	*The Statistical Account of Scotland, XII, Aberdeenshire* (Edinburgh, 1845), 'Parish of Fraserburgh', Revd J Cumming, 1840
Ordnance Gazetteer	F H Groome, *Ordnance Gazetteer of Scotland*, 6 vols (London, 1894)
OS	Ordnance Survey
OSA	*The Statistical Account of Scotland 1791–99, vol XV, North and East Aberdeenshire*, D J Withrington and I Grant (eds) (Wakefield, 1982)
RCAHMS	Royal Commission on the Ancient and Historical Monuments of Scotland
RIAS	Royal Incorporation of Architects in Scotland
RMS	Thomson, J M *et al* (eds), *Registrum Magni Sigilii Regum Scotorum*, 11 vols (Edinburgh, 1882–1914)
RPC	Burton, J H *et al* (eds), *Register of the Privy Council of Scotland*, 38 vols (Edinburgh, 1877–)
Prisoners of the '45	Seton, B G and Arnot, J G (eds), *The Prisoners of the '45*, 3 vols (SHS, 1928–29)
SHS	Scottish History Society
SP	Paul, Sir J B, *The Scots Peerage*, 9 vols (Edinburgh, 1904–14)
Wodrow	R Lippe (ed), *Selections from Wodrow's Biographical Collections* (Spalding Club, 1890)

Acknowledgements

We are grateful to all those in Historic Scotland we have dealt with between our first fieldwork in May 2002 and this publication, including Nick Bridgland, Ann McCrone, Ann MacSween, Peter Yeoman, Martin Brann and Mark Watson. We would also like to thank those who have read various versions of this text, particularly the late Ian Shepherd for his kind and helpful comments.

As ever, the staff of the libraries and archives we visited, or which have supplied illustrations, have been friendly and helpful. These include Special Collections, Aberdeen University Library; the National Library of Scotland; Tam Burke, Chris Fleet and Diana Webster at the National Library of Scotland (Map Library); the National Archives of Scotland; Kevin McLaren at the National Monuments Record; Helen Osmani at the National Museums of Scotland picture library; Heather Brunton at the Scottish Life Archive; and Pam Cranston and Norman Reid at Special Collections, University of St Andrews Library. We are grateful for permission to reproduce images from the British Library, the National Library of Scotland, the RCAHMS (RAF Aerial Photographs Collection), the National Museums of Scotland, the Scottish Life Archive, and University of St Andrews Library.

We would also like to thank all those we met and spoke to during our field trips to Fraserburgh, and Colin Martin for advice on the selection of images.

Introduction to the Survey

The named authors represent the core of a larger team, including David Green of the Department of Geography, University of Aberdeen, Neil Grieve of the Department of Town and Regional Planning and Chris Whatley of the Department of History, University of Dundee, and Kevin Hicks of CFA Archaeology Ltd.

Ali Cathcart, Charles McKean, Paula Martin, Tim Neighbour and Richard Oram visited Fraserburgh in May 2002. All but Ali Cathcart paid a brief second visit in November 2003. In March 2007, in appalling weather, the team visited Fraserburgh again for a few hours, in the company of Mark Watson of Historic Scotland, mainly to check for changes since this report was first written. As the original budget allowed for only one field visit, we carried out desk-based historical and archaeological research in advance, so that we arrived with a set of questions. We explored the town on foot, as thoroughly as possible, carrying with us copies of the relevant maps and town plans. Then, before leaving, we drove around the immediate hinterland.

We work as a team, looking for changes in the burgh morphology. We try to spot details and point them out, and bounce ideas off each other (often puzzling passers-by). We look at the backs of as many buildings as possible, and try to identify earlier building- and street-lines. Our aim is to understand the morphology of the town, and its various phases of development, within its physical landscape. Existing architectural guides highlight individual buildings, but we aim to see these buildings within their geographical and historical contexts.

After the field visit, more research was carried out on the history and archaeology in the light of a better understanding of the burgh, and the sections on architectural styles and building materials developed. The final section on the 'spirit of place' and the potential for further research and sympathetic development was the last to be written. The text contributed by five people has been edited and merged into one narrative, though individual voices will inevitably be apparent in places. The original report presented to Historic Scotland in early 2003 was subsequently rewritten in a revised format, and has been gradually developed since then in the light of helpful comments from external readers.

1   Use of the Burgh Survey

Continued evolution is the essence of urban life. Change is inevitable in towns and is what gives them their vitality. Yet it is the imprint of history that gives localities their distinctive character. Conservation is a matter of ensuring that the qualities that define a place are maintained while change continues to happen. Managing change requires an understanding of that character.

The Scottish Burgh Survey is a guide to the archaeological resource in towns published by Historic Scotland and the Council for British Archaeology. It helps to influence decision-makers and to set the research agenda on questions that may be answered by archaeology where development occurs. Publications in the latest series are at http://www.britarch.ac.uk/pubs/latest.html.

This third series of Burgh Surveys is intended to furnish local authorities, developers and residents with reliable information to help manage the archaeology and historic environment of Scotland's urban centres. It offers comprehensive and consistent base-line information against which research, regeneration and land-use planning objectives may be set. It also guides the general reader in researching the rich history and archaeology of Scotland's historic burghs.

In its role as a tool for local authorities to use in the planning process, the first point of reference in this volume is the development plan (map 9 and broadsheet) which depicts the extent of urban development at various stages, and the character map (map 10) which defines areas of distinctive character, some important views and vistas, and areas which seem to offer particular archaeological potential. It is often the case, however, that discoveries may yet be made outwith those areas, which will necessitate a reassessment of the state of knowledge of the burgh of Fraserburgh. Indeed the purpose of this book may be to provoke further investigation.

Further information about the archaeological potential of a site within the historic town can be found in local and national libraries and archives. The PASTMAP website (http://www.PASTMAP.org.uk) can also be consulted. This interactive website, supported jointly by Historic Scotland and the Royal Commission on the Ancient and Historical Monuments of Scotland, allows anyone with internet access to search data on Scotland's historic environment including the statutorily designated sites, scheduled monuments and listed buildings.

Both this Burgh Survey and the PASTMAP website provide information only. Where development is being considered, advice should be sought in all cases directly from Aberdeenshire Council Archaeology Service, Aberdeenshire Council, Woodhill House, Westburn Road, Aberdeen, AB16 5GB (archaeology@aberdeenshire.gov.uk).

2 *Character statement and executive summary*

The nature of Fraserburgh derives from its various periods of development: the original medieval settlements of Faithlie and Broadsea, the sixteenth-century new town, a proposed early nineteenth-century new town to the north, the post-1818 new town to the south, Victorian extension to the west, Edwardian extension to the south, and twentieth-century developments further west and south-west (**fig 1**). Faithlie is almost certainly the older settlement, although Broadsea seems to be of some antiquity. Shown as the 'Seatown' by General Roy *c* 1750 (**map 5**), Broadsea is relatively unusual among north-east fishing villages. It does not conform to the later pattern of rows

FIGURE I
Vertical air photograph (106G-SCOT-UK108-3281), showing the extent of the harbour in 1946 (Crown Copyright: RCAHMS, RAF Aerial Photographs Collection)

JAMB

FIGURE 2
Engraving of a courtyard
house, Gill Lodging, now
demolished (MacGibbon &
Ross, *Castellated and Domestic
Architecture of Scotland*, v,
83, fig 1199, 'House with
Courtyard and Arched
Gateway'). See fig 14 for
the preparatory sketch.
(Courtesy of the University
of St Andrews Library)

of cottages gable-end to the sea, but comprises a single double-sided street running slightly downhill along a promontory enclosing a bay to its east, and swelling into a market- or meeting-place at the centre.

Fraserburgh's most significant contribution to Scottish urban history was the laying out of Fraser's broch (burgh), the earliest of Scotland's new towns. Other new towns of the reign of James VI – Langholm, Peterhead, Campbeltown and a proposal for a new Edzell – shared with Londonderry the centrifugal plan of a central, enclosed market-place with routes leading off in the directions of the compass. Fraser's broch resembled none of these. Instead, Fraser laid out a *suburban* plantation. It takes the form of a grid of four streets by three, laid out at a different alignment to and just south of Kirk Green, in the angle between the route south to the Kirkton and the road west to Pitsligo and Rosehearty. Broad Street, which was incorporated as the eastern edge of the grid, was the reasonably level wind-sheltered market-place required by such towns. Roy's map shows it to have been tightly enclosed at both ends, and it had gained the status of the town's principal thoroughfare by the early seventeenth century.

It is difficult to assess the original character of Fraser's broch. Three streets, Cross Street, Manse Street, and School Street, lay parallel to Broad Street inland. Eventually, uphill from here, two further streets, Frithside Street and Mid Street, crossed them at right angles (see **map 8**). These were later joined by Hanover Street and Love Lane (said to have existed by 1713). Consequently, there are no long rigs, as in other Scots burghs, but backlands of abutting rectangular walled gardens of the new-town character that we associate with developments of 200 years later. Some larger houses were probably set back from the street, with courtyards in front, a style suited to Fraserburgh's square plots (**fig 2**).

According to the 1613 contract between Fraser and his burgh, the basic feuing unit was 28¼ ells (26.6m) wide and the same long, and at least two of the streets were 40 feet (12.2m) wide. For that date, such a plan was unique not just in Scotland, but also possibly in Great Britain. It remains to be discovered where Alexander Fraser acquired such a pioneering idea, but for a grid-iron town lying to one side of a market-place one might look towards the Iberian peninsula. This remarkable development represents the heart of present-day Fraserburgh.

Outside the parallelogram, probably because it followed the squint alignment of the existing road along the bounds of the Kinnaird Head castle policies, lay the High Street, some 40 feet (12.2m) wide, the fairly standard width of an early nineteenth-century smaller 'new town' suburban street. Possibly because it was on slightly higher ground, or because it was nearest to the Fraser jointure house of Kinnaird Head, High Street became the location of some of the town's principal buildings. Being on the edge of the grid, its north side provided the greatest scope for large houses and gardens (**map 5**). The ambitious nature of Fraser's project is perhaps best symbolised by his attempt to establish a university here.

As a burgh of barony, Fraserburgh's fortunes were for many years tied up with those of its baron, Fraser of Philorth. Situated on such an exposed headland, passed by much shipping, and also in an area of Episcopalian sympathies, Fraserburgh was garrisoned for much of the later seventeenth and eighteenth centuries. Unusually, the shore of Fraserburgh was for a long time the commercial heart of the town, until in the early nineteenth century banks and offices moved up the hill to Saltoun Square and adjacent streets. The pace of development in Fraserburgh began to accelerate rapidly after 1840, though the arrival of the railway in 1865 does not seem to have been as revolutionary an event as in some other towns. As suburbs were developed to the west and south, the commercial heart of the town also extended in a south-westerly direction. It was in these growing middle-class suburbs that new churches and schools were built. The wide streets and well-built cottages of the later nineteenth century were regarded as a natural and welcome extension of Fraserburgh's sense of its own progress. Many of the older buildings of Faithlie were removed for road and harbour improvements, while several of the older town-centre buildings were lost to redevelopment.

Fraserburgh's early development was challenged by Aberdeen, but, by the eighteenth century, its main rival was Peterhead, eighteen miles (29km) away, and a more prosperous port. Rivalry can be demonstrated in developments at the harbour, and in the development of a mineral well and baths in the early nineteenth century. Only at the very beginning of the twentieth century did Fraserburgh, briefly, overtake Peterhead as a herring port, and appeared to be growing faster than its neighbour. Today, with fishing in decline, and with its rail link long gone, Fraserburgh appears isolated, in contrast to its central role in the days of coastal shipping, but the town centre retains significant interest and potential.

Executive summary

The key points about Fraserburgh are:

➢ it is a late sixteenth-century 'new town' of a design unique in Scotland
➢ it is the home of Scotland's 'lost university'
➢ it is in a strategic location, so it was a garrison town for a surprisingly long time during the late seventeenth and eighteenth centuries.
➢ Broadsea, the adjacent fishing village, is of some antiquity, though poorly documented
➢ although neither the baths nor the related early nineteenth-century new town really took off, they have left a distinctive footprint
➢ it spent vast sums of money between 1818 and 1914 on developing its harbour, and was one of the busiest herring ports in Scotland
➢ it contains significant 1920s' and 1930s' local-authority housing
➢ as a burgh of barony, its fortunes were tied up with those of its founding family for over 400 years, making it an example worth further study.

Timeline

1504	Sir William Fraser of Philorth purchases Faithlie
1541–42	Charters to Alexander Fraser 7th, barony of Philorth, and fishing rights including Faithlie
1546	Charter to Alexander Fraser, Faithlie created burgh of barony with markets and fairs, and free port
1570	Alexander Fraser 8th inherits, and is said to have built Kinnaird Head Castle
1571–74	Building of new parish church, in new burgh
1576	New harbour built
late 16th c.	Building of tolbooth and erection of mercat cross
1588	Charter to Alexander Fraser, renewing 1542 charter
1592	Charter to Alexander Fraser, renewing 1542 and 1588 charters, but now to be called 'the burgh and port of Fraser', and for 'erecting an university'
1590s	Laying out of new town, building of Wine Tower?
1600	Charles Ferme appointed principal of university
1601	Charter to Alexander Fraser, Fraserburgh created burgh of regality
1605	Charles Ferme imprisoned. Effective end of university
1613	Charter, contract between Alexander Fraser and town of Fraserburgh, re Common Good etc.
1652–56?	Cromwellian garrison in Fraserburgh
1707	Presbyterian minister finally installed in Fraserburgh

1717	Episcopalian congregation finally evicted from parish church
1738	New harbour built
1746	Fraser not an active Jacobite but Philorth House sacked; Episcopal meeting-house burned down; Warld's End forfeited
1746–c 1785	Government garrison in Fraserburgh (and again from 1797)
1770	First bank branch, Aberdeen Banking Company
1776–77	Assembly rooms built above a warehouse
1787	First NLB lighthouse built on Kinnaird Head; new parish school on Links
1801	Building of Saltoun Inn
1803	New parish church
1804	First piped water supply
1805–06	First lifeboat
1807–11	North Pier built
1807	Development of Baths
1810	First turnpike road reaches Fraserburgh
1818	Harbour Commissioners established
1818–22	South Pier built; Commerce Street laid out
c 1830	Mid Pier rebuilt
1832	Fishing boats allowed to use harbour
1835	Bank of Scotland opened branch
1838	New parish school, Saltoun Place; North of Scotland bank branch opened
1840	Barony council replaced by Police Commissioners
1841	Gas company established
1850–57	Balaclava Pier built
1852	*Fraserburgh Advertiser* established
1853–55	New Town-house; restoration of mercat cross
1865	Railway arrived
1870	Adopted 1862 Police Act
1870	Fraserburgh Academy founded
1872	Broadsea absorbed within Fraserburgh
1875–82	Balaclava breakwater built
1877	Thomas Walker Hospital built
1881	Dalrymple Hall built
1882	Central School built
1883	Maconochie Bros, Kinnaird Head Preserving Works established
1884	*Fraserburgh Herald* established
1893	Burgh Commissioners (from 1900 Town Council) replace old barony council

1896	Fraserburgh becomes port of registry (FR)
1898	New South breakwater, dry dock in Balaclava Harbour, and other improvements
1899	New fish market built
1903	Fraserburgh and St Combs light railway opened
1904	Park and playing fields established; Consolidated Pneumatic Tool Works established
1908	Station Harbour built
1920	Start of council housing building programme
1923	War memorial unveiled
1940–43	17 bombing raids (53 killed, over 300 injured)
1945	Fish freezing introduced

3   Site and setting

Like many east coast towns, there was a logical reason for the location of Fraserburgh (**maps 1, 2 & 3**) when it was founded. Close to a headland passed by ships of all nationalities, it was part of a North Sea maritime network. Its exposed position was also strategic in national terms, and is reflected in the

MAP I
Location map: Fraserburgh
and Scotland

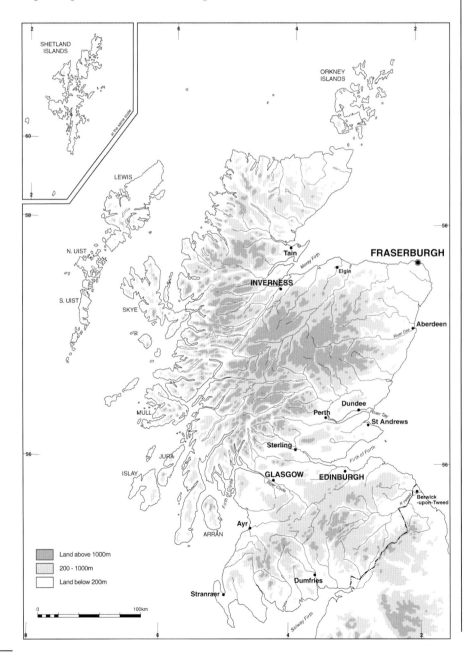

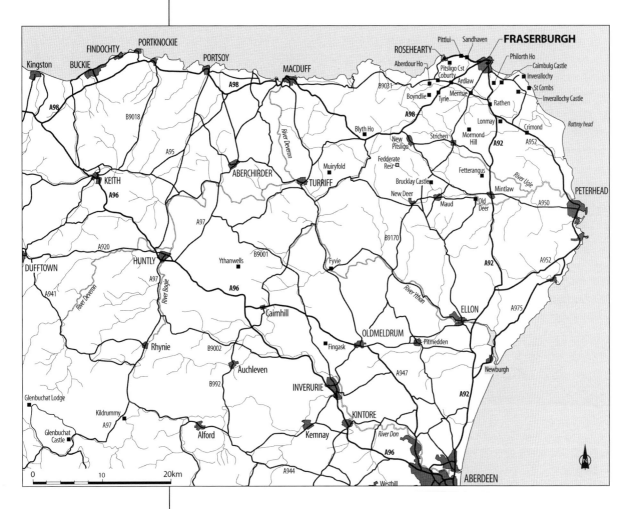

Fraserburgh's setting in
Aberdeenshire

long period during which it was garrisoned, and the acknowledged danger from pirates and foreign warships. When many other east coast ports declined, Fraserburgh invested in expanding its harbour, and benefited from being on the route to the northern entrance to the Caledonian Canal. The building of the railway network, however, and the development of road transport, changed Fraserburgh's situation from core to periphery in terms of economic activity. This paradoxically increased its economic reliance on shipping, and on the developing fishing industry, with rail and road networks available to distribute its catch. Seen in terms of the road network, Fraserburgh was not 'on the way to' anywhere else, and this is demonstrated by the fact that few eighteenth- and nineteenth-century travel writers came to it. Most went either directly from Aberdeen to Inverness, or took in some of the coast, but cut off this corner, for example by going direct from Peterhead to Banff.

Fraserburgh was laid out on a 'small plain', just south of Kinnaird Head, 'in a square formation'.[1] Its site was influenced by several natural factors: the sea to the east and north; a loch or marshy ground toward Philorth to the south (**map 4**); the loch of Fingask to the west; and the ridge of land

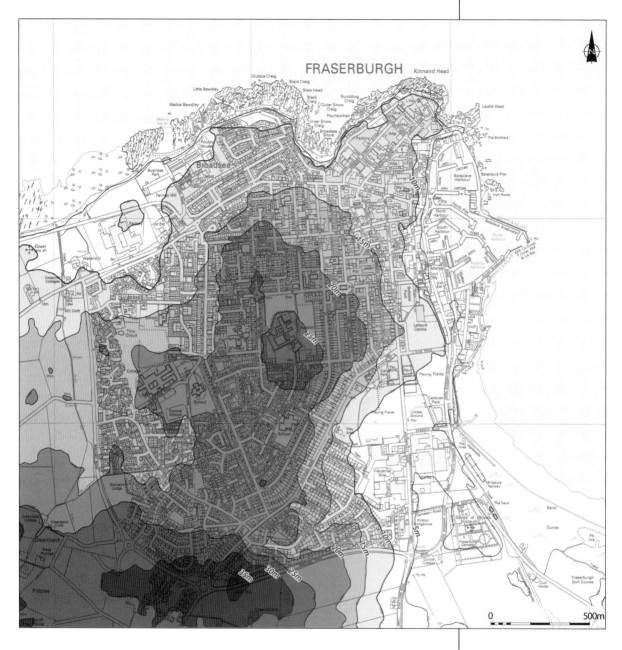

FRASERBURGH

MAP 3
Relief map of Fraserburgh

that continues from the promontory of Kinnaird Head, running south-west to the high point on which a windmill still stands (**fig 3**), and continuing out to the early settlement site at Pitblae. The land sloped from this ridge west down to the loch, and east down to the raised beach overlooking the later harbours. It protected the latter from the south-westerlies that can howl over the flatlands of Buchan. The final settlement factor was the availability of water in the Frith burn which, for centuries, acted as *de facto* southern boundary to the built-up area. The three earliest settlements within the town itself – Broadsea, Faithlie and Fraser's Broch – all therefore evolved

in response to their location, and to the need to minimise the effect of the prevailing winds.

As indicated by both surviving plans[2] and recent oral testimony, the old settlement of Faithlie huddled against the shelter of the steep slope of the raised beach, stretching along the shore from the Garvage Well at the north, eventually as far south as the Frith burn that once came down the line of Frithside Street (and whose outlet into the harbour can still be seen).[3] Its inland boundary was probably the lane that runs along the rim of the raised beach, now Braeheads and Castle Lane. The village consisted of a long two-sided street not dissimilar to Dundee's Seagate at that time, broadening out toward the south and the pier. Its principal landward connection was the main route north-west, which ran along the bounds of the Kinnaird Head Castle policies, in a straight line west to Pitsligo, and is, unusually, shown on Pont's map (**map 4**). The site of Broadsea is less favourable. Facing north, the bay is rocky, access was difficult at low tide, and all boats had to be pulled up above high-water mark when not in use. This must presumably imply a subordinate status to the far better harbour and beach of Faithlie.

FIGURE 3
Windmill tower, off Albert Street (Paula Martin)

MAP 4
Detail from Pont map 10 (Buchan), c 1590 (Reproduced by permission of the Trustees of the National Library of Scotland)

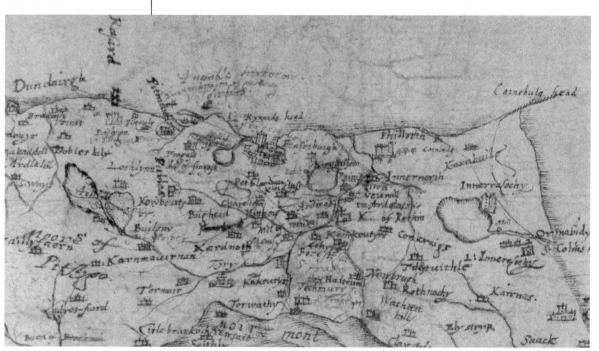

Building materials

Locally available building materials included granite, sandstone, and clay, with bents for thatch.[4] With the exception of grander houses in High Street, the houses are likely to have been one- or two-storeyed granite or clay bool cottages, roofed with thatch or tile, typically gable end on to the street.[5] Most of the older buildings have harling checks, implying that they were once harled. There is substantial use of a pleasant deep-orange-red brick for secondary features such as garden walls and chimneys (**fig 4**). It is likely that these were locally made, the clay probably obtained from the lands to the east of the Loch of Fingask where names such as Claypots and Lochpots abound.[6] In the mid-seventeenth century, Sir Robert Sibbald noted that the lands of the entire district were generally of a clay soil.[7] In 1784 a suburban villa, Brick Lodge, was built entirely of brick. As late as 1805, clay for brick and tile making was still being extracted from several locations including the Kinnaird Head estate,[8] although demand was such that by 1840 bricks also had to be imported.[9] The warm colour of the local brick needs to be appreciated, and its survival, even in garden walls, encouraged. Another possibility to be borne in mind by householders is the survival of clay in the pointing of walls and in the walling itself, known as clay bool when boulders are embedded in clay.[10]

Evidence of the detail of early buildings is slight. Carved stonework, perhaps in easily worked sandstone (for it could not have been in granite), proved too attractive for later generations to ignore. A carved stone WE/EK is built into the gable of No 14–16 Saltoun Square, and a carved lintel is built into the wall of the close leading from Broad Street to the Cheers Bar. It is very worn, but appears to have a monogram and lettering that includes 'ever [will] the good pro[sper]' (see Appendix 3). There is a fine dormer window head with strapwork, a crescent and three shields, and a carved stone BVM/GL 1817 lying at the east end of the church.

The finer seventeenth- and eighteenth-century buildings had sandstone dressings, though some smaller windows, particularly on the back elevations, have chunky granite lintels almost as deep as they are wide (**fig 5**). Many of the eighteenth- and early nineteenth-century buildings are constructed of whinstone, with sandstone dressings, the contrasting colours clearly deliberate as in the Station Hotel, Seaforth Street. After the mid-nineteenth century many buildings, especially in the main streets, were constructed of, or at least fronted with, the newly available polished,

FIGURE 4
A brick outbuilding, an example of locally made bricks (Paula Martin)

machine-cut granite (**fig 6**). There is some pink granite (for example, the seaward wall of the extension to the Town-house) that is probably local, a pink outcrop being very visible in Broadsea Bay. Toward the end of the nineteenth century there was resurgence in the use of whinstone and darker, brownish granite. The recording of local styles and materials would be helpful as a guide for repairs, conservation and particularly for any infill development.

FIGURE 5
A typical back wall of a town-centre house, with small windows and chunky granite lintels (Paula Martin)

FIGURE 6
The former Post Office, Commerce Street, 1907, an example of the use of polished granite on the street frontage (Paula Martin)

Place-names

Three names can be made out on Timothy Pont's *c* 1590 map of the Fraserburgh area (**map 4**). The most prominent is Fraserburgh, which was probably added later by Sir Robert Gordon.[11] Above it are the words 'Fraser's brouch' which, given Pont's predilection for using local nicknames and pronunciation, was probably what locals called it, and undoubtedly indicates that the origin of the town's nickname 'The Broch' lies in the original title of Fraser's burgh. The third, which may just be made out, 'Faith...', was almost certainly 'Faithlie'. Fraserburgh had its origins in a settlement at Faichlie or Faithlie, a name that probably derived from the Gaelic *faiche*, a meadow or field, which lay on the east-facing shore to the south of the rocky promontory of Kinnaird Head in the medieval parish of Philorth. The name Kinnaird derives from Gaelic *ceann na h-àirde* meaning 'end of the point of land'.[12] The boundaries of Faithlie were said to be the Moray Firth, Kinnaird and the Broadsea coast on the north, the North Sea to the east, Keithock to the south, while to the west the boundary ran 'along the burnside at Watermill'.[13]

Street names

Modern street names have been used in the text. Earlier names include Eastgait (Broad Street), Fishcross Street (Cross Street), Midgait (Mid Street), School Croft (School Street), and Watergait (Frithside Street). Puddle Street was renamed Hanover Street in the 1780s.[14] North Street became Back Street and then in the 1870s when it had become a shopping area it was renamed High Street.[15] In a 1613 Charter Broad Street is described as running from Frithside Street to the Cross.[16] On an 1818 Stevenson manuscript plan of Fraserburgh harbour, the southern end of Castle Street is labelled Kelman Street after the Saltouns' factor, Broad Street is renamed Philorth Street, and the north end of Shore Street is renamed Kinnaird Street.[17] The first identified mention of 'Kirk Green' is in a bond of 1835, which also implies that High Street ran right down to the Shore, incorporating what is now Kirk Brae.[18] The name of Kirk Green was changed to Saltoun Square when the inn was built in 1801. Windmill Street was renamed Albert Street in 1900.[19]

Notes

1   *RMS*, Thomson, J M, *et al* (eds), 38 vols (Edinburgh, 1877–1970), v, no 1525; *NSA*, XII, Aberdeenshire (Edinburgh, 1845), 'Parish of Fraserburgh', Revd J Cumming (1840), 253–4; J B Pratt, *Buchan* (Aberdeen, 1858), 155.

2   NAS RHP 45434, Stevenson harbour plan, 1818; NLS, Admiralty charts 1438 (1834) and 1439 (1858) all show a dense settlement in this location.

3   J Cranna, *Fraserburgh: Past and Present* (Aberdeen, 1914), 448; M W Melville, *Historical Walks around Fraserburgh* (Peterhead, nd), 8.

4   *OSA* 1791–99, vol XV, North and East Aberdeenshire, D J Withrington and I Grant (eds) (Wakefield, 1982), Revd Mr A Simpson, 'Parish of Fraserburgh' (1791),

168, 170; *NSA* 249–50; J Anderson, *General View of the Agriculture of Aberdeenshire* (Edinburgh, 1794), 20, the local granite 'affords the best material for building I have any where seen; and is managed by the masons of that country with surprising adroitness. It is so hard as to resist the finest tempered edged tool; yet they know how to split it into blocks with astonishing facility, and to cut it into the size and form they wish for', 30, the stones were not further dressed except on the fronts of buildings, where the stone was smoothed. *NSA*, Parish of Tyrie, 719, 'From these quarries have been taken the materials for building great part of the dressed work of the pier of the harbour of Fraserburgh, and for the ornamental work of the modern buildings in that town', aided by the turnpike road.

5   *Christian Watt Papers*, 90, 'when we were young … most of the houses along the Broadgate were gable on to the road, with a lot of little lanes swarming with humanity'.

6   D Murison and L Noble, *Names and Places: a history of place and street names in and around Fraserburgh* (Fraserburgh, *c* 1995), 18, 46.

7   Sir A Mitchell (ed), *Geographical Collections Relating to Scotland made by Walter Macfarlane*, 3 vols (SHS, 1906–08), iii, 224.

8   Philorth Papers: KC MS 3004 bundle 272, letter from H Kelman, the Saltoun factor, to James Thom of Huntly, 13 May 1805; Cranna, *Fraserburgh*, 438, refers to the prevalence of clay, and to a brick and tile works (undated) at Rosehill, almost opposite Corbiehill, on the Cairnbulg turnpike road.

9   *NSA*, 255; *Topographical, Statistical and Historical Gazetteer of Scotland*, 2 vols (Glasgow, 1842).

10   An assumption based on that fact that there was plentiful local clay, and clay bool technology for cottages was common in north-east Scotland, particularly around Garmouth. There are references to the 'Clay Castle' on the Shore (Cranna, *Fraserburgh*, 389), and stone and clay houses in Braehead (S Wood, *The Shaping of 19th Century Aberdeenshire* (Stevenage, 1985), 202, 223–4, from Police Commissioners Minutes). There are also two possible references in the *Christian Watt Papers*, 39, 'Philorth has an atmosphere all its own … combined with the stink of a seldom fired clay building', and 64, 'It was good to be home. There was something about 72 [Broadsea] that spoke to me. I am as much a part of it as the rumble stones of its clay walls'. The 1788 contract included the acquisition by the feuars of some land near the town 'to furnish Clay to the Feuars' Buildings'.

11   Pont manuscript maps, NLS, Adv.MS.70.2.9, see J Stone, *The Pont Manuscript Maps of Scotland* (Tring, 1978), and I C Cunningham (ed), *The Nation Survey'd* (East Linton, 2001). The handwriting attribution is from Chris Fleet, NLS.

12   W M Alexander, *The Place Names of Aberdeenshire* (Spalding Club, 1952), 55, 78; D Murison, *The Broch as it was* (np, 1990), 8.

13   Murison, *Broch*, 7–8.

14   Murison and Noble, *Names and Places*, 35.

15   *Worrall's Directory of Aberdeenshire*, 1877, 'Note – The name of Back-St is now changed to High-St'.

16   Murison and Noble, *Names and Places*, 12, 34, 65.

17   NLS MS.5850.59.

18   Murison and Noble, *Names and Places*, 12, 34, 65.

19   Murison and Noble, *Names and Places*, 3.

4 Archaeology and history

Prehistory

The Mesolithic of the east of Scotland is better known now than it was even ten years ago.[1] It was assumed for quite some time that settlement in the Grampians was very late in Scotland. However, a range of stray finds in this region has been dated to the Mesolithic and the raised beach, upon which much of Fraserburgh is founded, should be considered a likely repository of Mesolithic remains.[2]

Many prehistoric sites are recorded in the surrounding area. Chiefly found in the nineteenth century, the sites discovered have included burial mounds,[3] cairns,[4] cists,[5] and cemeteries.[6] Also recorded is a range of unprovenanced finds including flint arrowheads,[7] flint chisels,[8] stone axes,[9] and carved stone balls.[10] Many of the burials were accompanied by urns and some appear to have been inurned cremations. Aerial photography has revealed a number of sites as cropmarks, including enclosures,[11] ring-ditches,[12] and arrangements of pits,[13] some or all of which may be of prehistoric date. Details of the sites in the vicinity of Fraserburgh can be found by consulting the National Monuments Record of Scotland (NMRS) and referring to map sheets NJ96NE, NW, SE and SW and NK06NW and SW.

There is no evidence that a promontory fort was ever built on Kinnaird Head. In Fraserburgh itself, probably the earliest features so far recorded lie within the churchyard at Kirkton, where midden deposits and the possible footings of structures were uncovered during grave digging. John Cranna, harbour treasurer of Fraserburgh, writing in 1914, provides the most detailed account:

> it is held by many, and among others by the late Mr J M D Smith, sculptor, Fraserburgh, a man whose opinions and investigations are of considerable value, that ancient Faithlie was located near the cemetery – to be particular – to the south and east of the old churchyard. The kirk of Philorth was there … and where there is a village or town, it is natural that the church should be in close proximity to it. As a matter of fact the name Kirk-town, corrupted into Kirkton, forces one strongly to the belief that a town of some kind must have at one time existed in the neighbourhood of the churchyard.[14]

Cranna then quotes from an article by Mr Smith on *The Topography of Ancient Faithlie and some surmises theron*:

For around this part [Kirkton] there is indisputable evidence for a village. Often in the past years I had my attention drawn to a thick, hard, black loam, some three feet or thereby from the surface, and of about one foot in thickness, above and below which was pure sand, while shells of different kinds were occasionally to be met with scattered and impregnating this loam. What to make of this I could not conjecture, until the formation of the new cemetery, when, on the south side of this 1866 addition, in opening graves we came on numerous ash middens, with whole bucketfuls of shells mixed up with the ashes. In several instances these middens were built round with stones ... I was told by [the late Mr Burnett of Kirkton] that around the graveyard, to the south side, his men had come frequently on these ash middens in the process of their digging.[15]

Unfortunately, this account provides no indication of date and, while Mr Smith assumes that the middens relate to a settlement associated with the original kirk, the lack of ceramics or other artefacts means that any date from the Mesolithic to the end of the first millennium AD could be considered possible for such remains.

Roman

The first written reference to the area around Fraserburgh is on Ptolemy's map of the mid-second century AD, where Kinnaird Head has been equated with *Promontorium Taezalorum*. Ptolemy's information on the north of Scotland is considered most likely to have been derived from a Roman coasting voyage, possibly during Agricola's governorship in the later first century.[16] Several Roman marching camps have been recorded in the area to the south-west of Fraserburgh, for example, Muiryfold[17] and Ythan Wells[18]. None of these is securely dated, though they probably relate either to the Flavian (AD 80s) or Severan (AD 208–210) campaigns. A coin of Antoninus Pius, minted between AD 151 and 154, said to have been found on the beach at Muckhills, 'north-east of Fraserburgh towards Sandhaven', is the sole Roman find from the area.[19]

Early medieval, c 500 to c 1100

There is little definitive archaeological evidence for the period between the Roman Iron Age and the medieval era in the vicinity of Fraserburgh and certainly none within the burgh itself. There is likewise little by the way of clear historical record for this corner of north-east Scotland, and for northern Buchan in particular. What can be said is that down into the mid-ninth century this area formed part of the zone of Pictish culture that covered most of mainland Scotland north of the Forth–Clyde line. There is no concrete evidence for the political structures of north-east Pictland. A series of major fortifications occupies headlands strung along this exposed northern coast – from Burghead in Moray and Green Castle at Portknockie, through Cullykhan at Troup to Dundarg[20] – but none east of Rosehearty. Excavation results and stray finds from a number of these sites have indicated that they occupied the top level of a hierarchy of political and economic power down into the later ninth and early tenth centuries. The absence of a clearly recognisable equivalent site or sites from eastern Buchan presents an as yet unexplored archaeological and historical question.

There is sufficient evidence to show that there was a pattern of substantial agricultural estates scattered throughout Buchan and material evidence for an elite with disposable income. Place-names offer the clearest evidence for the settlement pattern, while sculptural remains indicate the presence of both patrons and skilled craftsmen. North-east Buchan, however, has few Pictish place-names, and the nearest surviving Pictish symbol stones to Fraserburgh are at Tyrie and Fetterangus.[21] There is a cluster of four *pit*-names in the vicinity of Fraserburgh: Pitblae (NJ 978650), Pitsligo (NJ 938670), Pittendrum (NJ 961670), and Pittulie (NJ 959676). Names of this type, where the generic *pit* is considered to be a Pictish term derived from the Latin *petia*, meaning a portion or piece (of land), are believed to record the former existence of important estate centres. The absence of Pictish symbol stones from the region may be a consequence of the underlying geology. It has been noticed that such stones are concentrated on areas of lighter, gravel-based soils in the north, and usually away from the coastline.[22] The soils of Buchan are generally heavy clays.

In line with the poverty of surviving evidence for the secular political structures of the region in the Pictish period, there is no great evidence for the spread of Christianity into the area. Tradition attributes the conversion of the Picts of Buchan to Columba, but the life of the saint written by Adomnan in the late seventh century gives no indication that Columba ever travelled so far east. It is more likely that missions sent out from Iona or its colonies in the course of the seventh or eighth century carried out the main task of conversion. There is a strong, but archaeologically unverified, tradition of an early monastery associated with these Columban missions at Aberdour (11km west of Fraserburgh) but the chief pre-twelfth-century monastery in the region, again with Columban links, lay at Old Deer (18km south of Fraserburgh), where an important community survived into the twelfth century and may have been the basis for the Cistercian abbey founded at Deer by William Comyn, earl of Buchan, in 1219.[23] There is some evidence for a number of other Celtic missionaries active in north-east Buchan from the late sixth century onwards. On the Links east of Fraserburgh, for example, a now-vanished knoll was supposedly the location of a chapel founded by St

Modan in the sixth century, which may have been the precursor of the old kirk of Philorth.[24] There were also some holy wells in the medieval parish of Philorth, one of which was dedicated and named after the sixth-century Celtic saint Marnan.[25]

By the middle of the ninth century, the southern shores of the Moray Firth were subject to attack by the Vikings. These Scandinavian raiders, more probably Norse (from primary colonies in Orkney and Shetland) than Danes, increased pressure on the northern Pictish area in the closing decades of the ninth century. While Caithness and Sutherland were subject to varying degrees of Scandinavian colonisation from the 880s AD through to the early 1000s, there is no evidence from either archaeology or place-names for any Norse settlement in the coastlands south of the Moray Firth. Raids, however, continued into the tenth century – and possibly later, coinciding with periods of political instability within Scotland or wider episodes of conflict between Scottish rulers and the Norse jarls of Orkney. There are records of a major episode of raiding in the reign of King Indulf mac Constantine (Idulb mac Castantín, reigned AD 954–62). One chronicle source records the destruction of a Viking fleet in Buchan at some point during the reign, but in AD 962 the king himself was slain at Cullen while repelling a Norse raid.[26]

The Vikings may have been drawn south by political upheavals within Pictland in the later ninth century. In the 840s, the Pictish kingship passed into the hands of Kenneth mac Alpin (Cinaed mac Alpín), a man of possibly mixed Gaelic and Pictish ancestry, whose successors asserted their mastery over a kingdom which stretched from Fife to the Moray Firth.[27] Gaelic influences had probably been growing in the region since the beginning of the conversion to Christianity of the Picts by Gaelic-speaking clergy from the kingdom of Dál Riata in what is now Argyll. Evidence from southern Pictland suggests that its ruling elite was already heavily Gaelicised by the early ninth century, before Kenneth's takeover, but the displacement of Pictish language and culture by the Gaelic of the Scots seems largely to have been a product of the new dynasty.[28] By about AD 900, the Gaelic kings of Scots had imposed their lordship over most of what had been Pictland, evidently displacing a native aristocracy in favour of their own warrior nobility. The vast majority of Buchan place-names are of Gaelic origin, which reflects a submerging or displacing of the older Pictish place-name pattern by a new language. Here, as in other parts of Pictland, this process of displacement can be seen clearly in the *pit*-names where, although the Pictish generic has been retained in the prefix, the specific element, the suffix, is uniformly Gaelic. It is a structure which may signal the takeover of a Pictish property by a new Gaelic master. At the head of the new social order was a *mormaer* (great steward), a man who ruled the province of Buchan with quasi-regal authority, and who possessed estates scattered throughout the region. On the evidence of the estates of the mormaers' twelfth- and thirteenth-century successors, the land on which

Fraserburgh later developed constituted one among several important estates in northern Buchan held by the new provincial ruler.[29]

In the twelfth century, Buchan emerged as an earldom under a line of earls of clearly Gaelic ancestry.[30] The last of these, Fergus, left a daughter, Margery, who was married to William Comyn, one of the chief councillors of King William the Lion.[31] The marriage brought William the earldom, the first of these great Gaelic dignities to pass into the hands of one of the twelfth-century colonial families which had been introduced to Scotland by David I. Under the Comyn lordship, Buchan was brought firmly within the political community of medieval Scotland. It provided that family with a strong reservoir of manpower throughout the thirteenth century, which the kings of Scots used to underpin their own authority in northern Scotland. In the early fourteenth century, however, Buchan was important to the Comyns in the struggle for control of the kingdom between the supporters of the exiled king, John Balliol, and the usurper, Robert Bruce. The consequence was the systematic devastation of the earldom and the forfeiture of its lords by the victorious Bruce.[32]

Later medieval Faithlie and Philorth

Little is known about Faithlie before the fourteenth century, other than that it had been a demesne estate of the earls of Buchan in the thirteenth century.[33] The adjoining lands of Philorth formed the core of one of the main constituent baronies of the earldom, but, despite this proximity, Faithlie itself was a component of the barony of Kingedward, whose main lands lay some 20 miles (32km) to the west. Following the forfeiture of the Comyn earls of Buchan in c 1314, Robert I divided the earldom among his supporters, one of whom was Hugh, earl of Ross, who received the superiority of both Kingedward and Philorth. When Hugh's son died in 1372 his lands were divided between his two daughters. Euphemia, the elder, married Walter Leslie, who received the style earl of Ross, and Johanna married Alexander Fraser of Cowie and Durris in Kincardineshire (grandson of Sir Alexander Fraser of Touch-Fraser (Stirlingshire), chamberlain of Scotland 1325–32, and his wife, a sister of Robert Bruce). In 1375 Alexander and Johanna received the barony of Philorth from Walter Leslie 'as compensation for the said lands of Ross' along with its principal estates of 'Kirktoun, Cairnbuilg, Inuerolochy'.[34] The toun and lands of Faithlie, however, in the barony of Kingedward, remained the property of Walter and Euphemia. Although retaining the superiority, in 1381 Walter and Euphemia granted away components of the barony, and in February 1382 Robert II confirmed their charter of the lands of 'Faythley' and 'Tiry' to one Andrew Mercer.[35] The Mercers held Faithlie until, on 15 June 1504, a charter of feuferme for Faithlie and Fyvie was granted by Sir Henry Mercer of Aldie to Sir William Fraser of Philorth.[36] Sir William died about a decade later and in 1516 his brother Alexander was infeft in the lands of Faithlie and Tyrie by Sir Lawrence Mercer of Aldie.[37]

For most of the fifteenth century the superiority of the barony of Kingedward and the lands of Faithlie remained with the descendants of the Leslie earls of Ross. In *c* 1437 that title, with all its dependencies, had passed into the hands of Alexander MacDonald, lord of the Isles. In 1475 John MacDonald was stripped of the earldom as punishment for his treasonable alliances with the English crown, but received back several components, including Kingedward. Throughout this period the Mercers appear to have retained the direct lordship of Faithlie under the MacDonalds. In 1478, however, John MacDonald granted the lands of Kingedward, including Faithlie, to Alexander Leslie of Wardis (Wardhouse), eldest son of Leslie of Balquhain. Alexander Leslie was James III's receiver-general, and this award has the appearance of a political manoeuvre. It is not clear whether Leslie's control survived the overthrow of James III's regime in 1488, and in 1490, as John MacDonald's grip on the remains of the former MacDonald empire crumbled, the lord of the Isles surrendered the barony of Kingedward to the crown. It was immediately granted to James IV's great-uncle, James Stewart, earl of Buchan. Shortly before September 1505, Buchan appears to have surrendered Kingedward to the king, with whom the superiority remained. The establishment of Fraser control over Faithlie appears to have been achieved around this time.

Despite the fact that the Frasers of Philorth did not hold Faithlie itself until the early 1500s, it is clear that throughout the fifteenth century they were establishing their position in Philorth parish and adjoining districts. In October 1408 William Fraser of Philorth received from Sir James Douglas, lord of Abercorn and Aberdour, the lands of 'Pitsligo, Pittully, Culbarty … Ardlaw … Durin with the miln thereof, Memsie with the mill of Bodiehell and Rathen' with other lands in the barony of Aberdour, which William's father Alexander had previously resigned. Three days later William received a charter of confirmation from Archibald, earl of Douglas, 'of all and haill the lands of over Pittourly and nether Pittourly' along with the others previously granted by his younger brother, James Douglas.[38] William Fraser's son Alexander was seised in these lands in 1420 by James Douglas of Balvenie.[39] James II incorporated all the lands held by Alexander Fraser of Philorth into a free barony, 'to be called the barony of Philorth', and to be held by Alexander and his heirs.[40] The Frasers of Philorth continued to add to their holdings and in 1469/70 Alexander received confirmation from John, lord of the Isles and earl of Ross, who then held the barony of Kingedward, of a grant from Thomas Graham of the lands of Scatterty and Byth.[41] So by the early sixteenth century the Frasers of Philorth held extensive lands. Was such consolidation of landholdings part of a larger, long-term plan for future development in the area? Certainly such a plan came to fruition during the sixteenth century.

The Burgh founded

In 1531 King James V issued a letter of safeguard to Alexander Fraser, 7th of Philorth, ensuring the protection of his estate for three years while he was on a pilgrimage to 'Sanct John of Amess'.[42] On his return from France, Alexander is said to have begun construction of a 'convenient harbour', with the view to making Faithlie a great port.[43] In 1541 James V issued a charter to Alexander of the barony of Philorth, including all the fishing within the barony as well as the lands of Faithlie, while 'the maner place and castell of Phillorth, now biggit or to be biggit, to be the chief chymmeis' of the barony,[44] which suggests that it was not only a harbour that Alexander Fraser had plans to improve. Indeed, this Alexander has been credited with building the mid-sixteenth-century portions of the castle of Philorth (now known as Cairnbulg Castle), the Frasers' seat two miles (3.2km) south of Fraserburgh.[45] In 1542 influence in this area was extended when Alexander received a crown charter for the fishing and the fish bait from the sea adjacent to his lands of 'Carnbulg, Faithlie, Pitcarlie, and Cowburty'.[46]

Little is known about this Alexander Fraser but it was said that he was a man of great 'energy and intelligence' who 'devoted himself to the improvement of his estate and the acquisition of further possessions'.[47] His building schemes were part of a grander plan which became clear in 1546 when he succeeded in having Faithlie created a free burgh of barony with the right to hold markets, practise various trades, elect town officials, have a jail, hold courts weekly on Mondays, Wednesdays and Fridays, and arrest thieves, while the usual privileges were granted to burgesses.[48] The new burgh was also allowed to hold two annual fairs, lasting for eight days from St John the Baptist's day (29 August) and St Michael the Archangel's day (29 September).[49] Alexander died in November 1569, and it was his grandson, also called Alexander, who benefited from his achievements.[50]

The village of Faithlie huddled on the shore, under the shelter of the raised beach. It is improbable that the Frasers would have encouraged a settlement here, so far from their seat at Philorth/Cairnbulg to the south-east, without some form of nearer presence, so the Frasers may have inhabited Kinnaird Head considerably earlier than 1570, the traditional date of its building.[51] Once Faithlie became a free port in 1546, the Frasers apparently erected a breakwater to improve the harbour, but it proved unsuitable.[52] How large the original community was is unknown, but it appears to have evolved rapidly between 1546 and 1588. In 1584 'William Pettindreich in Faithlie' was clearly a man of authority in the burgh.[53] In 1600 he was recorded as bailie of Fraserburgh, witnessing a deed of surety along with others including John Simpson, common clerk of Fraserburgh and notary public.[54]

Calm in the midst of conflict

It has been said that Alexander Fraser, 8th of Philorth, had even grander visions, but the 'means at his disposal' did not allow him to fulfil them.[55] This may have been true for the Frasers in the seventeenth century, but in the 1580s and 1590s it is clear that substantial funds were still available and that Alexander was able to undertake a series of major building projects despite the political turbulence of the time. The strength of the Frasers' finances at this date can be seen in their ability to absorb the double impact of Alexander 8th's entry fine and payment of what amounted to little more than a forced loan to the Protestant regime in Edinburgh, while continuing expenditure on the development of the burgh and other works. It is probable, however, that Alexander's ambitious schemes were funded by credit and loans, and that his inheritance was mortgaged heavily with near-disastrous consequences for his family later. Whatever the state of the Frasers' finances by 1600, however, it is clear that the 8th laird had succeeded in establishing his project at Fraserburgh on a secure footing.

Despite the apparent remoteness of this part of Buchan from the political epicentres of sixteenth-century Scotland, the Roman Catholicism of several of the leading families of the north-east, such as the Gordons of Huntly and Hays of Erroll, dictated that the Protestant government for the child-king James VI had to secure the loyalty, or at least the acquiescence, of this region. Although the army of the deposed Queen Mary had been defeated and scattered at Langside near Glasgow in May 1568, and Mary herself had fled into exile and imprisonment in England, her supporters, both Protestant and Catholic, had continued the armed struggle in her name. The civil war between the supporters of James VI (the King's Men) and Mary (the Queen's Men) was to convulse much of central and southern Scotland between 1568 and 1573, when Edinburgh Castle, the last fortress to hold out for the queen's cause, surrendered.

The conflict has been presented as a fight between Protestants and Catholics, Douglases and Hamiltons, pro- and anti-English factions, but none of these labels rests easily on either side, where family or confessional loyalties were often subordinated to personal allegiances. James Stewart, earl of Moray, regent for the young James VI, was personally aware of the complexities of north-eastern politics and between April and June 1569 had secured a series of bonds from the heads of the leading kindreds of the region, pledging support to the king's party.[56] At this time, Moray wrote to the heir of Philorth regarding the financial state of the country, expressing his certainty of the good affection Alexander had for the young James VI and mentioning the personal distress which the laird obviously would experience if there was any 'dishonour of your Prince and native country'. To this end Moray asked for a loan of one thousand pounds 'in this our sa urgent necesitie'.[57] This may have been nothing more than a piece of political opportunism designed to exploit Alexander's temporary legal weakness, as he had not yet been given sasine of his inheritance following the death of his grandfather. Considering Alexander's aims to promote Faithlie further it is likely that he complied in this wish, but such an outlay did not prevent him from continuing with the work on his own estate in the following year.

Alexander Fraser, 8th of Philorth, a mature adult in his early thirties, formally took over the estate on 23 March 1570, four and a half months after the death of his grandfather.[58] It is perhaps surprising that the hiatus was not longer, for on 23 January 1570 Regent Moray had been assassinated and a savage civil war had erupted. King's and Queen's Men established rival administrations and parliaments, each claiming to be the legitimate legislature.[59] The service as heir (in which the heir is formally invested with the property) of Alexander so soon after Moray's death may imply that his

FIGURE 7
Kinnaird Head, with Castle (centre), Wine Tower (right), and a doocot (left) since lost to coastal erosion (aquatint and engraving, William Daniell, 1822) (author's collection)

views inclined towards the King's Men and that they wished to secure his loyalty. The delay may have been a legal fiction, for according to family tradition the new laird is said to have laid the foundation stone of the castle on Kinnaird Head on 6 March 1570 (**fig 7**).[60] Alexander, 'imbued with the idea of making Fraserburgh a great port and place of trade and learning', is said to have positioned his castle in such a way that he could view the developments going on in his town.[61] If this tradition is correct, it also highlights the tranquillity of Buchan in contrast to the conflict being fought out in the central lowlands.

Kinnaird Head tower, however, would have been grossly anachronistic for an improving laird in 1570, as the Scottish economy entered half a century of prosperity. Architecturally, it has far more in common with the early sixteenth-century towers such as those designed by Con of Auchry in the 1530s.[62] We should look, rather, to other buildings in the inner or outer close of the castle for what might have been constructed by such a pioneering man in the 1570s. What now remains – an austere tower converted into a lighthouse in 1787, and the disconnected Wine Tower – are the relics of a more elaborate establishment. It is highly probable that Kinnaird had the customary inner and outer courts. Old drawings indicate evidence of a building, possibly a gallery wing, extending from the tower,[63] and thus forming an inner court, and a now-missing doocot and other buildings perhaps forming part of an outer court. Its later stables lay down by the edge of the town, and traces of these may still survive in the courtyard behind the Saltoun Arms Hotel (**fig 8**). The castle gardens appear to have extended equally far southwards.

So the outer courts of Kinnaird Head lay toward the town, and what is known as the Wine Tower almost certainly formed a corner of one of them (**fig 9**). This is a small, truncated, formerly harled, tower, its present appearance deriving from its conversion into a magazine in the late eighteenth century. It comprises a vaulted cellar (the magazine), and a tight, reasonably well-lit, highly decorated principal floor room above, with projecting carved bosses or pendants with Counter Reformation insignia (**fig 10**). It would originally have been plastered. There are traces of upper storeys. The twin-holed gunloop and the carved bosses imply the hand of Thomas Leiper.[64]

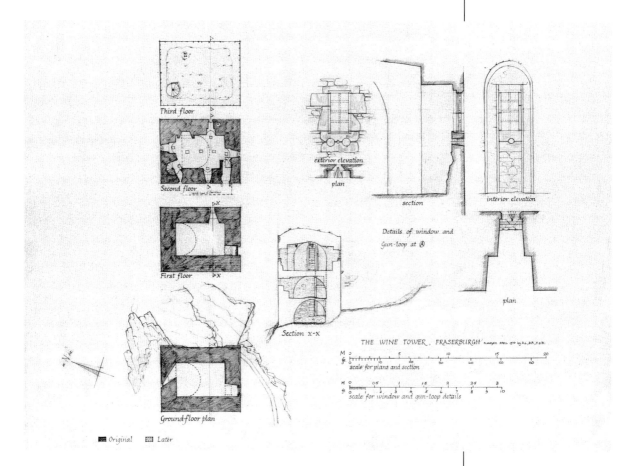

Third floor

Second floor

First floor

Ground-floor plan

exterior elevation

plan

section

interior elevation

Details of window and
Gun-loop at Ⓐ

plan

Section x-x

THE WINE TOWER, FRASERBURGH surveyed April 1976 by A.L., D.P., J.S.D.

scale for plans and section

scale for window and gun-loop details

■ Original ▨ Later

FIGURE 9
Measured survey drawing
of the Wine Tower,
1976 (Crown Copyright:
RCAHMS)

FIGURE 10
Two bosses from the Wine
Tower, photographed in
1976 (Crown Copyright:
RCAHMS)

Some have suggested that Fraser erected the main tower house to oversee the development of his new town. More probably he built himself this little pavilion with a viewing platform on top for that purpose – a rather more elaborate version of Edzell's summerhouse. If it were Leiper, that would imply a date in the 1590s which better suits the expansion of Fraser's Broch.

Parish and kirk of Philorth

The first act in the transformation of Faithlie to Fraserburgh may have been the relocation of the parish kirk to the plateau overlooking the harbour, more or less where the road from Pitsligo debouched, between 1571 and 1574.[65] Although Faithlie was earlier incorporated into the barony of Kingedward, it lay in the parish of Philorth. The pre-Reformation parish church was in existence by 1274,[66] and it was evidently considerably older. It stood in the old churchyard at Kirkton, which remained the principal graveyard of the burgh and parish.[67] There are no definite upstanding remains, although the location and plan of the church was identified in 1910 when the cemetery was extended.[68] There are no contemporary descriptions of the new building in Fraserburgh, but later tradition records that it was cruciform in plan, with a steeple probably intended to act as a day-mark for sailors.[69] It was 'understood to be a wonderful building for the age in which it was erected, and much superior to anything of the kind in the district at the time'.[70] Only excavations beneath the present church would reveal further information. It is survived by the detached, pyramid-roofed burial aisle decorated with armorial panels, immediately to the south of the present church, which Alexander Fraser had erected in 1623 (**fig 11**):

> I ordain my body to be buried at the south side of the Kirk of Fraserburgh, and an aisle to be built there, and a little vault to be built upon my corpse ... the aisle be vaulted and a chamber be built above the vault, to be a session house or chamber for the minister. The aisle to be thirty feet of height, and as much in length, and a steeple to be built on the aisle, and a bell to be put therein, and passage to be made on the east side, that the minister may go in thereat to the pulpit.[71]

As with the construction work at Kinnaird Head, the building of the new Protestant church was a sign of confidence and optimism, and underlines how the new burgh was developing despite the continuing national instability. Overtly, it is an indication of Alexander's commitment to the Protestant cause in the immediate aftermath of the assassination of Moray and the intensification of the war between the King's and Queen's Men. Following the final collapse of the Queen's party in 1573, general peace was restored to the kingdom and the controlling Protestant regime of the new regent, James Douglas, 4th earl of Morton, sought to draw a line under the previous five years of conflict. As part of this process, in 1574 a general bond declaring

FIGURE II
The Saltoun Mausoleum, on
the south side of the parish
church, built on to the 1570s'
church as a burial aisle in
1623 (Charles McKean)

support for the new political and religious dispensation in the kingdom was
circulated by the Morton regime for signature by the leading noblemen.
Alexander signed, confirming his allegiance to James VI and the Protestant
faith.[72] The completion of the church roughly coincided with this. Alexander's
Protestant credentials seem impeccable, but his public stance seems to be
directly at odds with the overt Catholic symbolism to be seen in the sculptural
embellishments of the surviving upper chamber of the Wine Tower, perhaps
datable to the 1590s, and may represent a display of pragmatism on his part at
a time when the ultimate outcome of the Reformation in Scotland was once
more plunged into uncertainty.[73]

Later sixteenth-century expansion

Alexander Fraser did not stop at the erection of Kinnaird Castle and the
new church. He also built, to the north of the church, a 'good' tolbooth.[74]
We do not know which was the main façade of Alexander's new church,
but the tolbooth probably faced the church, since its gable end faced what
is now Saltoun Square, thereby creating a significant open space between

them.[75] A more immediate symbol of the community's status as a trading burgh was its market cross. This was (and is) a grand affair, 'a hexagon, with three equidistant angular abutments; the area of the base is 500 feet; by 9 intrenchings the top is contracted to 23 feet, on the middle of which is raised a stone pillar 12 feet high. The British arms, surmounting the armorial coat of Fraser of Philorth, adorn the summit' (**fig 12**).[76] The area around the tolbooth and the church, with the Cross at its top, long known as Kirk Green or just The Green, was clearly intended as the focus of the expanded town. The town's first identified inn, during the late seventeenth century, lay at Braeheads, effectively just behind the tolbooth.[77]

Alexander's intention was not to improve the existing settlement at Faithlie, but 'to build a large and beautiful town, which he adorned with public buildings and streets of a width then almost unheard of'.[78] He induced skilled artisans, wealthy merchants, and relatives of his own who had entered into trade to settle in the town. The advantages resulting from this beneficent and far-sighted policy are felt to the present day', as can be seen from epitaphs in the graveyard.[79] It was to the harbour that Alexander next turned his attention.

FIGURE 12

Detail of the top of the mercat cross, Saltoun Square (restored 1988) (Reproduced by permission of the Royal Incorporation of Architects in Scotland)

It would appear that the site his grandfather had chosen for the harbour was unsuitable,[80] or that its breakwater had been damaged, and in 1576 Alexander decided to construct another one, in the area of the old North Harbour.[81] The result was what Pont called 'a noble harbour' and what Alexander Garden of Troup described in 1683 as the best artificial harbour on this part of the coast.[82]

In 1583 Alexander Fraser furthered his position in Faithlie when he purchased a third part of the town and lands from Robert Innes of Kinkell (who may have been an investment partner in his grandfather's original scheme).[83] Possibly as a result of this purchase and the many improvements that he was implementing on his estate, the crown looked to him again as a source of revenue. As in 1570, despite his considerable financial outlay on his properties, Alexander was clearly in a position to help underwrite royal expenditure. On 7 April 1588 he received a letter from King James concerning his proposed marriage and the expenses that this would entail, and the king's desire that negotiations would be carried out 'according to the honour and necessities of that errand'. To that end James was 'forceit to have recompse to the favourable guid will of sume spealis of oure nobilitie baronis and utheris our loving subiectis' and imposed a further taxation of £1000 Scots (about £83 sterling).[84] Either in an attempt to secure funds from Alexander or by way of reward for his generosity, two days later, following the resignation of all Alexander's lands, James granted him 'all and haill the lands of Faithley and Fyvie, with the part of Faithley and town and burgh of barony of the same', and renewed the earlier grant of 1546 erecting Faithlie into a free port and burgh of barony. Alexander and his heirs were also given the patronage of the churches of Philorth, Tyrie and Crimond.[85] Understandably the improvements at Faithlie were taking a financial toll, for on 30 May 1588 James VI granted to Alexander a licence to sell lands worth £10,000 'for help and support of his children and for performing of other necessary affairs and business as he shall think expedient'.[86] Having invested heavily in Faithlie, Alexander felt it necessary to continue his push for the advancement of this burgh, thereby ensuring that no other town in the locality could rival it.

In theory, Alexander Fraser's town might have just expanded around Kirk Brae and Broad Street or High Street. However in 1587, not far away, the Earl Marischal received authority to lay out a new town by Keith Inch, known as Peterhead (**map 2**). In 1592 Alexander was again the beneficiary of James's favour when another charter reaffirmed all privileges granted in 1588. The estate of Inverallochy, a recent addition to Alexander Fraser's estate despite his growing financial embarrassment, was included, as was the patronage of the parish church of Rathen. He was again granted 'all and haill the lands of Faithley and Fyvie with the port of Faithlie and town and burgh of barony thereof'. Interestingly, it added that from then on it would be known as 'the burgh and port of Fraser'.[87] Was he simply renaming a new town already begun, or had he, impelled by Peterhead, decided to make a new start? Competition was certainly in the air. The following year the Earl Marischal had Peterhead declared a burgh of barony, and at the same time founded Marischal College in Aberdeen. Competition would also be heightened by the growing opportunities for Scots abroad, particularly trading with the Baltic, and the increased potential for export.[88] Whatever the case, Alexander Fraser decided to lay out a grid-iron new town of four streets by three, incorporating Broad Street but not High Street.[89]

Fraserburgh University

This 1592 charter also contained a grant for the creation of 'a college or colleges within the said burgh of Fraser, and erecting an university'. Alexander was given the right to appoint rectors, principals and other necessary individuals and to make 'laws and statutes to the better government thereof'.[90] In 1597 an Act of Parliament was passed for the founding of the university and, with Alexander's approval, his patronage of the parish churches of Philorth,

Tyrie, Crimond and Rathen was granted to the University of Fraserburgh. He had been preparing well in advance for this, as the Act recognised that Alexander 'hes [begwn] to edifie and big vp Collegis', which had caused him 'exhorbitant and large expensis'. The Act likewise recognised that Fraserburgh had 'greatumlie florishit and incressit' as a result of Alexander's efforts, and that he had 'biggit ane sure hevin and port'.[91]

Alexander Fraser's foundation of a university is more than simply an indication of his pretensions or his ambitions for the community he had founded. Firstly, there was the religious symbolism of the move. At this period the Kirk saw the universities as the primary mechanism for securing the provision of an educated ministry and also for providing the kind of broad education for the laity that would help to extirpate the remnants of 'popery'. Secondly, there would be an economic advantage if Fraserburgh could establish itself as a conveniently located educational centre for students from the northern mainland and Northern Isles. Certainly these were the points identified by one seventeenth-century observer:

> The town of Frazerburgh lyes in the shire of Aberdeen, and Presbitry of Deer, a place remote from education very much. It was attended with difficultys to send youths from the Shires of Caithnes, Inverness, Murray and Ross, to the Colledges at Aberdeen, lying at a considerable distance. In that country, Popery was not yet much rooted out, and ther was a great need of a learned ministry, and a carefull education of the youth of the nobility and gentry, and better sort of the inhabitants, in literature. This was justly reckoned one of the best means to root out barbarity, superstition, and Popery, from that more remote part of the natioun; and, therefore, a little Colledge or Seminary for all kinds of learning was set up at Fraserburgh, to answer those good purposes.[92]

Opinion in the past has been divided as to whether the university ever actually operated as such, for it met strong competition from the University of Aberdeen, founded in 1495, and Marischal College, founded in 1593/94.[93] Nevertheless, in 1600 Charles Ferme, 'a man of obscure parentage but exceedinglye pious', who had been appointed minister of Philorth in 1598, was made principal of the new establishment, and four other masters were appointed.[94] It took the coercion of the General Assembly, however, to secure Ferme's acceptance of the post.[95] There are reports of five academic sessions being completed before Ferme's opposition to James VI's religious policies led to his imprisonment in 1605. No successor is recorded and the whole project appears to have failed after Ferme's forced departure. Ferme's academic credentials are not in doubt, for he was later to be offered the principalship of Edinburgh University, and it is likely that some significant progress had been made in consolidating the project under his direction. Ferme returned to Fraserburgh in *c* 1609, but there is no suggestion that he resumed the principalship and by the time of his death in 1617 the grand plan seems to have been defunct.[96]

Alexander Fraser was also said to have made 'considerable progress' in relation to building work to house the university. But it may never have been completed and some accounts claim that the college was 'soon used as a quarry for materials for the construction of other buildings'.[97] One building erected for the university was subsequently used as accommodation for junior branches of the Fraser family.[98] Fraserburgh University lay at the high point, where High Street crosses over the ridge at the edge of the town, near a well, probably just to the east of Barrasgate where, according to oral testimony, vaulted cellars now filled with concrete survive beneath the tarmac. The College buildings may have extended further west to the edge of Broadsea, and carved stones are said to be embedded inaccessibly into the rear of the Alexandra Hotel.[99] There are records of a three-storeyed square or rectangular tower, possibly resembling the Cromwell Tower of King's College Aberdeen, or the northern tower of Aberdeen's now-demolished Marischal College.[100] Being on the height of the ridge running from castle to windmill, it would have dominated the principal land entrance to the town. The street-name 'College Bounds', however, dates only from c 1875.[101] The minister in 1791 noted that the 'good carving of Moses and the ten commandments on free stone found in the College of Fraserburgh', recently incorporated into the new schoolhouse, was 'said to have been intended for the altar-piece of its chapel'.[102] This seems highly improbable given the religious climate of the 1590s, and it seems more likely that it was designed to be set above the principal entrance to the College.

The challenge of Aberdeen

The extent of the town at the close of the sixteenth century is unclear but the general picture seems to have been one of steady expansion and a burgeoning economy. The growth of Faithlie town and harbour, its creation as a free burgh of barony, and the subsequent liberties granted, however, brought Faithlie and the Frasers into conflict with Aberdeen. On 18 January 1564 the provost, bailies and council of Aberdeen took action before the privy council against Alexander Fraser 7th, 'anent the preuilege vsurpit be him of ane fre burght in the toune of Faythlie, contrar the libertie and ald preuilegis of this burgh'.[103] In 1573 they complained to Regent Morton that Alexander Fraser 8th had loaded a Flemish ship at Faithlie 'in hurt and preiudice of the priuulege of this burght, commoditie, and jurisdictioune of the samen'.[104] The council of Aberdeen obviously felt threatened by the rapid rise of Fraserburgh, with its developing port and the creation of a university which might rival King's College.

Aberdeen's petition seems to have made little impact, for in April 1601 James VI confirmed and expanded upon his 1588 and 1592 charters in a wide-ranging award to Alexander Fraser.[105] Fraserburgh was established as 'a free port, free burgh of barony and free regality', which considerably expanded its status and jurisdiction. Despite this sign of royal favour to Fraser, Aberdeen was clearly unwilling to give up the struggle. By 1605 the Aberdonians had taken their plea to the Court of Session, arguing that the creation of what was by then called Fraserburgh as a free port and burgh of regality had been illegal. The next year they charged Alexander and 'his tennetis of Fraserburght … to desist and ceis frome vsing of merchandice, paking, peiling, losing, and laidning'.[106] In 1616 they continued to assert that Fraserburgh 'lyis within the precinct and liberties' of Aberdeen, but although 'the said mater sould be prosequite and followit out to the finall decisioun', Aberdeen appears to have abandoned this quest later in the seventeenth century.[107]

Seventeenth century

The development falters

For just over three decades, Alexander Fraser's plans for his burgh appear to have progressed comparatively smoothly while, superficially at least, his personal prestige also grew. Alexander's standing reached its height between August 1594, when he was knighted on the occasion of the baptism of James VI's first son, Prince Henry, and 1596, when he and John Leslie of Balquhain were elected as Commissioners to Parliament for Aberdeenshire.[108] By 1605, however, Fraserburgh's development began to stall when Fraser's creditors closed in, and there was a succession of setbacks that all but halted further growth. The first blow came with the departure of Ferme from the university. He was evidently never replaced as principal and the academic community appears to have withered away swiftly. When King's College, Aberdeen, was evacuated to Fraserburgh during a plague epidemic in 1647, the Aberdeen masters and students were accommodated with ease, possibly in part of the former college buildings. There is no indication that the university at Fraserburgh was itself still functioning at that date, and the early seventeenth-century 'Grammar School' may have been housed in part of the complex.

The collapse of the university scheme would have been a serious blow to the prestige of Fraser's project, but potentially greater threats followed swiftly. The same year saw Aberdeen mount its most serious challenge in the Court of Session, litigation that was to drag on for several years. Although this ultimately came to nothing, the threat which it posed should not be underestimated. The provost of Aberdeen who instigated the legal challenge was Thomas Menzies of Durn, builder of Fordyce Castle in Banffshire and owner of commercial interests in both Aberdeen and Banff. The Menzies family were kin of the Frasers, Alexander's grandfather having married Catherine, a daughter of Gilbert Menzies of Findon, a previous Aberdeen provost.[109] The Menzies family, moreover, were longstanding associates of the

Gordons of Huntly, whose current head, George, 1st marquis, stood high in favour with James VI. Local political and commercial interests may have been combined in the challenge.

The slump in Fraserburgh's fortunes as a result of the Frasers' financial crisis lasted until after 1610. The clearest sign of revival came in 1613 when Alexander Fraser drew up a new contract to define the political relationship between his family and the town. Now in his mid-seventies, his finances in ruins and major portions of the estate that he and his grandfather had so assiduously built up mortgaged or sold off, Alexander sought not simply to provide for the future financial stability of the community but also to safeguard this remaining jewel in his family's shrunken fortune from his creditors. While many of Alexander's more grandiose plans had come to nothing – there was evidently to be no attempt to resuscitate the university – the development of the burgh as a self-governing community proceeded apace. The 1601 charter of confirmation had authorised Fraser to create and elect bailies, treasurer, dean of guild, councillors and free burgesses. From that date until 1840, successive Frasers of Philorth nominated the barony council, with the laird as nominal provost.

It is unclear how many burgesses there were in the early 1600s. While the 1601 crown charter remained the basis upon which the council was organised, the council's powers and duties were redefined by the new contract of 1613 (registered 1627), which handed over customs, harbour and market dues, rights to gather bait, and some land, to form the Common Good. It is possibly this event that is commemorated in the 'good carving of Moses and the ten commandments' traditionally associated with the university and now preserved in the porch of the South Church.[110] Its subject, Moses handing down the laws, might better be considered as an allegory for Fraser's bestowal of privileges on the burgh, and the panel to have come from some civic structure. The feuars were all burgesses and later guildbrethren.[111] The contract was signed by 32 burgesses, indicating a flourishing community, and mentioned bakers, brewers, fleshers, fishermen, fish sellers, bleachers, weavers, dyers, masons, blacksmiths, wrights, knitters, saddlers, barbers, tailors, tanners, shoemakers, all the ingredients of a small but economically secure commercial community.[112]

Alexander Fraser's intention that his burgh should develop as a centre for seaborne trade appears to have been realised. In 1656, the port had four ships. They were only of 20 tons each, but it is a significant number compared with nine in Aberdeen, and one each in Peterhead and Inverness.[113] The 1696 Poll Tax returns underscore the extent of the burgh's maritime activities. Pollable individuals included 22 merchants, one skipper and 21 seamen, as well as a minister, schoolmaster and notary public.[114] The burgh's emergence as a commercial centre was confirmed by the existence by the late seventeenth century of an inn at the north corner of Saltoun Square Lane.[115] Success can also be measured by the construction of several large town-houses by prominent lairds from the surrounding area, whose business interests clearly demanded residences in Fraserburgh.

Although houses generally lined the street edge, larger houses and public buildings were probably set back from the very first. For example, once the Episcopalians were dispossessed from the parish church in 1717 they established themselves on a double plot set back from Mid Street. The early town-houses probably took the customary form of a courtyard comparable to the Baird of Auchmeddan Lodging in Banff. The initialled and dated reset 1687 date stone in the delectable Gordon's Court, No 32 Mid Street, may recall the town-house of Saltoun's factor (**fig 13**).[116] The Gill Lodging, *c* 1700, probably lay on the south side of the High Street with an entrance archway to a courtyard and substantial lodgings facing each other, with 'an imposing outside stone stairway leading to the upper flat'.[117] An armorial stone – PG and BS, 1746 – recorded Patrick Gill, tacksman of the mill of Fingask and his wife Barbara Spence (**fig 14**).[118] There was, apparently, a similar building at the head of the town, by 1914 a curing yard. 'It had quite the same imposing appearance, with remnants of the outside stair and other relics of grandeur, which showed much the worse of the wear, before it was knocked down'.[119]

FIGURE 13
Late seventeenth-century stone, dated 4 May 1687, reset in 1885 in Gordon's Court, Mid Street (Richard Oram)

FIGURE 14
Gill Lodging in the MacGibbon and Ross sketchbook, which notes a 1749 skewputt as well as the 1747 armorial that was moved to Rothes in 1907. This is a preparatory drawing for the published engraving (see fig 2) (Crown Copyright: RCAHMS)

A building on the north side of High Street, virtually beside the College by the entrance to Barrasgate, had 'several steps and iron hand-railings leading from the pavement up to the door'. Its existence may be recorded now by a sole *in situ* skewput dated 1761.[120] So although the evidence is slight (the late nineteenth-century herring-based prosperity having been very harmful to the old High Street), there is sufficient to conclude that Fraser's Broch had evolved into a substantial, well-built town of good quality and some distinction.

While the town propspered, the Frasers did not. The growing financial crisis hinted at by the crown's 1588 licence to sell £10,000-worth of land threatened to overwhelm Alexander from the mid-1590s. Portions of the estate – Aberdour, Scattertie, Tibertie and Utlaw – were effectively protected from his creditors by their alienation to his eldest son, Alexander (future 9th laird), to whom Pittulie was also granted in 1595–96 on the occasion of his marriage.[121] The bulk of the property remained exposed, however. Soon after the drawing up of the 1613 contract with the burgh, the position became critical and Alexander surrendered his estates to trustees empowered to sell off as much as was necessary to clear his debts and to infeft his eldest grandson, Alexander (future 10th laird), in the residue.[122] In 1615–16 the bulk of the barony was sold, revealing the scale of the debts accrued by the 8th laird in the pursuit of his ambitions. Significantly, the purchasers were all his close kin, indicating an effort to rescue the head of their line from ruin and to preserve the Fraser family's dominance of the locality.[123] Equally significant, however, was the fact that the superiority of Fraserburgh and two-thirds of the lands of Faithlie were retained in the hands of the Philorth Frasers.

Alexander Fraser, 8th of Philorth, died in 1623. His longevity meant that his son, Alexander, 9th laird, was already well into middle age when he succeeded. He was well connected – in 1595 he had married Margaret Abernethy, daughter of George Abernethy, 7th Lord Saltoun, and grand-daughter of one of the leading Catholics of the later sixteenth century, John Stewart, earl of Atholl[124] – but his heritage was significantly truncated. His position was further circumscribed by the fact that the bulk of what remained of the Philorth estates had been settled on his son, Alexander. As a result any ambitions he may have had were never to be realised and there is no indication of any notable development at Fraserburgh during his lifetime.

Rebellion and occupation, 1638–60

Alexander, 10th of Philorth, was confirmed during his father's lifetime in possession of the residue of the estate that had been placed in trust for him by his grandfather. In 1628 the trustees resigned their trust into the hands of the King's Commissioners in Scotland and Alexander's ownership was confirmed by crown charter on 15 March 1628.[125] On his father's death in *c* 1636 he obtained the rest of the Fraser heritage and succeeded to the Philorth title which, nominally at least, had been his father's.

Alexander's succession coincided with the eruption of the religious and political crisis that had been gathering in the face of the policies of Charles I. The new laird seems to have been a committed member of the growing political and religious opposition to the king. He subscribed to the National Covenant at Aberdeen in 1638, and participated in 1639 at the General Assembly of the Kirk in Glasgow at which the Episcopalian structure of the church, set in place by James VI, was overthrown and Charles I's religious policies systematically denounced. Fraser speedily demonstrated that his commitment to the Covenant was more than political posturing. In 1639 he joined Montrose's Covenanting army during its campaign against the royalist Gordons in the north-east, and commanded a force that attacked the Gordon houses of Kellie and Gight.[126] Despite this early activity against the crown, Alexander, like many north-eastern lairds, was moderate in his political and religious views, and seems to have been alienated by the increasingly extremist policies of the Covenanting regime. His moderatism led to his participation in 1647–48 in the Engagement, the agreement between Charles I and the less-radical Covenanters. In return for the support of a Scottish army against the forces of Parliament, the king would accept Presbyterianism in Scotland and give it a three-year trial in England. In 1648, he led a regiment of the Engagers' army into England, but escaped its defeat by Oliver Cromwell at Preston on 17–20 August. Alexander remained a committed supporter of the royalist cause and after the execution of Charles I in January 1649 declared his allegiance to the young Charles II. When Charles arrived in Scotland in June 1650, Alexander was swift to confirm his loyalty by advancing large sums of cash to the penniless king, cash which the still-burdened Philorth estate could ill afford. In 1651 he led a regiment in Charles II's army at Worcester and was captured after the rout of the royalist force.

Throughout this turbulent period Fraserburgh is effectively invisible in the historical record. This is primarily a consequence of the strongly Edinburgh-centric nature of the political and ecclesiastical affairs of the time, but the 10th laird's early commitment to the Covenant and military activity makes it unlikely that the burgh was entirely unaffected. Indeed, as later events suggest, it is probable that the port was actively engaged in the importation of arms and ammunition from Sweden and the United Provinces to supply the army of the Covenant. The burgh, too, would have been deeply affected by the shifting fortunes of its superior. Fraser's support for the Engagement would have seen him suffer exclusion from holding any office in both the government and military under the Act of Classes introduced in January 1649 by the extreme Covenanter regime now in power. This exclusion would have been a severe blow to Fraser's finances, but he was still capable of raising money to make substantial advances to Charles II in 1650. Of greater consequence for the position of Fraserburgh was the capture of Alexander at Worcester in September 1651. Following the conquest of

Scotland by Cromwell's forces during 1652, the Philorth estates would have been burdened by heavy fines and taxed to pay for the English troops quartered in the district. Fraser, moreover, would again have been excluded from holding public or military office and the jurisdiction he exercised over his burgh would have been suspended, depriving him of a much-needed source of revenue from which to pay his fines.

No details survive of the scale of the English garrison in Fraserburgh and its locality, but it is clear that it was an active military force quartered in an area of continuing hostility to the occupying power. In September 1656 a detachment of Cromwellian troops in Fraserburgh seized a consignment of arms and ammunition that had been shipped in to the port.[127] This was just one of several such seizures in that year, with other cargoes being taken at Aberdeen and Elgin, and also at Crail, a distribution that underlines the continuing Royalist activity in the north-east after the Cromwellian conquest of the country. Aberdeenshire in 1653–54 was still a centre of strong resistance to the English occupation.[128] It had been only in 1654 that the Royalist garrison of Kildrummy Castle had been forced to surrender and a Commonwealth force installed in its place. Continuing opposition to the Cromwellian regime might also be reflected in the election in 1658 of the Marquis of Argyle as MP for Aberdeenshire in the Commonwealth parliament, since Argyle was hostile to General Monck, Cromwell's Commander-in-Chief in Scotland.[129]

Restoration to revolution, 1660–88

The Commonwealth experiment had barely bedded in when it was swept away at the Restoration of Charles II in 1660. The Restoration settlement not only overturned the changes effected in Scottish government after 1651–52, but sought to turn the clock back to the position before 1638. The most profound effect was on the Church, which saw a return to the full-blown Episcopacy of the 1630s. Those synods which were dominated by hard-line Presbyterians were dissolved. The synod of Aberdeen, however, was encouraged by Charles to present an address to him on the subject of the future form of worship and church government, for its sympathies were strongly Episcopalian.[130] Despite his original commitment to the Presbyterians and the National Covenant of 1638, Fraser of Philorth, together with most of the Fraser family and their neighbours in northern Buchan, embraced the restored Episcopal church and remained Episcopalians thereafter. The conversion was not restricted to the nobility, for Episcopacy took a deep hold among the population in general and retained strong support into the late eighteenth century and beyond.[131]

The 10th laird may have benefited financially from the Restoration of the monarchy in 1660, for the family finances were sufficiently strong for him to begin the building of a new House of Philorth to replace the former ancestral caput at Cairnbulg. The recovery was short-lived, however, for before the close of the 1660s Alexander had fallen heir to the poisoned chalice which was the Saltoun inheritance. In 1669, Philorth claimed the title Lord Saltoun on the failure of the senior male line of the Abernethy family. The Saltoun title, held by the Abernethies since 1445, passed to the Frasers through the marriage of Alexander, 9th of Philorth, to Margaret Abernethy. Her heritage consisted of little more than the title, as the family estates had been sold off in the face of mounting debts. The 10th laird of Philorth was retoured (a legal term relating to inheritance of property) as heir to the Abernethy estates in April 1670, took his seat in Parliament on 9 August, and was confirmed in the Saltoun title by Act of Parliament on 22 August.[132] The Frasers of Philorth had joined the peerage of Scotland but this new dignity threatened ruin.

It was not just a title that new 10th Lord Saltoun had inherited; it was also the morass of litigation that had finally overwhelmed the Abernethies. He was immediately plunged into a long and costly series of lawsuits concerning the residue of the Abernethy estates, primarily the lands of Balvenie in Banffshire. After twenty years of debilitating struggle, Fraser lost the action.[133] The crisis was compounded by the character of his heir Alexander who was, according to family tradition, weak-willed, profligate and surrounded by unscrupulous friends who drained him of his money before his death in 1682. Like his grandfather before him, with debt threatening to overwhelm the Philorth estate, Lord Saltoun made over what remained of his property to his grandson William. He retained certain rooms for himself in the House of Philorth and the castle on Kinnaird Head, but also possessed a lodging in Fraserburgh itself, in which he died in August 1693.[134] This marked the end of a chapter in the Frasers' history for, although still crippled by his grandfather's debts, the 11th Lord Saltoun was to begin to turn around the family fortunes and to open a new phase in the development of Fraserburgh.

Turning tides, 1688–1715

Like many of the leading political figures of north-east Scotland, William Fraser was equivocal in his attitude to the Williamite revolution of 1688–90. Certainly, there is no sign that the Frasers had been alienated by the regime of James VII (James II of England). Indeed, in 1681, during the then James, Duke of York's, period of residence in Scotland, William Fraser had obtained from him the command of an infantry company.[135] Neither he nor his grandfather, however, became involved in the first Jacobite rising that ended at the battle of Cromdale in May 1690, but support for the overthrown king was strong within their properties. In 1693 his kinsman Charles Fraser of Inverallochy, 4th Lord Fraser, was tried before the High Court of Justiciary in Edinburgh, charged with having the previous year proclaimed King James at the cross in Fraserburgh, drunk his health and that of Prince James Francis (the Old Pretender), and cursed William of Orange and all his adherents, for which he was fined £200 Scots.[136]

The personal commitment of William, 11th Lord Saltoun, can be seen in such acts as his marriage in October 1683 to Margaret Sharpe, daughter of the assassinated Archbishop of St Andrews, James Sharpe, one of the great hate-figures of the Presbyterians.[137] Saltoun's stance was shared by many of his neighbours and tenants, and was to make itself manifest in the strong resistance shown to the new regime in Edinburgh after 1690. The traditional historiography of this period tends to present the political and religious changes which accompanied the overthrow of James VII and II as wholesale and rapidly achieved. His remaining supporters – the Jacobites – were swiftly marginalised and then effectively neutralised by May 1690, while there was an almost overnight transformation of the Kirk from an Episcopalian to a Presbyterian structure. Aberdeenshire, however, demonstrates the superficiality of that view. It remained dominated by strongly Jacobite families, such as the Forbeses, Frasers, Gordons and Leslies, and steadfastly ignored efforts to introduce Presbyterian ministers. Only two representatives of the whole Synod of Aberdeen attended the 1690 General Assembly in Edinburgh which sought to ratify the new religious settlement, while only one minister from the synod was present at the 1692 Assembly.[138] After that date, the numbers of Presbyterian ministers in the Synod of Aberdeen increased steadily, but in northern Buchan many pre-1690 incumbents remained in possession of their charges.

The Frasers' inactivity in 1688–90 may have stemmed from the continuing weakness of the family's finances rather than acceptance of the new regime. The litigation over the Saltoun inheritance was drawing to a close, but in 1689 William was obliged to sell the estate of Memsie to cover debts, followed in 1690 by a portion of Rathen.[139] William's involvement in the Company of Scotland and its failed colonial venture at Darien,[140] in particular, may have confirmed him in his opposition to William of Orange's government. Despite the financial lifeline which the Union settlement offered, Saltoun was among the peers in 1706 who remained opposed to the Union Bill.[141]

The political and religious upheavals of the later seventeenth century had a lingering effect on the prosperity and general life of Fraserburgh, but there is no hard evidence that the shifting fortunes of the burgh's superiors had a direct impact. Despite the succession of financial crises that struck the Frasers throughout the seventeenth century, it is clear that they were at pains to avoid losing control of Fraserburgh itself. Although one-third of Faithlie had been alienated in 1616, the Frasers maintained a majority interest in the burgh. Indeed, it is probable that the income derived from Fraserburgh was what largely kept the Frasers of Philorth and lords Saltoun from being overwhelmed by their debts. Although evidence is fragmentary, it is clear that the north-eastern ports enjoyed some foreign trade.[142] Connections with Scandinavia and the Baltic remained strong, and Fraserburgh was certainly involved in the flourishing timber trade with

Norway.[143] Most ships either went to Norway in ballast or did a three-way voyage, usually to Holland first with agricultural products such as grain and hides. If there was anything at this period exportable directly to Norway it was probably grain. By 1705 Fraserburgh was doing well enough to be taken under the wing of the Convention of Royal Burghs. Along with eight others, it was granted trade privileges in return for a contribution to the royal burghs' tax roll.[144]

Eighteenth century

The eighteenth century represented a period of protracted change for the burgh which was not entirely positive. The post-Union political climate was highly charged and in some areas, including much of Aberdeenshire, the religious upheavals of the 1690s had not yet been fully resolved. The strong support for Episcopalianism and Jacobitism in this part of Buchan went far deeper than the personal beliefs of a handful of leading noblemen. While flirtation with Jacobitism could, to an extent, be associated with the political and economic problems experienced by the nobility of much of lowland Scotland, religious nonconformity was not a recent development and cannot be attributed to any one economic factor. The townsfolk of Fraserburgh maintained a strong attachment to Episcopacy. The incumbent minister, a man of Episcopalian sympathies, died in 1703, and his son, more overtly Episcopalian, tried to succeed him. He was not confirmed by the Presbytery, which in 1706 ordered him to be ejected. In 1707, when members of the Presbytery of Deer attempted to induct a Presbyterian minister in Fraserburgh, they were set upon and chased away by 'a rabble of people who threw stones and dub or mire upon them', but, after another attempt, the new minister was installed later that year. The parish church was damaged in the riot, and repaired only in 1710.[145]

With William, Lord Saltoun, maintaining a very low political profile, leadership of the Jacobite interest locally fell on Alexander Forbes, 4th Lord Pitsligo, head of a staunchly Episcopalian branch of that family. The north-east proved to be a major centre of Jacobite support in 1715, but Saltoun's death in March 1715 probably saved his family from disastrous involvement in it. Instead it was Forbes of Pitsligo who led a substantial body of Buchan men to serve the Old Pretender.[146] Peterhead, under the leadership of Thomas Arbuthnott, had been the first of the north-eastern burghs to proclaim James Francis Stuart as 'King James VIII and III', and it was there that the Pretender eventually landed in December 1715. At Fraserburgh the new Lord Saltoun is said to have half-heartedly attempted to prevent the public proclamation of the Pretender as king, but to have backed down in the face of the threats of an armed band from Peterhead.[147]

Jacobitism and military occupation, 1715–1815
'The justice of the Government is as a foul stank'[148]

By the time James Francis Stuart landed at Peterhead, the rebellion had all but collapsed following the indecisive battle of Sheriffmuir on 13 November 1715. He was to sail again into continental exile from Montrose on 4 February 1716. The government took a generally lenient line with the defeated rebel nobility, imposing fines and other restrictions rather than resorting to wholesale forfeitures. More severe punishment was meted out to the principal Jacobite leaders such as the Earl of Mar and the Earl Marischal, whose estates were forfeited, and lords Derwentwater and Kenmure, who were executed. There were other casualties, in particular Episcopalian clergy, who were suspected of support for Jacobitism. In Fraserburgh the Episcopalian congregation was finally evicted from the parish church in 1717 as part of this punitive policy.

Lord Pitsligo, who had served prominently in the 1715 rising, also, at the age of 67, joined that of 1745–46. In the aftermath of the collapse of that rising, northern Buchan witnessed a punitive campaign by government troops as savage and destructive as the better-known repression of the Jacobite clans of the central and western Highlands. As a consequence Pitsligo was forfeited but, unlike many of his fellows, refused to find refuge in exile, and lived in hiding on his former estates. His property, however, was systematically plundered and the House of Pitsligo ransacked and burned by Flemish mercenaries in the service of the Hanoverian regime. These troops, who had a reputation for brutality, had been landed from a contingent of Admiral Byng's blockading fleet anchored in the roads at Fraserburgh. The victims of their depredations were not only those Jacobite lairds, such as Forbes of Pitsligo, Cumming of Pittulie and Fraser of Inverallochy, who were 'out' in the '45, but also Episcopalians such as Lord Saltoun. Although he had not participated in the rising, he was suspected of Jacobite sympathies, and Philorth House was ransacked. A contemporary account records the carriage of plunder from the houses of Pitsligo, Pittulie and others through Broadsea and Fraserburgh to be transported south by sea. 'Daily going through Bretsie was cartloads of plunder from the Castle of Pitsligo on their way to Fraserburgh, where they were schipped from the harbors if room permitted in Bynges schipps. So as not to break the setts, cartloads of cheeres would go on one schipping, sureting tables and oil pictures on one other, the hich ranking officers having first pick of the speeles'.[149]

Some of the Flemish troops were quartered in the school in Broadsea, where it was recorded that they 'every morning lit the fire with books and irreplaceable documents'.[150] A force was quartered in Fraserburgh for the duration of the operation and a garrison remained in the town until the late 1780s or early 1790s.[151] In the aftermath of Culloden, Lieutenant-Colonel Lord Ancrum had been charged with the establishment of a series of garrison posts throughout Buchan. At Fraserburgh, he ordered construction of a guard-post at the western end of the High Street, opposite the College Tower, with both carriage and pedestrian gates to police the movement of traffic along the main road running to the west. A second guard-post ('the Barrack guard-post'), also with gates, stood at the southern end of Cross Street. The main garrison was established at the southern entrance to the burgh. By the time of its withdrawal after *c* 1785, the military had evidently constructed a substantial complex of buildings, with a house for the commanding officer – the 'Colonell's house' – behind which stood a three-storey barrack block.[152]

This, however, was not the limit of the garrison's presence, for the military commandeered other property in the burgh. The former town-house of the Frasers of Philorth, on the site now occupied by the Saltoun Arms Hotel, was taken over as officers' quarters. Behind it, in 'the Saltoun Close', entered from the High Street, was the steading associated with the castle on Kinnaird Head and the so-called 'Kinnaird Head Garden', both of which were taken over by the army. Land outside the town was used as grazing for the military's animals and as garden plots for the troops. An extensive area of the burgh's rigs and common grazing ('the Links') stretching from the Pittulie crossroads on the main road west, south over Gallowhill to Dennyduff House (which stood in the vicinity of the Thomas Walker Hospital in Charlotte Street), was steadily encroached upon and the townsfolk edged out. By the 1780s the army had divided the whole area into a series of parks and Lord Saltoun eventually gave the burgh a large area of the sandy bents along the foreshore south of the burgh to make up for the loss.[153]

Fraserburgh clearly did not escape unscathed from the brutality of the occupying troops: 'We lived through a rain [sic] of terror and Fraserburgh had seen a time as never before, knowing deep in our hearts never in our time would we ever be the same again'.[154] It is evident that the Fraserburgh area endured a long-lived and deeply resented military occupation. Contemporary memoirs describe 'an atmosphere of subjugation' and, even in the 1760s and 1770s, 'most cruel, ruthless and brutal persecution', religious as well as political.[155] In May 1746, as the government tightened its grip following the collapse of the rebellion, Orders in Council were issued instructing firm action against 'Non-Jurant Meeting-houses', followed by specific instructions to the Scottish authorities to enforce the new policy.[156] This assault on the Episcopalians was a result of the perceived link between Episcopacy and Jacobitism, and the assumption that non-jurant clergy were Jacobites who preached anti-Hanoverian politics to their flocks.[157] In Fraserburgh in 1746 the Episcopal meeting-house in Mid Street was burnt down on the orders of Lord Ancrum. The homeless congregation, prohibited from assembling in groups of more than four, then met in various houses, including their minister's home in Middleburgh, outside the town, until they were able to provide themselves with a new church in the milder climate of the 1780s.[158]

Apart from the targeting of the Episcopalian meeting-house and the ransacking of the homes of local lairds involved in or sympathetic towards the Jacobite rising, Fraserburgh appears to have escaped the widespread forfeitures after 1746. Only one property within the burgh, Warld's End in Dalrymple Street (**figs 15 &16**), owned by John Gordon of Glenbuchat, one of the key Jacobite commanders in the '45, was seized along with the rest of his estate. The subsequent litigation continued for many years, with Glenbuchat's son-in-law, James Dalgardno of Milnhill, who had had no involvement in the rebellion, claiming that the property had been assigned to him in 1743 as part of his marriage contract. Counter-claims from various creditors, including the Duke of Gordon, who maintained that the Fraserburgh property was part of the security against a wadset (pledge for the money borrowed) owed by Glenbuchat to him, led to the disposal of at least a portion of the property, including the Fraserburgh house, by public roup (auction) in 1766.[159]

It is not known how many Fraserburgh men participated in the '45. The most prominent individual identified was Alexander Gill, a shipmaster, who held a commission as a lieutenant in Lord Pitsligo's regiment of horse. His

FIGURE 15
Warld's End, Dalrymple
Street (Crown Copyright:
RCAHMS)

FIGURE 16
Measured survey drawing
of Warld's End, 1976 (Crown
Copyright: RCAHMS)

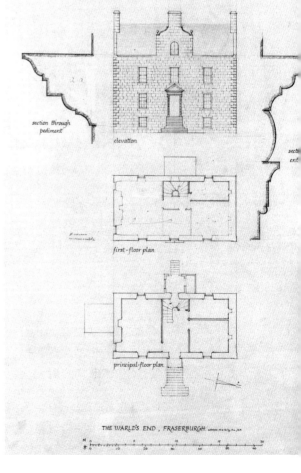

THE WARLD'S END, FRASERBURGH

fate is unknown.[160] Published records note that George Brown, jailer of Fraserburgh, made only one return to the authorities listing three Jacobites imprisoned there, all of whom were discharged in September 1746.[161] A further five Fraserburgh men were listed as being involved in the rebellion.[162] There were casualties, too, from among local families. David Lascelles joined the rebellion aged fourteen or sixteen as valet to Charles Fraser of Inverallochy, and was killed at Culloden.[163]

The importance of sea-borne traffic around the north-east coast of Scotland had been tellingly revealed in the role played by the region in the wars and rebellions of the seventeenth century. The openness of this part of the coast to hostile naval operations had also been exposed in 1715 and again in 1745. On the latter occasion, however, the government had been swift to react and Byng's squadrons had very effectively sealed off access to the region by sea. During the Jacobite army's northward withdrawal after the battle of Falkirk, government ships had shadowed them and were used to evacuate loyalists from Inverness. The 24-gun HMS *Glasgow* and three sloops were deployed to blockade the Moray and Cromarty Firths, where they intercepted three French merchantmen with cargoes of arms and men for the Jacobites. The *Glasgow* remained on blockade duty in the area until September 1746, and it was as part of a naval operation that the harrying of the Jacobite households of northern Buchan was undertaken.[164] The naval presence in the Moray Firth did not last beyond the end of 1746. Britain's growing imperial commitments required redeployment of the vessels elsewhere, but garrisons were established on shore to deal with any further Jacobite threat.

The removal of the warships left the sea-lanes exposed to attack and in the course of the Seven Years War with France (1756–63) merchantmen in the northern sector of the North Sea fell prey to foreign privateers. The problem worsened in the last quarter of the eighteenth century during the succession of wars between Britain and France and her allies. French privateers were attracted to the Buchan coast by the volume of shipping passing Kinnaird Head, knowing that the Royal Navy was busy patrolling the Channel and maintaining communication with the colonial campaigns.[165]

It was the late 1780s before the garrison was withdrawn from Fraserburgh and the barracks at the southern edge of the town sold off.[166] By 1797, however, Fraserburgh was once again a military depot with a regular garrison. The outbreak of the Revolutionary and subsequent Napoleonic Wars with France after 1789, led to a very real fear of a French landing.[167] Popular tradition identified the soldiers' quarters as a block of buildings in Barrack Lane, perhaps reusing the post-1746 barracks, but it is possible that the post-1797 arrangements are being confused with the more substantial mid-eighteenth-century complex.

At the height of the 'invasion scares' in 1803, when Napoleon had assembled an army some 150,000 strong at Dunkirk and massed his fleet at Boulogne, the Fraserburgh Volunteers were set up, and applied for somewhere suitable to store their ammunition. The council was 'of opinion that the [Wine] Tower in the Castle Park would be a very secure place'. Lord Saltoun's agent agreed, but inspection revealed that the roof leaked, so the building was overhauled and most of the windows bricked up for security.[168] From 1803 until the end of hostilities in 1814 most news from Fraserburgh in the *Aberdeen Journal* was confined to reports on the drilling and inspections of the Fraserburgh Battalion of Volunteer Infantry, the Fraserburgh regiment of Local Militia, and the Fraserburgh Volunteer Artillery Company.[169]

Despite the fears of central government there were no insurrections in Scotland inspired by the French Revolution. There were, however, a number of 'popular disturbances', driven primarily by economic factors, which served to add to the tense political climate. One of the most significant factors behind these disturbances was the dislocation of the international grain trade with the Continent because of British involvement in the wars against France. In Scotland, rising prices and local scarcity of grain prompted a series of food riots between 1780 and 1813, mostly in two main areas, Dumfries and Galloway and the east coast from Largo in Fife round to Dingwall in Ross. The last such riot occurred on 6 March 1813 at Fraserburgh, when a mob led by one George Murison attacked the premises of merchants involved (or believed to be involved) in the export of meal, grain and potatoes. Like earlier riots elsewhere around the country, it was caused not so much by local shortages but by fears that the export of local supplies by merchants seeking to profit from shortages elsewhere in the country would lead to higher prices and scarcity at home. At Fraserburgh, the rioters turned back carts which tried to approach ships in the harbour, then closed off all access from the town to the harbour.[170] There was no identifiable political agenda behind the disturbance, which petered out once tempers cooled, though the suspected ringleaders were still pursued by the authorities. After the raw emotion of the mid-eighteenth century and evidence for a local radical tradition, it was a rather anticlimactic end to a turbulent period in Fraserburgh.

Enterprise, expansion and improvement, *c* 1720–*c* 1820

The strategic value of this coastal district, however, was not just military or naval, for its commerce was to develop rapidly through the eighteenth and early nineteenth centuries, and the lords Saltoun, as superiors and nominal provosts, were to remain at the forefront of efforts to secure and develop Fraserburgh's share of maritime trade. Although this was an era of improvement in land management and agriculture, for Lord Saltoun it was the sea that held the key to Fraserburgh's prosperity. In 1726 Daniel Defoe had commented that 'the country of Buchan, is, indeed, more to be taken notice of from what is to be seen on the sea-shore than in the land; for the country is mountainous, poor, and more barren than its neighbours'.[171] He observed that Aberdeen, but also all the ports along the Aberdeenshire coast, were benefiting from the development of commercial fisheries. 'The herring-fishing is a common blessing to all this shore of Scotland, and is like the Indies at their door; the merchants of Aberdeen cannot omit the benefit, and with this they are able to carry on their trade to Dantzick and Konigsberg, Riga and Narva, Wybourgh and Stockholm, to the more advantage'. Potential for further development was hinted at in his comment that Buchan Ness 'is generally the first land of Great Britain, which the ships make in their voyages home from Arch-Angel in Russia, or from their whale-fishing-voyages to Greenland and Spits-Berghen in the north seas'.[172] Fraserburgh, as an already-established port on what was otherwise an exposed section of coast, seemed well placed to capitalise on this developing trade.

Evidence for Fraserburgh's wider maritime trade in the early eighteenth century is fragmentary. There is, however, good evidence for its involvement in the busy coastal trade around north-eastern Scotland, the Moray Firth and beyond. In 1718, for example, John Stewart, an Inverness-based merchant, instructed his agent that 'barks' to carry meal from Banff to Portsoy should be found in either Banff or Fraserburgh.[173] Four years later, Stewart recorded that 'The ship *Ann* is not yet arrived at Findhorn that I hear of, but doe suppose that she be at Fraserbrugh, a harbour 60 miles from thence, where are severall oyr shipes at present bound up this frith, where they are deteaned by hard gales of westerly winds'.[174]

Fraserburgh was clearly functioning as a harbour of refuge on an otherwise exposed coast. The town, however, was also operating as a significant outlet for agricultural produce from its rural hinterland. In May 1729, for example, Stewart wrote that one of his vessels was taking on a cargo of meal at Fraserburgh for sale in the Western Isles, and that he was seeking to secure 500 or 600 more bolls of meal at the port.[175] The inference is that the cargo amounted to around 1500 bolls (9000 bushels or 327,600 litres), which indicates a substantial trade in grain. The export of agricultural produce from the town's rural hinterland remained significant well into the nineteenth century, but it was a low-key activity locked into local and regional trading patterns rather than wider international trade.

A good harbour was imperative for the commercial development of the burgh, but it was not until 1738, with the building of a 'bulwark' (probably on roughly the same position as the North Pier of 1811) and a 'pier' (probably on the site of the first part of the Mid Pier), that the late sixteenth-century harbour was redeveloped.[176] This new harbour, which was probably of great benefit to Byng's seamen in 1746, and can be seen on Roy's map of *c* 1750 (**map 5**), formed the first stage in a programme of commercial development along the shore. In 1791 the minister described the harbour as 'small, but good ... Vessels of 200 tons burden enter at present', and claimed that there was a reasonably good roadstead outside the harbour. At that time the harbour was a trading facility, not a fishing port. Fishing had, nevertheless, become an important part of the local economy before the 1790s, under the Frasers, who had been granted the rights to it in the sixteenth century, but the operation was based entirely in the separate village of Broadsea.[177] Cod and lobsters caught by local fishermen were exported to London, but large commercial Dutch busses (ships) dominated the industry, taking their catch to the Netherlands. Fishing from Broadsea was carried out in small open boats, which had a roughly ten-mile range, but further development was hindered by the lack of a good harbour.[178]

Although not yet a fishing port *per se*, Fraserburgh was well established before 1820 as a significant player in the fish export trade. By 1810, at least 4000 barrels of herring per annum passed through the port, but this was trivial compared to what was to come. The expansion of the commercial herring fisheries around the coast of Scotland has been attributed largely to the increase of the government's herring bounty in 1815 to 4 shillings (20p) per barrel, but the appointment in that same year of the first Fishery Officer to cover the area from Peterhead to Banff indicates that the fishery was already significant in scale and value.[179] Herring fishing had long been carried out on a small scale, but the bounty encouraged its commercial development. The season was short, between July and September, and the fishery used boats of different form to those employed in inshore fishing, and drift nets rather than lines. While some fishermen turned to this work for the season, there were others, especially among the crews, who were not full-time fishermen, but worked on the herring boats as a break from other occupations.

Growth was rapid after 1815, despite the size of boats needed, the cost and fragility of the nets, and the short season, which made herring fishing capital-intensive. A trade directory in 1825 listed eleven fish-curers and three fishery officials based in the town. Most of the catch was cured by pickling or drying, and exported to the West Indies, though a gradually increasing amount went to northern Europe and Russia. By the time the bounty was abolished in 1830 it had served to increase the scale of the fisheries significantly. Its withdrawal was compounded in 1833, however, by the abolition of slavery in all British possessions, for herring had been a significant element in the slaves' diet. Overall, the result was a short depression, from which the trade began to recover in 1835, and from then into the 1840s, catches rose and new markets were found in the expanding northern European cities.[180]

Fraserburgh had been conceived in the sixteenth century as a trading port, and mercantile operations continued to dominate its economy until well into the nineteenth century. The *Old Statistical Account* provides a snapshot of the trading activity by *c* 1790, listing seven vessels of 50 to 100 tons involved in coasting and foreign trade.[181] The 1797 *Encyclopaedia Britannica* described Fraserburgh as possessing a 'small, good harbour, made and kept up by the proprietor and the town', which could take vessels up to 200 tons and enjoyed a small North Sea trade.[182] Development may have been hindered, however, by circumstances outside the control of the burgesses. The Customs House was 44 miles (70.8km) away in Aberdeen, reinforcing the domination of the area's trade by Fraserburgh's old rival.[183]

In the early nineteenth century plans were set in train for a massive extension of the port facilities. A report and plans commissioned from John Rennie were delivered in 1802. In 1804 a subscription raised almost £2000 (£800 from Lord Saltoun alone) to build this harbour, to provide low-water piers and better shelter. Despite the subscription, funds were insufficient

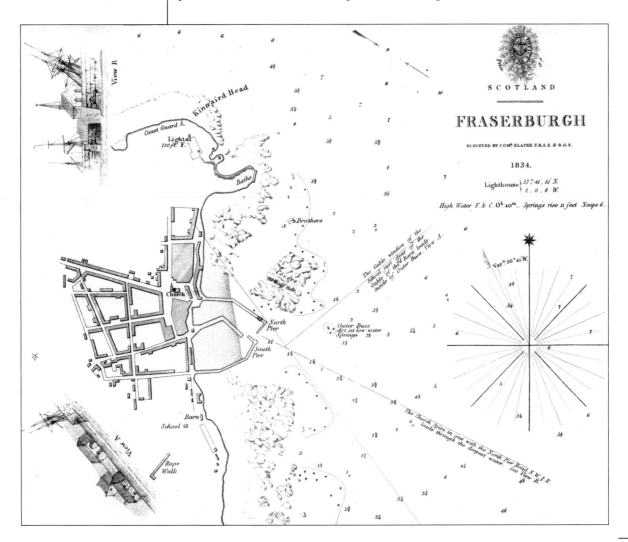

to develop the whole plan at once, so the burgh started on piecemeal improvements. In 1807 William Stewart, who had been involved in building the Crinan Canal, took up a salaried post to oversee the development of the harbour, and by the time of his departure in 1811 the 300-yard long North Pier had been built at a cost of over £11,000 (**map 6**).[184] The *New Statistical Account* comments that the North Pier was not considered satisfactory. Rennie had also proposed a pier and breakwater on the line occupied by the later Balaclava Pier and Breakwater, but funds had not been available at that time. When they did become available, the council, in association with Alexander, 16th Lord Saltoun, consulted Robert Stevenson, and in 1818 started to build the South Pier that he had recommended. Work on this project was completed *c* 1821–22.[185] Developments in infrastructure and an increasing volume of trade led to the establishment in 1818 of Harbour Commissioners, chaired by the baron bailie.[186]

The growing movement of shipping demanded greater protection for vessels and crews. The first lifeboat was provided in 1806 by public subscription, with Forbes of Pitsligo making a substantial donation.[187] A lifeboat house, shown on Robert Stevenson's 1818 harbour plan, was built beside the old harbour.[188] The hazards of the headland north of the port had been recognised when the Northern Lighthouse Board was established in 1786, and the first lighthouse they authorised was built on top of the old castle on Kinnaird Head, and lit on 1 December 1787 (**fig 17**).[189] In 1830 the light was improved and the surrounding keepers' accommodation added by Robert Stevenson.[190]

It is uncertain how much of Fraserburgh's trading fleet was locally built. The *Old Statistical Account* states that 'shipbuilding has been attempted here, and has succeeded well, especially since the peace of 1783'.[191] A later shipbuilder, John Dalrymple, established a business in the early 1800s, which continued to *c* 1830.[192] A commercial directory in 1825 listed four

FIGURE 17
The lighthouse on Kinnaird Head (Paula Martin)

boatbuilders, who would have serviced the needs of the growing fleet of small fishing vessels, but only one shipbuilder. In 1803 a rope- and sail-works was established on a site now partly overlain by Bellslea Park but at that date some distance beyond the southern edge of the town (**map 6**). It lasted until *c* 1865, when the arrival of the railway allowed the cheaper, mass-production outputs of the large rope- and sail-works in industrial centres further south to reach the Fraserburgh market.[193]

The industrial base of northern Buchan remained restricted despite the efforts of improving landlords such as Forbes of Pitsligo. Quarrying was carried on to a limited extent, probably mainly for local use. In the 1790s 'limestone' was quarried at Broadsea and along the Water of Philorth, but this seems to have been a generic term used loosely to describe any fine-grained stone and refers probably to sandstone. Ironstone sources had been identified, but remained unexploited largely because of the unavailability of coal to fuel the smelting of ore. This lack of coal was a product of the high levels of duty imposed on the movement of the fuel north of the Red Head in Angus, an imposition that was lifted in 1793. Kelp burning to produce an alkaline ash used in a variety of industrial processes, such as glass- and soap-making, was also recorded, but it never developed to the extent of the Hebridean industry. Its production appears to have ended on the east coast by the early nineteenth century. The only significant manufacture mentioned in statistical sources was linen yarn, using imported Dutch flax,[194] and it is possible that this industry provided Fraserburgh with some of its later eighteenth-century prosperity.

The development of linen manufacturing in the north of Scotland was largely a product of the efforts of the Commissioners of the Annexed Estates, the board set up in 1755 to administer the properties forfeited by leading Jacobites, including Alexander, 4th Lord Pitsligo.[195] The Commissioners were concerned principally with the Highland estates that had been seized by the crown under the 1752 Act of Annexation, and had first embarked on a radical policy of social, economic and religious reorganisation. Industrial development was a key component in this policy, but few projects they initiated had achieved any significant success before the board was dissolved in 1784. To what extent either the Annexed Estates board or the Board of Trade and Manufactures was responsible for the emergence of linen manufacturing in northern Buchan remains unclear, but it is evident that by the 1790s linen was a significant element in the economy of Fraserburgh's hinterland.[196] The area around Strichen, 11km south-south-west of Fraserburgh, was noted by *c* 1800 as a centre of linen manufacture.[197] There is no evidence, however, for linen weaving being undertaken on an industrial basis in Fraserburgh.[198] A small business, weaving wool rather than linen, was owned by William Noble in the late eighteenth century, but was bankrupted when the cheap output of the Lancashire mills flooded into Scottish markets.[199]

Despite the limitations of Fraserburgh's trade, it would seem that by the middle of the eighteenth century the economic benefits of the 1707 Union were making an impact even in this provincial port. The rebuilding of the harbour in 1738 may have been the trigger for future development, perhaps accelerated by Fraserburgh's status as a significant garrison town after the '45. From about 1750, the burgh experienced a period of sustained economic growth, accompanied by redevelopment. In 1752 the guildry built a warehouse (Merchants' House),[200] the start of a concentration of commercial buildings around the Shore. In 1766–67 Shore House (**fig 18**) was built on the opposite side of the Stinking Stairs to the Crown Inn (itself highly significant and concealing an older cottage behind), just beneath Braeheads. Of finely dressed granite on a commanding site, Shore House contained spacious assembly rooms on the upper floor, and served as both business and social centre.[201] In 1781, however, the council was still trying to raise money to pay for it, and gave a prize at a horse race to help raise funds.[202] In 1770, a branch of the Aberdeen Banking Company opened nearby, beside the old post office.[203] Ten years later, this cluster of buildings was completed by the construction of the present Harbour Office at the shore end of the Mid Pier

FIGURE 18
Shore House, Shore Street,
built 1766–67
(Charles McKean)

FIGURE 19
Harbour Office, at the
head of the Mid Pier,
built 1780, its quality still
showing despite unfortunate
alterations (Paula Martin)

(**fig 19**).[204] Overall, the picture is one of steady, if unspectacular, development. The Shore remained the town's principal business centre until it moved up to Broad Street and Saltoun Square in the 1830s.

On the south of the town, the post-1745 Barracks appear to have occupied all the land between the main road to Aberdeen (later Saltoun Street, on which the garrison had erected a gate) and the raised ground just behind Warld's End. Thus they probably occupied the land lying inland from and belonging to Warld's End, the town-house of the forfeited Jacobite, John Gordon of Glenbuchat (see **figs 15 & 16**). It seems likely that Glenbuchat's land sloped uphill from the Shore toward the ridge, and that the military levelled it off, creating a terrace immediately behind his mansion, which may itself have been refashioned in its present substantial and elegant form at about this time as the Governor's House. Although said to date from *c* 1767, it is almost certainly earlier or incorporates much of an earlier structure.[205] As the century progressed, the Barracks' importance dwindled and its site provided an opportunity for future urban redevelopment.

Commercial optimism was also evident in plans for developing the town as a tourist destination. In the late 1760s a mineral well had been discovered at Peterhead and a moderately successful spa was established. The *Old Statistical Account* had noted that there were fine mineral springs in different locations in Fraserburgh, but 'an excellent one, of a chalybeate nature, resembling the waters of Peterhead, but reckoned by judges more fit for weak constitutions, was discovered, a few years ago, on the south east corner of the town'.[206] By 1791 this was being marketed along with 'public rooms for Company'.[207]

The next development was the creation of two cold baths cut from the rocks below Kinnaird Head, which filled with seawater at each high tide. Then came buildings which, to judge by plans (**map 6**) and Daniell's drawing of them, comprised a long, low, two-storey building occupying the east side of the promontory; it had a pitched roofed, a central bow and projecting pavilions. It seems that the town had achieved its goal of challenging Peterhead, for in 1807 the *Aberdeen Journal* praised Fraserburgh's facilities as:

> the neatest and completest set of Baths erected and in a delightful situation for air and walking [which] ... do credit to the architect as well as to the spirit of the promoters, and particularly the Magistrate of the place, a very intelligent active, and public spirited character ... Scarcely can anything be imagined neater than the Warm and Cold Baths and the dressing places for either. The mineral Water too is light and not unpleasant to the taste, and the medical gentlemen assert very efficacious.[208]

The 'magistrate' credited may be either the young 16th Lord Saltoun or the baron bailie, William Kelman,[209] although another inspiration could have been Saltoun's mother, Margery Fraser, who, with her father, Simon Fraser of Ness Castle, administered the estate during her son's minority.[210] By 1808 there were baths, pump-room and bathing machine, all ready for visitors.[211] Fraserburgh was described in a guide to the watering-places of Scotland in 1822 as a bathing centre of consequence, 'well provided in every requisite', with 'numbers resorting to it in the summer season'.[212] The baths survived on limited local custom for some time, but eventually failed as a commercial venture, the area made much less attractive as the herring fishing grew and the harbour expanded northwards.[213]

Landward communications beyond the immediate hinterland were greatly enhanced when the first turnpike road reached Fraserburgh in 1810, providing faster and easier overland access. Perhaps this encouraged the developers of the baths to hope for a matching growth in tourist traffic. Local landowners and the burgh's traders also looked on the road as a means of stimulating the overland transport of agricultural produce, especially grain, meal and potatoes, and the output of cottage industries (such as linen spinning) to the port for carriage by sea.[214] The improvement of the road westward from Fraserburgh towards Banff in 1816 further enhanced the town's prospects.

Social and cultural life diversified in tandem with the commercial development of the burgh. Freemasonry, often associated with nonconformist politics, made an appearance when Solomon Lodge was established in 1765, but it had collapsed by the end of the century, leaving no surviving records.[215] The lodge was resuscitated in around 1806, holding its meetings in the old Town-house. It seems to have prospered initially, taking sasine of a property at the north side of The Green in 1818, as well as other land down by the

Shore, but closed again in 1837.[216] The failure of freemasonry to establish itself locally may have been due to the success of an alternative forum. The 'Gardeners' Friendly Society of Fraserburgh', a gentlemen's club formed for social and benevolent purposes, was established in 1791 and proved a great success. In 1801 it used its fundraising strength to build the Saltoun Inn (later the Saltoun Arms Hotel) as a commercial enterprise (**fig 20**).[217] In 1777 the first meeting of subscribers to the Buchan Golf Club was held in Fraserburgh.[218]

In the quieter political and religious climate of the later eighteenth century, the Episcopalian congregation was able to re-establish its presence in the burgh. A new 'neat' chapel had been built by 1791, when the charge was held by Alexander Jolly, the future Bishop of Moray.[219] This revival coincided with the re-emergence of the most prominent of the dispossessed local Episcopalian families, the Forbeses of Pitsligo, who bought back their former estates from the government.

The expansion of the burgh's population was beginning to place pressure on the available supplies of water. The lade running behind Frithside Street does not seem to have been intended as a source of drinking water, its primary functions being to drive a mill down by the present Mid Pier and to scour out the harbour, but it probably serviced the domestic needs of that end of the town. As part of his contract with the town in 1787, Lord Saltoun

FIGURE 20
Saltoun Arms Hotel, Saltoun
Square (Paula Martin)

appears to have secured the partial rerouting of the lade, but it was still supplying the harbour mill in the later nineteenth century.[220] The lade was the only open source of running water in Fraserburgh and there are very few recorded public wells in the burgh.[221] In 1804 a water system using wooden pipes was installed to meet demand, running from near Pitblae farm, at that date 2km south-west of the town, to a reservoir on the West Links. The early date of this provision suggests that the lack of water was a serious concern and may have been seen as threatening the development of the burgh.[222]

Another indication of an expanding population is the provision of a new burgh school. The exact location of its precursor, first mentioned in 1601,[223] has not been identified. Tradition implies that the seventeenth-century grammar school had occupied part of the old university property, but a late reference to the 'old school' infers a location at one or other end of Hanover Street. At the beginning of the eighteenth century a new school was built at the southern edge of the town near Brick Lodge.[224] This is presumably the school which gave its name to School Street. The new school needed repairs by 1735 and was described in 1748 as 'ruinous', but it was not until 1787 that a replacement was built on the Links, on the site later occupied by the South Church (**map 6**).[225]

These developments were part of wider significant changes in the burgh's appearance. The minister in 1791 commented that 'many new houses have been erected within these few years … neatly built, and covered with slates or tyles'.[226] It is not entirely clear what motivation lay behind the plan for Fraserburgh's proposed extensions, or two new towns, to north and south. On the other hand, it would have been surprising if the town had *not* contemplated such expansion. After all, it was in the centre of the north-east Scotland improvement landscape dotted with many new towns such as Strichen, which probably depended upon the port. Just a few miles to the east lay the estate of the pioneer Sir William Forbes of Pitsligo, who had bankrolled much of Edinburgh's New Town and built the village of New Pitsligo. Links between Fraserburgh and Forbes are demonstrated by the latter's substantial contribution to Fraserburgh's lifeboat in 1805.[227] Moreover, the parish's population, predominantly urban, increased by over 30% between 1755 and 1801 (**fig 21**).[228]

Whether or not it was associated with the baths – and embryonic plans including a Bath Street imply that it was – a proposal for a Fraserburgh new town emerged in the early 1800s in the Kinnaird Castle policies. The spine was to be a wide new road – Castle Street – planned to sweep through the lands to the north from Saltoun Square virtually to the tower on Kinnaird Head (**maps 6 & 7**).[229] A cross street, which might have been laid out by the 1790s, was renamed Duke Street after a visit by the Duke of Clarence in 1826.[230] In 1807 the *Aberdeen Journal* found 'the town … not only neat and clean, but considerably enlarged and the foundation laid for more extensive

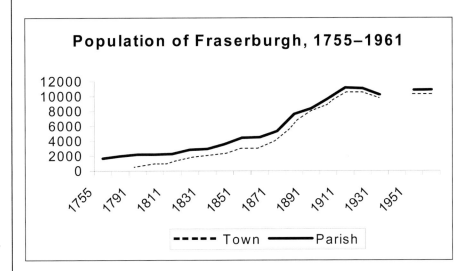

FIGURE 21
Graph showing the
population figures for
Fraserburgh town and parish,
1755–1961

improvements'.[231] However, the ambition implied in plans of streets stretching north and east to the bathing facilities remained largely unfulfilled. Only Castle Street was built in the neo-classical manner, and that only partially by the 1840s[232] (much was lost to bombing during the Second War). Only the courtyard buildings on the corner of North Street, and the range of simple classical, two-storey houses with wide segmentally arched pends, survive to indicate the formal urbanism that was intended. Houses on North Street are, for the most part, later cottages of the mid-nineteenth century, whereas those on Duke Street, and in the lanes north and south of it, are larger, and retain the strong character of the earlier period.

Part of the ethos of improvement involved attempting to rename some town centre streets (see p.16, Section 3). The new names did not stick, however, apart from the renaming of Kirk Green as Saltoun Square.[233] Expansion at the western end of High Street is marked by the naming of Caroline Place after the Prince Regent's slighted and divorced wife, Caroline of Brunswick (1768–1821). The new developments included a more regular street-plan imposed over the earlier arrangements. Love Lane, said to have existed by 1713,[234] possibly represents a late seventeenth- or early eighteenth-century expansion that pre-dates the regular laying out of Commerce Street, Saltoun Place and Seaforth Street. Commerce Street, as far west as School Road, was laid out between about 1818 and 1820, at an early stage in a southern extension of the town.[235] It may have been developed from an earlier approach to Brick Lodge, a large suburban villa built in 1784 in private grounds at the south-western corner of the town.[236] The line of Cross Street may have been straightened in the late eighteenth century, at which time Hanover Street may have been created or developed from the realignment of an earlier lane.[237] There were also significant developments along the harbour frontage. By 1818 the grounds of World's End had become Dalrymple Street (**map 7**).[238]

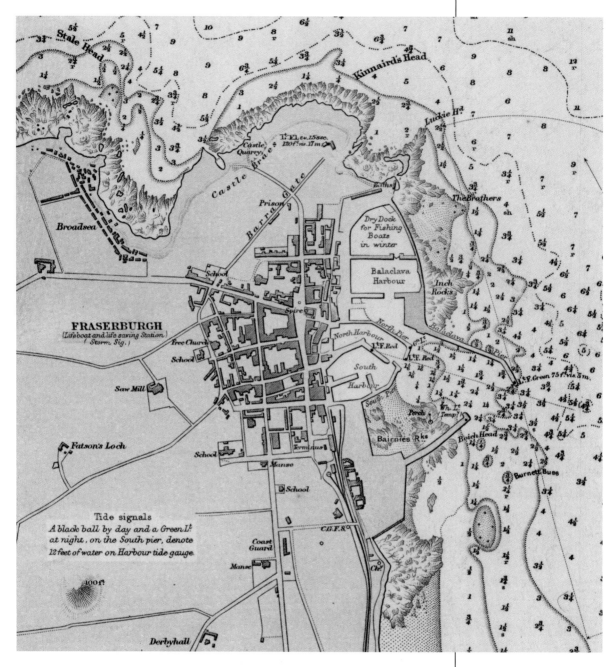

Central to this spurt of civic improvement, however, was the transformation and probable northward enlargement of Kirk Green, at the head of the town, into a suitably imposing classical town centre, renamed Saltoun Square.[239] The first step was the construction of that essential accessory of a modernising town, the 'new and elegant' inn. In 1801 the Gardeners' Friendly Society of Fraserburgh commissioned local mason Alexander Morrice to build the Saltoun Inn (**fig 20**). With its two parlours, dining room, six bedrooms and kitchen, large hall and drawing room, and garret, along with offices, garden and stable yard,[240] it provided a fashionable place in which the burgh's commercial classes could transact business, probably replacing the assembly rooms on the Shore. Although its roofscape dates from the later nineteenth century, its lower two floors are earlier, dating from 1801, if not to the earlier building on the site, Saltoun's former Town-house. The original Kinnaird Head Castle stables were reused as its back court. At about the same time, Nos 14–16 Saltoun Square, also probably designed by Morrice, were erected as the head to the Saltoun Arms' left shoulder, facing down Broad Street (**fig 22**). Although later used by freemasons and a bank, the fact that its window embrasures once reached down to ground level implies that they were originally open arcades, and that the building might therefore have been intended for a market, a smaller version of that recently constructed in nearby Peterhead.[241]

The Presbytery had provided a new manse for the minister in 1758, but the recently refurbished parish church was still adequate for the needs of the congregation.[242] By the early nineteenth century, however, during what

FIGURE 22
Nos 14–16 Saltoun Square
(Paula Martin)

was to be a peak period of rebuilding for Scottish parish churches, the Kirk Session of Fraserburgh was claiming that its old parish church was dilapidated and unsuited for the growing population.[243] Its replacement, also designed by Alexander Morrice, was opened on the same site in 1803 (**fig 23**). The spire, aligned to close the vista down High Street, was also intended to serve as a navigation mark for seamen (see **map 6** and broadsheet).[244] Local tradition recounts that its construction was delayed for lack of funds, and it was eventually built shorter than the original design, to save money.[245] A new manse was added in 1818, to the south of the town, on the road to Peterhead (**fig 24**).[246]

FIGURE 23
Parish Kirk, Saltoun Square, built 1803
(Charles McKean)

FIGURE 24
Manse of 1818, No 7 Saltoun
Place (Paula Martin)

Early nineteenth century, c 1820–40

The confident expansion of the burgh accelerated from 1820. Although Alexander, 16th Lord Saltoun, retained his family's controlling interest in the affairs of the burgh, he was a professional soldier and spent little time at home. His military career spanned 50 years and he saw distinguished service in the Peninsular War (1811–14), at Waterloo in 1815, and in the military occupation of France (1815–18), culminating in the Opium Wars in China in the 1840s.[247] In his absence, oversight of burgh affairs fell increasingly to the baron bailie, typified by Lewis Chalmers, who dominated the political and commercial life of Fraserburgh in the 1820s and 1830s.[248] While he may have been a largely absentee landlord, 'The Waterloo Saltoun' maintained a close interest in his ancestral properties and remained committed to the further development of the burgh.

The principal development was the speculative laying out of new areas of gridded streets outwith the old burgh core, the opening up of the south end of Broad Street, and the replacement or first provision of most of the major public buildings that are so much a feature of the modern townscape. Population growth was one factor in this physical expansion, emphasised by the moving of the parish school in 1838 from the Links to larger premises in Saltoun Place,[249] but a burgeoning population (see **fig 21**) was in itself an indication of increasing prosperity and the consequent expansion of employment opportunities. The new development is characterised by the movement of the commercial heart of the town up from the harbour to the Broad Street, Saltoun Square and Commerce Street areas. To an extent, this trend had begun in the early 1800s with the building of the Saltoun Inn. This may have served as a catalyst for further commercial developments throughout the 1820s and 1830s, in particular the rapid proliferation of banks. A trades directory of 1825 identified one banker, one broker and an agent to the Sea Insurance Company of Scotland.[250] In 1830, a Savings Bank was established,[251] and after more than 60 years as the only bank in Fraserburgh, the Aberdeen Banking Company was joined by two more. The Bank of Scotland opened a branch in 1835, probably on premises belonging to its agent Lewis Chalmers,[252] and in 1838, as part of a period of intense competition between Aberdeen-based banks, the North of Scotland Bank opened an office in Saltoun Square, probably in the building now occupied by the Registration Office.[253]

The southern new town had probably been triggered by the opening of the turnpike road in 1810 and then the need to provide better and less steep access between the town and shore after Robert Stevenson's 1818 harbour improvements. The south end of Broad Street was opened up and the lower end of Frithside Street was hugely widened, presumably to cope with increased harbour traffic. Its mouth facing the Shore was built with appropriate grandeur. The recessed, shallow-bowed frontage in fine dressed granite is typical of this phase of new-town architecture.[254] In due course, the symbolic corner of Broad and Frithside Streets was adorned with an even finer bow – the swelling columned façade of one of the most splendid neo-classical buildings in north-east Scotland, the 1835 offices of the Bank of Scotland – in the superb Grecian corner-turning manner of the masterly Aberdonian neo-classical architect Archibald Simpson (**fig 25**).

FIGURE 25
Former Bank of Scotland,
built *c* 1835 in the style of
Archibald Simpson
(Paula Martin)

Most of Commerce Street was probably developed in the 1820s, although Nos 5–7, at the Shore end, appear to have been an older warehouse.[255] Building was discontinuous, and only Commerce Street itself, with the customary rounded corners facing the harbour (**fig 26**), was wholeheartedly of the period. There was a particular impact on the old town centre. In order to provide a seamless join between the turnpike road at Saltoun Place and the old town's squint geometry, the original width and alignment of Fishcross Street seem to have been altered to suit that of Saltoun Place, probably *c* 1823–28 to judge by the evidence of an increase in property transactions.[256] Much of Fishcross Street's original southern end was demolished and rebuilt, although faint traces of its original alignment are still discernible. The new buildings were not grandiose: two-storeyed well-proportioned granite houses, those in Saltoun Place very dignified in detail (**fig 27**). The three-bay villa built as the Manse at No 7 Saltoun Place (see **fig 24**), set back from the road, is particularly elegant. When, in mid-century, Seaforth Street was opened up through the Barracks ground, it followed the grid, being built parallel to Saltoun Place in an approximate continuation of Broad Street. Development never fully extended to the south – not even to a full city block – and it was only squared off with the opening of Victoria Street in 1857. The new southern Fraserburgh had to await the arrival of the railway for further impetus.

FIGURE 26
Rounded corners on
buildings at the foot of
Commerce Street
(Paula Martin)

By 1832, Fraserburgh was regarded as being 'on the whole neatly and regularly built'.[257] Neat building and regularity, however, did not necessarily indicate a high standard of public hygiene, for in the same year Fraserburgh was particularly badly hit by the cholera epidemic that swept through the country.[258] By 1840 'a considerable number of new houses have been built within these few years; and new openings are making, and new streets are laid off, according to a plan, which was resolved upon about twenty-five years ago. There are now 180 tenements'.[259] The development of Fraserburgh's landward communications, which had begun with the building of the turnpike roads from the south and east in 1810, was completed in the late 1830s. By 1840 there were turnpike roads from Fraserburgh to Aberdeen, Peterhead, Banff and Strichen.[260] There were three tollhouses on the outskirts of the burgh: Aberdeen Road; on the site now occupied by the War Memorial, High Street, built in 1816 (the Broadsea Toll that made way for Denmark Street); and Strichen Road, built in 1840 (**map 13**).[261]

FIGURE 27
Houses in Saltoun Place
(Paula Martin)

The town's elite had broken out of the first new-town streets of Frithside, Cross and Mid Streets, with banks and business offices moving away from the Shore, while shops, merchants and vintners were more or less split evenly between the Shore, Broad Street and the rebuilt Cross Street. As a further harbinger of change, Cross Street had also become the principal focus for trades and manufactures while, unsurprisingly, Shore Street was garnering its fish curers and coopers.[262] At the end of the 'improvement period', therefore, Fraserburgh was in good heart, and by the 1840s it was prospering.

Commercial success did not occur in a vacuum, and the key to Fraserburgh's prosperity was the progressive improvement and enlargement of its harbour, described in 1825 as 'a small but excellent harbour, which will admit vessels of 300 tons … defended from the sea by two large piers, lately built, at an estimated cost of about £20,000'. It was also 'well adapted for the reception of vessels that are wind bound, as they can make this port when they cannot come near any other on this part of the coast'.[263] In 1832, a gazetteer recorded that 'During the last war, a large harbour was constructed here, to serve as a place of retreat for British ships of war, which might suffer from stress of weather in the North Sea … in consequence, Fraserburgh has risen from comparative obscurity to a port of considerable importance'. The works cost about £50,000, paid for by the government, Lord Saltoun and private subscribers. It was observed, however, that 'the situation … of the town, with the sea stretching in three directions, and a land neighbourhood occupying only the remaining quadrant of the circle, perhaps precludes the prospect of Fraserburgh ever becoming a great port'.[264]

Despite such concerns, the present Mid Pier was rebuilt in about 1830 at a cost of £30,000, and was described soon afterwards as 'broader and even superior to the other two, within which vessels lie in perfect safety during the most violent storms'.[265] The gamble paid off, as harbour revenues increased rapidly. The scale of the development was vastly in excess of the volume of trade passing through the port and, while some of the work was speculative, part of the expansion may have been linked with the growth of the white fish trade. The scale of the trading ventures out of Fraserburgh had been growing progressively from the mid-eighteenth century. The absence of a customs operation in Fraserburgh had been deemed a hindrance to trade in the 1790s.[266] In 1825, a commercial directory identified eight shipowners, and noted the presence of a Custom House with four staff, and eight coasting vessels.[267] There were regular sailings to London, as well as Peterhead, Aberdeen and Leith.[268] Agricultural surpluses – grain, potatoes and cattle – were being shipped out, mainly to London, with the main imports being coal, salt, lime and household goods. The eight trading vessels were in 1840 of between 45 and 155 tons.[269]

Early Victorian expansion c 1840–70

From around 1840 the pace of development in Fraserburgh began to accelerate rapidly. The parliamentary and government reforms of the 1830s continued, bringing increased political weight to the emerging commercial elites even in provincial communities such as Fraserburgh. Scottish politics and religion were linked inextricably, and tensions within the Church of Scotland had been growing steadily over issues ranging from the powers of patrons over congregations in the appointment of ministers to the liability of the Kirk to the jurisdiction of secular courts. In 1843 the tensions erupted into the Disruption, a full-blown rift when 474 ministers out of a total of c 1200 left the Church of Scotland and formed the Free Church. Although there were numerous smaller denominations already in existence, this was the first significant schism in the Kirk's history, and its legacy of division was to leave an indelible imprint on Scottish society and townscapes.

In 1844 Lord Saltoun returned from service in China.[270] Despite receiving a hero's welcome, however, he returned to a burgh which, like the rest of the country, was riven by religious discord. As an Episcopalian, Saltoun was not personally affected by the 1843 Disruption, but it presented him with a difficult social and political situation which required careful handling. Having sounded local opinion, Saltoun granted the Free Presbyterians, who had been holding services in the open air in the natural arena at Broadsea boat shore, a vacant plot on School Street to build a new church.[271] Other church building followed. In 1853 the Congregationalists, who had established a presence in the burgh soon after 1800, built Mid Street Congregational Church.[272] The Congregationalists also split in the 1840s, when the Evangelical Union established its own congregations. In 1854, the Fraserburgh Evangelical Union built Manse Street Congregational Church, now the Bethesda Church.[273]

Possibly as a signal of recovered confidence after the traumas of the Disruption, a new parish manse was built in the early 1860s on the west side of the junction of the Aberdeen and Strichen roads, outside the spreading southern suburbs.[274]

Administrative reform and its consequences also reached Fraserburgh in the 1840s. The old barony council was superseded in 1840 by police commissioners after the partial adoption of the General Police Act of 1833.[275] The rest of the powers in the Act were adopted in 1850, providing the commissioners with the authority to enhance public facilities and, in particular, to improve water quality. In 1845 a new supply had been led from Smiddyhill Farm to a reservoir at the junction of Manse Street and Hanover Street. This was supplemented in 1851 when a new reservoir was constructed at Greenbank, to the south of the town, from which the water was distributed in clay pipes, soon replaced with cast-iron ones. In 1865 the arrival of the railway led to increased demand for water, so the Great North of Scotland

Railway laid on its own supply, and sold the surplus to the town. An outbreak of cholera in 1866 highlighted inadequacies in the existing supply system, and, as a temporary solution, cartloads were brought in from a dammed stream at Glenbuchty to the west of the burgh. The unsatisfactory water supply was contrasted unfavourably with Aberdeen and Peterhead,[276] but it was not until 1870 that the deficiencies were remedied.

Changes in the burgh's administration, along with commercial success, led to the provision of a suitably new and impressive Town-house in 1853–55.

FIGURE 28
Town-house, Saltoun Square,
built 1853–55 (Paula Martin)

The old tolbooth had staggered on in an increasingly ruinous condition until demolished in 1852.[277] The replacement was designed by the brilliant young Thomas Mackenzie, who exploited its location at the junction of Saltoun Square and Kirk Brae by giving it a principal façade to each (**fig 28**).[278] On the corner he placed a cylindrical entrance tower. Above the door stands a statue of the 'Waterloo Saltoun' (1785–1853), presented after his death by his nephew, the 17th Lord Saltoun, and unveiled in 1859. Far grander than its predecessor, and sophisticated Italianate in appearance, the Town-house had a rear wing offering a covered market on the ground floor and a meeting room above. [279] The wave of civic pride that followed council reform can also be seen in the restoration of the Mercat Cross in 1853.[280]

This programme of public and institutional building formed one element within a wider physical expansion of the burgh. The planned development of the northern new town does not seem to have made any significant headway before the mid-1840s,[281] when North Street was laid out, but by *c* 1862 there were still several undeveloped plots available there for house building.[282] The brunt of new fishing activity – gutting, curing and packing, and buildings for associated trades and temporary accommodation for seasonal workers – took place within the Castle Parks known as 'Castle Braes' and 'Cairds Hill', an area of high ground which lay towards the northern end of the ridge running out to Kinnaird Head.[283] So former grazing land, overlooking the eastern side of Broadsea Bay, was overrun by industry mixed with new cottages. By 1858 Barrasgate Road had evolved from a track from the University site at the western end of the High Street through the Castle Parks to Kinnaird Head,[284] and a further burst of development in the 1870s followed the laying out of Quarry Road (after the clay quarry had closed in 1875). When Denmark Street was laid out in 1875, it overlay part of Bath Street, which had presumably never been built on.[285] The prison was also located here by 1852 (**map 7**),[286] perhaps an indication that it had become the rough end of town,[287] and in 1863, Strachan's Female Industrial School was built on the corner of Barrasgate Road and High Street to provide reformatory training for women.[288] Its reused buildings survive.

The older buildings of Faithlie stood in the way of the 1850–57 harbour improvements and, eventually, the Balaclava Harbour, so most of the eastern side of the village – a dense agglomeration of fisher cottages (many occupied by widows), some curing yards, an inn, and a few tradesmen – was removed. In their place, there was an improved harbour, harbour buildings and sheds, and a widened Shore Street.

In 1875, it was reported that 'numerous improvements have been made in recent times; elegant and comfortable houses have been erected, and new streets laid out on a symmetrical plan'.[289] The principal developments at the south of the town were Seaforth Street and Victoria Street, both started in 1857 (**fig 29**), the southern extension of Saltoun Place by 1865, and the western section of Commerce Street in 1873.[290] In the west of the town, School Street was also extended northwards, parallel to Manse Street (originally it only ran between Commerce Street and Frithside Street).[291] An indication of the speculative and possibly entrepreneurial aspect of this episode of growth, and the probable class of the expected residents of the new houses, may be seen in the introduction of a piped gas supply. In 1841 the Fraserburgh Gas Light Company was established, its premises occupying a large yard between Seaforth Street and Shore Street north of Commerce Street (**map 8**).[292] The railway arrived from the south, through the Links, in 1865, but it was accompanied neither by great industrialisation nor by the urban housing in an 'industrial corridor' at the south end of town that one might have expected. It was probably the consequence of Fraserburgh's lack of local coal supply. However, the Customs House moved close by, to occupy the former offices and stables of World's End at the junction of Dalrymple Street (named after John Dalrymple, a Fraserburgh shipbuilder) and Commerce Street.[293] There were further extensions to the harbour, the reclamation of much foreshore, some sheds and minor industries and the Railway (later Station) Hotel.

Prosperity, confidence and a civic pride gave Fraserburgh all the attributes of a thriving provincial centre in the 1850s and 1860s. The consolidation of banking provision was one key indicator of commercial success. In 1849 the Union Bank of Scotland had acquired the Aberdeen Banking Company, and by 1851 had replaced its old premises with a new office at the corner of Commerce Street.[294] Business opportunities in the rapidly expanding commercial sector in Fraserburgh, buoyed up by the steady growth of the herring trade, were sufficient to attract a fourth bank, the Aberdeen Town and Country Bank, which by 1867 had opened a branch in Mid Street.[295]

FIGURE 29
Victoria Street, looking west
(Charles McKean)

The town's nineteenth-century history showed a distinct shift in social composition. Perhaps as a consequence of the town's specialisation in fishing, by the mid- to late nineteenth century more of the elite lived beyond the town's boundaries than had in 1837, only returning at the end of the century with the construction of new suburbs to the south-west. Banks, offices and ship-owning businesses, however, had increased by some 500% over the same period, and the commercial sector by just under 200%. By 1867, the slow growth of Broad Street to become the commercial, shopping and banking heart of Victorian Fraserburgh was finally complete.[296] The period also saw the emergence of two high-profile symbols of the success of Fraserburgh's business classes. In 1852, the *Fraserburgh Advertiser* was established, providing the town with one of the badges of nineteenth-century economic success.[297] While the newspaper was a public symbol of prosperity, more private was the second revival of freemansonry in 1863. On this occasion, with a significantly enlarged pool of potential members, the lodge thrived.[298]

All this development was not founded on optimism alone, but was fuelled by the steady broadening of the commercial and industrial economic base of the town. Traditional areas experienced substantial growth. The export of agricultural produce continued, and from the 1830s there was a growing trade in cattle, both those raised in Buchan and those rested and fattened up in transit from Orkney. This trade was lost when steam boats allowed the transport of such animals direct to London.[299] The tide-mill at the harbour ground meal, much of which was shipped to London.[300] Other traditional businesses such as sail- and rope-making continued, until the impact of the railway was felt. Fraserburgh also consolidated its economic base through the development of industries and crafts to service some of the other trades, and building construction secured the future of its sawmills and timber yards.[301] The eighteenth-century windmill, which is still such a prominent feature of Fraserburgh's skyline, enclosed by later buildings off Albert Street, provided power for the sawmill (**maps 7 & 8**) (see **fig 3**). One major arrival was a bone mill, at the northern end of the north new town between Castle Street and Shore Street, where it had easy access to the harbour and fish-processing area (source of much of its raw materials), and where the prevailing winds would carry odours away from residential areas.[302] Problems with water supply may have limited the development of water-dependent trades or industries through the early nineteenth century. Until the middle of the century, most brewing was probably carried out on a domestic basis, and Fraserburgh's inns may still have been producing much of their own supplies. A commercial brewery was eventually established at Watermill on the Banff road west of Broadsea, where there had been a mill since the later seventeenth century (**fig 30**).[303]

FIGURE 30
Waterside Mill,
photographed by J R Hume
in 1976 (Crown Copyright:
RCAHMS)

Another indication of commercial optimism in the town can be seen in the revival of shipbuilding around 1840. Webster's shipyard at the South Harbour was a substantial operation, which for many years employed an average of 50 men. In 1849 Webster launched a 180-ton ship, but there then followed a lean period until business improved again in 1853, with an order for a ship of 317 tons, the largest ever built in Fraserburgh. Webster's success marks the start of the 1855 to 1880 heyday of the coastal sailing fleet – in 1856 the total registered tonnage at Fraserburgh was 7035 – although the years 1858 to 1861 saw another depression that hit smaller yards hard. Webster's survived that downturn in demand, their last ship being launched in 1887; thereafter they turned to boatbuilding.[304]

With Fraserburgh's registered shipping heading for the 7000-ton level in the 1840s, the existing harbour facilities were already at breaking point. With competition in the coastal trade high, especially with regard to Peterhead, there was recognition that Fraserburgh would lose out on commercial opportunities should the harbour not be expanded. As a result bailie Lewis Chalmers junior lobbied hard for a new harbour extension to the north. The existing north harbour enclosed 3½ acres, the south harbour 5 acres (**map 6**), but the proposed extension would more than double that capacity by providing an additional 14 acres. Work began in 1850, but the half-built structure was demolished by storms during the winter of 1851–52. Work resumed only in 1856–57 under a new contractor, and the new structure was named the Balaclava Pier, in commemoration of the battle in the Crimean War (**map 7**).[305] In 1858 what was now a Royal National Lifeboat Institution boat was moved to a new base in the Balaclava harbour.[306]

The growth in fishing was in part responsible for the enlargement of the harbour, with the northern sector of the Balaclava Harbour becoming the location for the main fish-yard, but the improved port was still considered to be principally a trading operation, and in the 1870s was engaged primarily in the export of the agricultural produce of the burgh's hinterland and the import of coal, timber, lime, tiles, bricks, salt and general merchandise.[307] There may have been some doubts as to the wisdom of such a massive expenditure on Fraserburgh's harbour at a time when the ever-expanding rail network was drawing closer to the town, but it may have been a pre-emptive move and any future decline in coastal trade would be expected to be offset by increased fishing revenues. The impact of the arrival of the railway in 1865 on coastal trade may have been blunted by the quality of the harbour facilities, but by the 1870s the numbers of ships working regularly between Fraserburgh and Aberdeen, Leith and London had begun to decline.[308]

Although the emphasis in harbour operations was still weighted in favour of trade rather than fishing, the latter figured increasingly prominently in the success of the port. In common with other ports between the Tay and the Moray Firth, whaling emerged in the 1850s as a significant industry. It flourished only briefly, but provided much employment both on ships and on shore through the 1850s and 1860s, though on a smaller scale than at Peterhead.[309] Broadsea (**fig 31**) had no harbour, so the size of fishing boats was limited to those which could be pulled up to the top of the beach. In 1832 the Harbour Commissioners decided to allow fishing boats to use Fraserburgh harbour.[310] A recognisable fisher community had developed in the Garvage area of northern Faithlie by the 1840s and 1850s, but it was probably the building of the Balaclava Harbour that marked the beginning of a decisive shift away from Broadsea. [311] At both Broadsea and Fraserburgh white fishing was carried on for most of the year, still using long lines, baited with mussels by women and children, but it was the herring fishing that was to become the mainstay of the fishing economy after *c* 1840. In 1818 there had been 90 boats, in 1840 there were 220, and in 1863, 227.[312] By 1879 half the Scottish east coast fleet was based in Aberdeen, Fraserburgh or Peterhead. A major boom followed the coming of the railway in 1865, which helped to get fish to wider markets.[313] It was clear that the gamble of investing in harbour development in the 1850s had more than paid off, despite a market depression in the late 1850s.[314]

Much of the finance for harbour improvements was provided by the herring curers, who bought the catch either at a fixed price in advance or at quayside auctions. Either way they controlled the business, and became the dominant force in the town.[315] Although often condemned for their greed and exploitation of the fishermen, their buying policies brought a stability to the industry that it had lacked in the earlier nineteenth century.[316] By the later 1850s, the scale of the herring-gutting operation had reached industrial proportions. Large gutting stations were being set up on the Links to the south of the harbour, while some of the biggest curing firms (such as Bruce's,

FIGURE 31
Old cottages in Broadsea,
later nineteenth century
(Scottish Life Archive,
reproduced courtesy of the
Trustees of the National
Museums of Scotland)

which controlled 60 boats) established premises in the town.[317] The rapid growth of business in the 1860s, however, was to pale to insignificance in comparison with what followed in the 1870s and 1880s.

Without question, it was the railway that provided Fraserburgh with the link into the national transport system through which the output of the gutting yards could be carried to the markets of the south.[318] The added incentive of rapid access to an enlarged market served in turn to encourage further investment in the infrastructure of the port and fishing industry.[319] There had been a project as early as the 1840s, at the height of the initial 'Railway Mania', to build a line from Dyce to Ellon, Mintlaw and Peterhead, with a branch from Mintlaw to Fraserburgh, but it had collapsed. A revised scheme tabled in 1854 would have left out Fraserburgh, stopping at Strichen. This prompted the Great North of Scotland Railway to revive a proposal to run a line to Fraserburgh from Maud (whose line opened 1861). Lord Saltoun's support was won by the concession of a private station for Philorth House, and the extension opened in 1865 with Fraserburgh as the terminus of the Formartine and Buchan branch of the Great North of Scotland Railway (**fig 32**).[320] In general, the impression given in contemporary sources is that although the benefits of a line were recognised, there was no special pressure to lay a track to Fraserburgh early or in preference to somewhere else. The completion of the spur line to Peterhead in 1862 did not prompt any hand-wringing in Fraserburgh, whose own line took a further three years to complete. Instead, the main initiative seems to have come from the rail companies and the line evolved as part of their wider network. Perhaps, as Fraserburgh had so much coastal trade, there was less pressure to bring the railway than there was in inland towns.

FIGURE 32
The railway station opened in 1865 and was partly covered by a train shed, carried on the trackside by an open colonnade. The tower behind is the Dalrymple Hall. Photograph taken in 1962 (Crown Copyright: RCAHMS, Rokeby Collection)

Dramatic growth 1870–1914: the herring boom

Despite a growing body of reforming legislation, for most of the nineteenth century the Frasers continued to dominate the burgh's political life through their right of appointment to the key offices in the burgh's affairs. The principal of these was that of baron bailie, in effect the head of the council, 'Commissioner for Lord Saltoun' and, *ex officio*, chairman of the Harbour Board.[321] The last third of the century saw profound changes in Fraserburgh's fortunes, the character of the town, and its system of government. According to an 1867 directory 'Lord Saltoun is hereditary provost, but His Lordship has most generously decided on giving up his rights to the inhabitants, and steps are being taken to obtain an act of parliament for securing these rights'.[322] After 350 years the superior's role was already largely nominal, for Alexander, 17th Lord Saltoun, played little active part in the burgh's affairs and displayed none of the acumen in estate management that his uncle and predecessor had employed to such good effect.

In common with many of Scotland's smaller communities, it was William Lindsay's 1862 General Police and Improvement Act that provided the mechanism for change. This act, designed to enable communities of more than 700 inhabitants to make their own laws governing building and sanitary requirements, was adopted in 1870.[323] In 1875, the police burgh covered about 350 acres.[324] The old barony council lingered until 1892, nominated by Lord Saltoun and administering the Common Good. The final stage in the transformation came with the Burgh Police (Scotland) Act 1892. Adopted in Fraserburgh in 1893, this act established an administration consisting of nine Burgh Commissioners (including a provost and two bailies). The provost thereafter also became, *ex officio*, chairman of the Harbour Board. In 1900 the Commissioners were renamed the Town Council. The Common Good was still managed separately, by a committee now renamed the Feuars Managers, which was provided with a new code of conduct in 1894.[325]

It would be quite wrong, however, to think of the Frasers' appointees as placemen holding sinecures. They were usually highly competent, experienced and well-connected local businessmen or lawyers. Indeed, it was largely the baron bailies of the nineteenth century who drove forward much of the redevelopment and expansion that both underpinned and was a consequence of the commercial success of the burgh. One such, and a guiding hand behind much of the dramatic development of Fraserburgh in the 1870s and 1880s, was Sir Alexander Anderson, chairman of the Harbour Commissioners from 1873 until his death in 1886.[326] Perhaps the ablest of Saltoun's baron bailies, Anderson provided the drive behind the development of the harbour facilities from 1875 onwards, which was to give Fraserburgh its pivotal role in the burgeoning herring trade (**fig 33**).[327]

A sense of civic duty and pride, as epitomised by Anderson, has been presented as a characteristic of late nineteenth-century public life. Coupled with a growing social awareness among the political classes as a whole, and reinforced by a raft of legislation governing what would now be described as 'public health' issues, this outlook could have a major impact on the development of civic institutions. The cholera epidemic of 1866 may have been one of the catalysts for the adoption of the 1862 Police Act in Fraserburgh in 1870. The epidemic had shown up the deficiencies of the water supply, the quality and quantity of water being a perennial problem that the town had made efforts to overcome as far back as 1804. In 1870 a new supply was brought from the Glashiemyre Burn, about four miles to the west of the town, and, in 1877, one of the new elected barony council's first projects was the installation of a new drainage and sewage system.[328] This still proved insufficient, and, moreover, it did not supply Broadsea. The system was again extended in 1883, drawing water from Ardlaw and Tyrie Mains, and the situation was eased, but it still could not cope with the extra people and demands of curers during the fishing season. Eventually in 1910 a new water scheme was provided from Fedderate.[329]

Water and sanitation were to become major concerns of the town authorities after 1870 when 'The herring boom hit Fraserburgh like a thunderbolt', and the existing facilities proved inadequate for the needs of the industry. Gutting and packing operations spilled out on to the streets, and one contemporary account recalls how 'pickle [was] running down the back street to the auld Kirk'.[330] Prices favoured the curers and, with a glut of labour available, wages in both fishing and fish processing remained low. Fishers, too, were caught by having committed themselves to herring fishing, which required a heavy capital investment in specialist craft and equipment which were unsuitable for catching white fish. Few could now afford to carry out both herring and white fishing. The coopers, too, were affected by the seasonal nature of the dominant industry, with little demand for their barrel-making skills in the winter months. There were, of course, major beneficiaries of the boom, most notably the curers.[331]

The scale of the herring industry was huge – at its height in 1907, some two and a half million barrels of fish were exported to the Continent. The shoals were to be found around the north and east coast of Scotland and as far south as East Anglia at different times of the year. The gutting and packing of the fish was traditionally done by young girls, who came from fishing villages all round Scotland, and they spent the season travelling from Stornoway in the north to Great Yarmouth in the south.

Many of the problems stemmed from the transient nature of the workforce, with thousands of boat crews, gutters and packers following the herring shoals around the country. Even the carters and cart-teams employed in moving the barrelled fish were migrant labourers, usually drawn in from farms in the rural hinterland. In the 1870s the curers, who relied on these hired teams, built temporary bothies for the men and stables for the horses in the area behind Saltoun Place, later swept away when Grattan Street was laid out in 1893,[332] but the bulk of the labour force had to find its own accommodation. In 1891, a Church of Scotland officer, Georgina Robertson, reported on the appalling living conditions common in the northern part of the town between Denmark Street and Castle Street, into which the great mass of transient workers was crammed in rented accommodation. In particular, she drew attention to the conditions endured by the female gutters.

> I have frequently visited them in their lodgings, and as I am conversant with sanitation and the Laws of Health – being a Member and a Lecturer of the National Health Society of 53 Berners Street, London – I would respectfully call the attention of the Local Authorities to the comfortless and insanitary condition of the majority of these lodgings, many of the girls' rooms being unfit for human habitation – smoky, dirty, draughty, without cupboards or shelves and only one bedstead for every three girls. According to the Bye-Laws, the cubic space of 250

feet has been granted, but the girls have to live, cook, and wash as well as sleep, and the space in many cases is insufficient. The worst of the places are in Hunter's Lane; the Barracks in Shore Street, a place behind the Oak Tree Inn, Shore Street – Denmark, Barrasgate and Castle Street. But the most crying evil is the want of WCs or such conveniences, near the lodgings and in the Curing Yards. In the latter there is generally one, but the girls decline and rightly too, to share in common with the other sex, consequently the Beach and outskirts of the Town are in a disgusting condition. There have been many ailments among the fisher folks arising from the want of these conveniences, and the sick people are put to great straits, which of course, has aggravated their diseases. Two extreme cases I can cite: No 10 Castle Terrace, small house at the back, and 25 Lance Lane. The complaints from the people were more urgent than ever I have heard before; they said they were treated like 'Beasts', although they came out of comfortable homes they had to put up with any sort of treatment, and pay high rents too. These high-rented rooms tend to overcrowding. Widows with married sons and daughters and lodgers, besides, all living and sleeping in one room, sometimes as many as 12. These matters in the interests of decency and morality, as well as the physical health of the people require to be remedied.[333]

In her memoir of life in Fraserburgh in the nineteenth century, Christian Watt recalled that 'the Broch was an interesting place during the fishing. You could hear the Fife accent, the Shetland, the Gaelic and every other, twenty thousand folk crammed into anywhere, washing houses, garrets, lofts and outhouses'.[334] The scale of this migrant workforce, which even drew workers from Norway, had a tremendous and not always beneficial impact. In summer 1874, while there were around 2000 'Highlanders', mainly Lewismen, in the town in pursuit of employment as hands on the herring boats, there was a near riot. Opinion differs as to the cause of the disturbances, with one view blaming curers for cheating the hired men of their share of the bounty, while another suggests disappointed expectations at the small settlement paid for the 'early fish', ie all catches up to 20 July.[335] Disgruntlement and strong liquor combined in a potent brew that exploded into violence when the pubs closed on the night of 1 August. The local police were too few to control the deteriorating situation and could do little more than watch helplessly as a mob of drunk and violent Highlanders descended on the Town-house, smashed in its doors and windows and made ready to burn down the building. Members of the local volunteers drew guns and ammunition from the armoury, intending to check the rioters by force if necessary, but the intervention of the Chief Constable of Aberdeenshire, who happened to be in the town, dissuaded them from any precipitate action. Further violence was ended by a downpour of rain, and the arrival the following day of a detachment of Gordon Highlanders enabled the police to restore order. Over the next few days, the ringleaders of the riot were rounded up and several were imprisoned.[336]

The 1874 riot had caused nothing worse than property damage, but the situation had been such that lives could easily have been lost. Little was done to ameliorate the conditions that had contributed to the outpouring of anger. Indeed, the extremes of wealth and poverty that arose from the herring boom in Fraserburgh were, if anything, to become even further accentuated in the last quarter of the century. Social division became increasingly polarised, particularly once the elite of Fraserburgh began to abandon their houses in the old town for new villas in the modern suburbs that sprang up to the south and west, well away from the harbour. This process, which had started in the 1850s and 1860s, led to a virtual doubling of the town's footprint. The continued development of the port and the expansion of herring fishing with its concentration of processing activities to the north and east of the old town centre caused the rate at which the town extended outwards to quicken after 1870.[337] The original rectangle of streets expanded to include Broadsea, which in 1872 was joined to Fraserburgh for administrative purposes,[338] and overwhelmed some of the small private estates that had lain outside the burgh core. The drift of the prosperous middle classes away from the historic heart of the town led to the progressive decline in status of the older areas, which degenerated largely into overcrowded slum housing of the type described above.[339] By the 1890s 'recent shoreward improvements and northward extensions have also tended to enhance its [the urban layout's] symmetry'.[340] Nevertheless, in the early 1900s, the pressure on housing for the poorest segments of the population, especially during the herring season, remained acute.

Fraserburgh did not join to any great extent in the development of seaside holiday resorts in the later Victorian era. There were, however, some incidental developments which had a tangential impact on the tourist trade. The most important of these came in 1903 when the Fraserburgh and St Combs Light Railway was opened.[341] Its primary purpose was to serve fishermen in Cairnbulg, Inverallochy and St Combs, allowing them to bring their catches in to the market in Fraserburgh, but it quickly developed tourist traffic, transporting golfers to the popular courses at Philorth and St Combs (White Links).[342] New, quality hotel accommodation was provided with the opening of the Alexandra Hotel in the High Street in 1899, the Grand (Temperance) Hotel at the lower end of Broad Street in 1904, and the Bellslea Temperance by 1904.[343] Their main customers, however, were probably not holidaymakers but fish-buyers, including foreign merchants or their agents, who were coming to Fraserburgh in increasing numbers as the herring fishery expanded.

Too often in the past, Fraserburgh's late nineteenth-century economy has been presented as wholly fishing-oriented. In *c* 1870, however, it was described as 'the seat of a considerable provincial trade' and in 1875 it was reported that 'the annual export of grain, meal, potatoes, butter, and other agricultural produce, is large, and the imports of coal, timber, lime, and goods for shopkeepers, are also large'.[344] This mix continued in the 1890s, when there was a large trade importing timber, coal and salt and exporting fish, fresh and cured, grain, empty barrels, and potatoes.[345] The timber trade, first noted in the later seventeenth century, evidently remained significant into the later nineteenth century, with John Webster, shipbuilder, owning a substantial yard for storing imported wood at the head of the North Pier. The yard, referred to locally as 'The Logs', was a well-known meeting-place and unofficial playground until it was swept away in the redevelopment of this part of the harbour towards the end of the century.[346] There was still a substantial non fish-related trade, which supported sixteen registered vessels, two of them steamers.

The town was at the same time described as 'the chief seat of the herring fishing industry in Scotland'.[347] Salt herring was exported mainly to Scandinavia, Germany and beyond. An 1886 commercial directory lists local solicitors, merchants and fish curers acting as vice-consuls for Denmark, France, Sweden, Norway and the German Empire.[348]

White fishing was also carried on steadily, and staged a recovery that was enhanced by the building of a new fish market in 1899 at the South Harbour.[349] Fraserburgh had achieved a notable, if largely symbolic, victory over its old local rivals. The original port of registry for local boats had been Banff, but this was later moved to Peterhead. In 1896, however, Fraserburgh (St Combs to Rosehearty) became a port of registry in its own right, with the boats now bearing the letters FR instead of PD.[350]

By the mid 1870s the harbour was once again too small. A loan of £60,000 from the Fisheries Board allowed the Harbour Commissioners to extend the Balaclava Harbour with a new breakwater. Made of concrete, this was started in 1875, and finished in 1882, by which time deepening had also become necessary as larger ships were introduced, and there was a risk of losing the largest boats to Aberdeen. By 1896 the concrete needed major repairs. From 1879 to 1887 work continued steadily to deepen the North and South Harbours and repair the North and South Piers. This opened up the harbour to large steamships, offering facilities as good as Aberdeen.[351] In 1894 Fraserburgh was described as 'now one of the finest and most commodious harbours on the east coast of Scotland'.[352]

The herring trade was so good that the Balaclava Harbour soon needed deepening, so in 1893 a new loan was sought, and the work was finished in 1897. The following year saw the completion of a new South breakwater costing £80,000, a dry dock at the head of the Balaclava Harbour, and the widening of the Balaclava Pier, providing an extra 14 acres of space. By 1900, following £308,000 of expenditure on developments (compared with

Peterhead's £300,000), Fraserburgh had a very large harbour which could shelter 1000 fishing boats. In 1902 it had more boats and more profit than its old rival, but the strength of demand for herring persuaded the Harbour Commissioners that yet more investment and expansion was required. In 1904 booms were installed at the entrance to the Balaclava Harbour, and in 1905–06 the harbour entrance was given extra protection. By this date, however, the existing facilities were again working to their full capacity. As a result, work began in 1908 on the new Station Harbour, enclosing and deepening the area between the South Pier and the South breakwater (**fig 34**).

One of the factors precipitating further development was the introduction of steam drifters which led to the concentration of the local fishing industry in Peterhead, Fraserburgh and Buckie.[353] The Fraserburgh and North of Scotland Steam Trawling Co Limited was floated in 1898, but had trouble breaking into a sector already dominated by the trawling port of Aberdeen.[354]

FIGURE 34
Aerial view of Fraserburgh Harbour, 1948 (Crown Copyright: RCAHMS)

The best year for harbour revenue was 1907, when £21,156 was netted.[355] When work began on the new Station Harbour in 1908, revenues were already beginning to fall, but the Harbour Commissioners could not have foreseen the crash that was to destroy the herring industry within thirteen years, but there were signs that the boom had already peaked before the outbreak of war with Germany in 1914. Fraserburgh's commercial elite had positioned their port at the forefront of the Scottish fish trade through a long-term policy of investment in the facilities that brought wealth. Indeed, between 1738 and 1913 the total cost of harbour works was £481,400. In 1904 it was said that 'Fraserburgh bids fair to outstrip Peterhead in population as she long since did in the matter of the great summer herring fishing', and in 1903 the harbour revenues were 25% more than at Peterhead, where arguments were going on about how and where to extend their harbour.[356] Ultimately, however, Peterhead became the greater fishing centre because of its broader-based economy.

Recession and crash were far from the minds of Fraserburgh's commercial classes in the 1870s and 1880s, and the town's prosperity drew in outside investment. The buoyant local economy and the profitability of the herring trade encouraged another major Scottish bank, the Clydesdale, to open a branch in Broad Street in 1875, in a grand Italianate building.[357] Such inward investment is a clear sign of general awareness throughout the Scottish business community of the wealth being generated in this remote corner of the country, but Fraserburgh itself was making a series of statements of confidence in its own economic future. One such was its newspapers. Most of Scotland's large commercial centres had only one, or at most two, newspapers at this date. It is noteworthy, therefore, that Fraserburgh had four at the beginning of the twentieth century. In 1884 a second newspaper, the *Fraserburgh Herald*, joined the *Fraserburgh Advertiser*.[358] By 1886, the *Herald*'s printers had recognised a possible niche market and introduced a weekly newspaper, *The Fisherman*, described as 'the only paper in Scotland devoted entirely to the fish trade, and the best medium for advertisements of everything connected with that important industry'.[359] *The Fisherman* appears to have ceased publication by 1911, possibly as a result of competition from the *Herald*'s rival, the *Fraserburgh Advertiser*, which had launched its own weekly, the *Fraserburgh Herring Circular*. This flourishing newspaper industry provides a clear indication of social change and levels of disposable wealth.

Churches

The prosperity of the 1870s was reflected in an exuberant burst of church building, providing a distant prospect of spires concentrated particularly on the south. The old parish church received a new timber ceiling in 1873, a vestry in 1874, an organ in 1892, and the whole building was then overhauled externally in 1898, with structural alterations and renovation of the interior.[360] A new window in the east gable was gifted by Sir George Anderson, Treasurer of the Bank of Scotland, in memory of his parents.[361]

However, the real wealth lay outside the established church and the old town centre, in nonconformist denominations in the suburbs. A United Presbyterian church was built in Saltoun Place in 1875,[362] followed by the West Parish Church in the Hexagon island site at the west end of Victoria Street in 1876 (see **fig 29**). Axially placed to close the vista up Victoria Street, it was designed by Edinburgh architects David MacGibbon and Thomas Ross at a cost of £4,000.[363] In 1877–80 the Baptist Church joined it just downhill.[364] The third in the same street was the soaring South United Free Church, built 1878–80 to the designs of the Aberdonian maverick J B Pirie (**fig 35**).[365] This, the finest of Fraserburgh's Victorian churches and perhaps the most striking in north-east Scotland, faced up Victoria Street from Seaforth Street. The clock on the steeple was another gift from the benevolent George Anderson.[366] The last of this group, St Peter's Episcopal, on one corner of the Hexagon, was designed by John Kinross in 1891 in memory of Bishop Jolly (1755–1838).[367] The congregation's eighteenth-century building in Mid Street was then taken over by members of the United Free Church, who swiftly replaced it with the current West Church.[368] A Roman Catholic Church was built at the corner of Commerce Street and School Street in 1895–96 principally to serve migrant herring workers.[369]

FIGURE 35
The South Church, Seaforth
Street (Charles McKean)

Education

After the Disruption in 1843, responsibility for education had been taken away from the parish. The strong Episcopalian tradition in the town then led to the building of St Peter's Episcopal School, opened in 1854, though its Victoria Street building was not completed until 1859.[370]

Intended to fill the gap between school and, for the privileged few, university was the Fraserburgh Academy opened in 1870 in Mid Street. Built and endowed by a local merchant, John Park, it also ran evening classes. In 1909 a new Academy building was erected between Finlayson Street and Dennyduff Road.[371]

The 1872 Education Act paved the way for compulsory, state-provided elementary education.[372] The first of the new state-funded schools, replacing the old school in Saltoun Place, opened in 1882 and was extended considerably in 1891. This, the Central School in Charlotte Street (opposite the top of Commerce Street), still stands, with the schoolmaster's house to the south.[373] In 1901 the old Broadsea School was replaced partly by an Infant School in Dennyduff Road, then in 1908 the Broadsea and Strachan schools were combined and relocated to a new building in College Bounds known as the North School, which catered for the children of Broadsea and the expanding northern suburbs of the town.[374] Also in 1908 a Technical School was built to provide a basic secondary education and training in the trades for those who did not progress to the Academy.[375]

There were other improvements. One of the earliest of these was the opening in 1894 of Broadsea Village Hall on the corner of George Street and College Bounds, which gave a focus to a community that had lost its status as a separate village in 1872, but which still retained a strongly distinct identity.[376] The description of 'fine, large, substantial houses built on the most modern lines' down on the shore presumably referred to later Victorian tenements like those at the bottom of Kirk Brae.[377]

During the second half of the nineteenth century, the town virtually doubled its footprint, and the pace of change was such that after 1870 'the old configuration of the town' was regarded as 'trampled down' and 'the burgh boundaries and suburbs [enlarged] to an extent that would bewilder a long-absent native'.[378] Commerce Street was extended westward in 1873,[379] and the alignment of Victoria Street extending beyond the Hexagon and downhill to the west governed a new western grid over the ridge. Its wide avenues swept north to Broadsea.

In the 1870s, the Reverend P McLaren 'gave a considerable impetus to house-building in Charlotte Street' by forming a Building Society whose members consisted of 'steady, respectable, well-doing tradesmen'. This development echoed Edinburgh's *Colonies*, in the way that tradesmen and craftsmen were assisted with the finance to build.[380] Charlotte Street[381] projected westward across Frithside Street, hitherto the western edge of the town. Windmill Street/Albert Street followed, and then Finlayson Street[382] was laid out in 1896 but took a long time to fill up. Yet by 1902, development was moving west again to Dennyduff Road.

The enormous city blocks of western Fraserburgh have no counterpart in the older phases of the town's development. The streets are too wide for the two-storeyed buildings to contain the space, rendering their pavements very vulnerable to wind on a blustery day. Whereas that had often been the case in new towns (for example, Stewartfield or New Pitsligo), this abandonment of appropriate scale was less common in cities, and not at all in evidence in, for example, Aberdeen. It suggests that there may have been a different reason: namely that the wind was being encouraged through these new streets to assist with drying – presumably nets. Yet the layout of this district implies that it was built for those who wished to remove themselves from the old town centre and its industries. For, rather than extending the streets of Fraser's Broch westwards to frame the western expansion, the sole connection between this new district and the old lies through Victoria Street to the south and High Street to the north.

The town then surged north-west to swallow up Broadsea. Noble Street was laid out in 1890, and George Street, named after George Duke of York in the year of his marriage, 1893.[383] Both comprised substantial one-and-a-half storey fishermen's houses in crisply cut facing granite. Save College Bounds, which was quickly established as a shopping street extension to the High Street, these streets were generally occupied by trades related to fishing – curing sheds and cooperages with an intermingling of cottages.[384] So north Fraserburgh had assumed the character of the working quarter of the town.

Development beyond the south end of Fraserburgh took off toward the end of the century. Saltoun Place South (beyond Victoria Street), Saltoun Place Lane and Alexandra Terrace were all begun in the late nineteenth century.[385] The numbers of gentry and professionals living and working in Fraserburgh increased by 350% between 1867 and 1911, but whereas their presence in the old town centre remained static or went into slight decline, the majority of the town's new élite moved to houses in the new southern suburbs.[386] By 1911, they were concentrated into only a few streets – Grattan Place opened in 1893 (now Grattan Street and named after 18th lord Saltoun's wife Mary Grattan-Bellew), Victoria Street, Saltoun Place and Strichen Road.[387] Although Maconochie Road/Place was laid out in 1906, Queen's Road (Queen's Street until 1950) in 1909, and Seaforth Street was extended in 1911, no building plot appears to have been taken up before the First World War.[388] Just before the outbreak of war the town expanded south-west with houses and bungalows of a different order of affluence to the houses of Charlotte and Albert Streets.

FIGURE 36
Two examples of Edwardian houses, King Edward Street / Grattan Place, with cast-iron work and stained glass (Paula Martin)

Substantial Edwardian houses with fine stained glass and good timberwork stretched south along King Edward Street, Grattan Place and Strichen Road (**fig 36**), and it was hereabouts that the principal inter-war private sector houses were to emerge.

The most striking change to Victorian Fraserburgh, however, was the transformation of Back Street. As the more prosperous inhabitants had drifted westwards to the wide new avenues of Charlotte, Albert and Finlayson Streets in the 1870s, so must the commercial centre of town have moved to respond to it. By 1877, Back Street had been renamed High Street, and by 1911 it had overtaken Broad Street as the principal shopping street of the town.[389] Some of Fraserburgh's most ancient buildings that had lined it were replaced by commercial property constructed of sharp brown granite.

Both population and institutions were quitting the congested older streets of Fraser's broch for more spacious new ones. To judge by its public buildings, Charlotte Street had to be the principal thoroughfare of the western expansion. In addition to its school, it gained the privately funded Thomas Walker Hospital in 1877.[390] The Public Library, however, added in 1905 to the southern corner of the Hexagon, between King Edward and Victoria Streets, acted as a signal that the elite of the town were moving from the western streets to the south.[391] Other public buildings, fulfilling a wide range of functions from meeting-places to medical facilities, were also constructed during this period of great prosperity and conspicuous philanthropy. Perhaps the most important was the Dalrymple Hall (The Café), built in 1881 as a commercial venture, mainly with money from Captain John Dalrymple. It contained café, dining room, newsroom, library, museum, school of art, recreation room, public hall and baths, and the sheriff court was held there once a month.[392]

Specific provision of facilities for organised sports came comparatively late. It was only in 1904 that playing fields were provided to the south of the town, on ground formerly occupied by gutting sheds and bothies. The centrepiece of the park was one of Glasgow's Saracen Iron Works prefabricated iron fountains (**fig 37**) (moved to its present site in 1923, after the War Memorial occupied its former site).[393] In 1906 an extension was built at the back of the Town-house to house a Police Station.[394] This era of dynamic civicism was rounded off in 1909 with the establishment of a second Masonic Lodge, 'Fraserburgh', a development that proclaimed the expansion and prosperity of the town's commercial classes and business elite, who still dominated lodge membership at that date.[395]

FIGURE 37
The Saltoun drinking fountain, 1999. This was first erected in 1904, with an intricate domed top, a product of Walter MacFarlane and Co, Saracen Foundry, Glasgow (Crown Copyright: Historic Scotland)

While fishing dominated the local economy in the late nineteenth and early twentieth centuries, other industries were present, but most of these were heavily reliant on the herring trade, either as suppliers of materials or as processors of by-products. These included two breweries, several rope and sail yards, sawmills, a manure factory, a fish-oil works, fish-curing works, and a fish-canning works.[396] The most important of these was the Kinnaird Head Preserving Works in Bath Street, founded in 1883 by the Maconochie Brothers. Initially it canned herring during the season, mainly for export, but from the end of the nineteenth century it produced army rations, establishing its reputation during the Boer War and providing the famous 'Maconochie rations' to the British armed services in two World Wars.[397] The presence of this factory was to provide a substantial prop to the remaining locally based fishing industry after the collapse of the herring trade.

In common with most of Scotland's smaller east coast towns, no significant heavy industrial sector had developed by the late nineteenth century. Shipbuilding, which provided a stimulus for the development of engineering-based industry elsewhere, had declined earlier in the century as the local yards could not compete with the cheaper products sliding down the slipways of the Clyde, Forth and Tay. Scott and Yule boatbuilders survived into the early twentieth century, building fishing boats, including some steam drifters, but they were neither major employers nor consumers of materials to a degree that required the development of support industries.[398] Nevertheless, some new industries were implanted in the early 1900s, possibly attracted by the land available in Fraserburgh for development and by abundant labour. Foremost among these newcomers was the American-owned Consolidated Pneumatic Tool Works, established in 1904 on the Aberdeen Road.[399] At first it manufactured only pneumatic drills but it later diversified into other pneumatic tools, most notably the hammers used for building Sydney Harbour Bridge, and after 1914 its output included portable power-tools for use in the munitions trade.[400] It was one of the few businesses in the town to weather the traumas of the post-1918 depression.

Few could have predicted that this exuberant burst of confidence born of prosperity would end in only a few years time as Europe slid into war. It has been commented that the massive development of the harbour at Fraserburgh, and the strategic importance to the national food supply of the herring fishing through the port, ensured that the town would hold a vital place in Britain's wartime effort. There were signs of this strategic role earlier in 1914, when an Admiralty inspection team visited the town, followed by an announcement that the Faithlie Basin of the harbour was ideally suited as a base for a destroyer flotilla. This would have entailed giving this section of the fishing port over to twelve warships. The Admiralty's interest in the harbour was matched by that of the German fleet, whose offer of a courtesy visit was politely rejected by the Harbour Commissioners. Despite this flurry of activity, however, there were few in Fraserburgh who believed in 1914 that war was inevitable.[401]

War, slump, stagnation and war, 1914–45

Like much of the rest of Britain, prosperous Fraserburgh greeted the outbreak of war with the German Empire in 1914 with a mixture of surprised confusion, enthusiasm and confidence that the conflict would be over by Christmas. Two days before the declaration of war on 4 August 1914, 257 naval reservists from the area had received their papers summoning them to join the Navy. The mobilised men assembled at the harbour, where, watched by a large crowd, they were paraded and then marched to the station to board a train for Portsmouth. The exercise was repeated the following day, when a further 230 men were called up.[402] The impact of this cannot be under-estimated, for those involved constituted around 10% of the permanent male population of Fraserburgh. Around 300 territorial reservists quickly followed, mainly white-collar workers such as bank clerks and accountants, and large numbers of other men were to be called up or enlisted in the months following the outbreak of war.[403]

There was an even more ominous consequence of the opening of hostilities. Fearing the destruction of the vital fishing fleet at the hands of the German navy and the risk that smaller German warships might use such vessels as cover for mine-laying operations or attacks on harbour facilities, the Admiralty ordered the confinement to port of all fishing boats. This immediately ended the employment of the large transient labour force of crewmen, gutters and packers, who quickly left Fraserburgh to return to their homes. Three weeks later, the Admiralty lifted the ban but with few crewmen remaining, only a handful of boats ventured out. Locals were recruited to process the catch, but the produce of the 20–50 boats that had risked going to sea was insufficient to keep the entire local workforce employed. The result was widespread unemployment, with much of the port and its facilities left to stand idle.[404]

By the early autumn of 1914, the government had begun to implement measures designed both to alleviate the local dislocation of the economy caused by the war and to gear up production in vital areas. As part of this, the Maconochie Brothers fish-processing factory was designated an official producer of rations, which led to rapid recruitment of additional workers as output increased, while other workers were drafted for employment in the construction of new naval facilities at Rosyth.[405] Despite such initiatives, however, the fishing industry remained in crisis, denied safe access to its traditional fishing grounds. The price of fish began to rocket and, by summer 1915, boats were venturing out in larger numbers, cramming into the restricted inshore areas along the Buchan coast. Towards the end of the year, however, as German attacks on fishing vessels declined, more and more boats were persuaded to venture out and large numbers of the fleet operated in the west coast and East Anglian herring seasons. For these vessels, the high prices guaranteed great wealth – around £2,000–3,000 for two months' work – exceeding even the levels of the pre-war boom years, but little of the money reached the hands of the Harbour Board, who were now struggling to find funds to maintain the new piers and jetties that they had built.[406]

From 1916 onwards, the Admiralty gradually relaxed its restrictions on fishing off eastern Scotland, and by the end of the season in September some 121,000 crans of fish had been landed at the port. Nearly half of this catch was sold fresh, being transported south by rail, with only 45,000 crans being cured. Significantly, however, there was little demand for cured herring among the British public and, although a small-scale export trade with Scandinavia was maintained, this in no way compensated for the loss of the huge German and Russian markets. Stockpiles began to accumulate in Fraserburgh's curing yards, and by 1918 there were an estimated 45,000 unsold barrels. Despite these warning signs, as the war ground towards its conclusion during 1917 and 1918, the government began to prepare for a return to pre-war conditions, confident that the fishing industry would swiftly revert to its old patterns of trade and prosperity.[407]

The consequences of war and revolution in Europe, however, had destroyed the foreign trade on which the town had grown rich. Buoyant domestic wartime demand for herring had secured the livelihoods of hundreds, if not thousands, of workers, but long-term survival needed a quick reopening of European markets. Any hopes that peace might bring a return to the pre-war patterns of trade, however, were rudely shattered by events in Russia, where the Bolshevik Revolution had swiftly closed the largest market. In four years, the herring fishery had enjoyed unprecedented economic highs and lows, and ended the war at the peak of a boom, but, with no guarantee that prices would be maintained, Fraserburgh's economy faced an uncertain future. The idea that at the close of the First World War 'rusting trawlers and rotting nets littered the ports from Stornoway to Lerwick, and from Wick to Anstruther', however, is rather exaggerated.[408] Herring prices remained artificially high and there was heavy demand for boats, suggesting that there was some confidence that foreign markets might be regained. In 1919, however, the import of foreign foodstuffs to Britain returned to its pre-war patterns and, after four years of a fish-dominated diet, people not surprisingly turned to other foods; the result was that the price of herring collapsed from a high of £6 per cran to only 5 shillings (25p) by the end of the season.[409]

The First World War may have destroyed the herring industry, but fishing in Fraserburgh had not died altogether. Nevertheless, the scale of its contraction was immediately obvious: in 1914, the fleet had numbered around 290 vessels, by 1918 about 160 remained. Some of the missing vessels had been requisitioned for navy service and lost in the war, while others would eventually be returned, but no timetable was offered for their restoration.[410] Indeed, losses continued, with at least five Fraserburgh vessels being sunk or destroyed in 1919. The uncertainty over the future of the industry led many owners to sell their vessels and leave the business while there was still a chance to make a profit. The lack of confidence was underscored in 1920 when there were no bidders for the 324 ex-service steam drifters the government offered for sale.[411] Disastrously low catches in the 1920 season were a final nail in the coffin of the industry, and in 1921 suggestions of a massive vessel-decommissioning programme began to circulate. It was not just the owners and crews who faced an uncertain future, for the decline threatened workers in the gutting and processing businesses, and, as demand for cured fish continued to fall, in the cooperages where the barrels for packing the fish were made and maintained. By the end of 1921 there were 1,350 unemployed in the burgh – some 20% of the adult population. The only expanding operation was the town's Employment Exchange, which had to move to a larger building.[412]

The year 1921 was a watershed in the fortunes of Fraserburgh as a fishing port. That year, rather than 1918, marked the clear collapse of the herring fishery. Although herring catches continued to play a part in the economic life of the town for many years yet, and were to recover to some extent in the 1930s when there was a revival of the European market, its role was to dwindle progressively during the twentieth century. The 1920s witnessed a further contraction of the fleet, with around two-fifths of vessels taken out of commission. At the same time, however, there was a growth in the white fishery, which had languished in the shade of the herring fishery since the failure of the Fraserburgh and North Scotland Steam Trawling Company. After c 1930 the introduction of seine netting transformed white fishing, which came to dominate the harbour and remained the mainstay of its port activities into the 1980s. [413]

The boom years had kept a number of boatbuilding yards in business in and around Fraserburgh. Wilson Noble's yard was one of the largest, but the important Sandhaven-based company of J & G Forbes also used the old Scott & Yule yard in Fraserburgh.[414] Both companies thrived during the war years, mainly supported by Admiralty contracts, but that lucrative sector all but disappeared in 1918. The yards' problems were compounded by the flooding of the market with cheap second-hand ex-service vessels, and by 1923 Forbes had closed its Fraserburgh operation. Wilson Noble, however, was buoyed up in 1919–20 by one last Admiralty order followed by a locally-placed order to build a cargo vessel for the newly established Fraserburgh Shipping Company. Set up by a local business consortium, this company planned to revive the port's former busy coastal trade, and this vessel was meant to be the first of several. It proved, however, to be the first and last, as the company failed to establish a niche in the market.[415] Noble's yard, however, survived, albeit on a much-reduced scale, and regained a degree of prosperity through Admiralty orders for motor minesweepers during the Second World War.

Perhaps one of the clearest indications of the impact of the collapse of the herring industry can be seen in the near total absence of large-scale building projects in Fraserburgh in the immediate post-war period. Apart from some shop refashioning, a smart polished granite commercial infill at Nos 36–38 Broad Street, the rebuilding of Hanover Street, and a new Freemasons Hall, near the site of the Brick Lodge, in 1934,[416] the inter-war period made little impact on the town centre save in one major respect – depopulation. The one significant new addition to the social landscape was the Picture House in Mid Street, built in 1921, which marked the town's embracing of the new form of mass entertainment (**fig 39**). The 1920s may have been 'Roaring' elsewhere, but in Fraserburgh there was no economic boom. Public services, however, steadily improved, and in 1935 electricity came to the town.[417] There was one new addition to the burgh landscape, the War Memorial. The traumas of 1914–18 received their official commemoration on 9 September 1923 when the memorial was unveiled amidst great public ceremony on the site at the junction of Saltoun Place and St Modan's Road previously occupied by the public fountain. Crowds of around 6000 had followed the procession of local dignitaries and representatives of various organisations from Saltoun Square to the memorial, which carries the names of the 411 local men who died.[418] The scale of the carnage among the town's young male population had been horrific, and few families in Fraserburgh had not lost a close relative.

The one bright spot on the town's economic horizon after 1918 was the Consolidated Pneumatic Tool Company. Following the outbreak of war in 1914 it had found its tools greatly in demand as the British munitions industry geared up for wartime production, and the closing off of foreign competition ensured that the company achieved a dominance in the market place. Having carved a significant niche for itself in this highly specialist market, it embarked on a programme of rapid expansion in the inter-war years. By 1939 the company had established branches in South Africa, Australia, India and France, and it was a major supplier to the British arms industry. At the outbreak of the Second World War, Consolidated performed a key role in the manufacture of military equipment, in particular supplying the fuel pumps and booster controls for the Rolls Royce Merlin engines used in the RAF's Spitfire fighter-planes. The existence of an already highly-skilled workforce, coupled with the relative remoteness of Fraserburgh from the main industrial centres of Britain, which were vulnerable to German bombing, led to the

rapid expansion of munitions operations in the town after 1939. Two new factories were opened, producing Bofors guns, Howitzer gun-units, and turret rings for the main British battle tank, the Churchill. At its peak, the military-industrial complex employed around 2400 people, over 1000 of them women.[419]

Handsome private bungalows stretched intermittently southward along Strichen Road, but not in huge quantity. By contrast, western Fraserburgh's edge was overwhelmed by suburban expansion in the form of subsidised houses, cottages and flats following the 1919 Housing Act. [420] Conditions in the centre had clearly become unacceptable,[421] and the town was quick off the mark in using the legislation to erect new houses: in April 1920, a council housing estate in a rather fine garden-city layout was proposed for the vacant land between Dennyduff and Mid Streets. Designed by the Fraserburgh architects and engineers D & J R MacMillan, it followed the most fashionable model with generous gardens.[422] Although the plan was not followed to the letter, it was in spirit, as can be seen from the two-storey semi-detached houses along Gallowhill Road by Walker and Duncan in 1937.[423] These houses were built in granite with simple modern Scots detail. They also had generous gardens and surpassed private sector houses in their individuality and quality (**fig 40**). There also was a decanting to Queen Mary Street, Union Grove and Viewfield Road in 1922, and Hamilton Road and Moray Road in 1932. Gray Street was built in 1933, and Jubilee Crescent (named in commemoration of George V's Silver Jubilee) in 1936. The town then built itself a fine new western gateway at Watermill Road with handsome, splayed (angled) council houses in red granite.

FIGURE 40
Public sector housing,
Gallowhill Road
(Paula Martin)

What distinguishes inter-war Fraserburgh is the sheer quantity of house building, whose quality was redolent of a new confidence promoted by new industry. Unfortunately, confidence took the form of an unnecessarily large scale: a landscape of enormously long, sweepingly wide suburban roads like Queen's Road and Alexandra Avenue, without local facilities, or any sense of enclosure or protection from the Buchan winds. Small architectural details of doors, windows or rooflines are quite overwhelmed by this large scale. Nonetheless there are enclaves of high quality: notably, the little 1938 cul-de-sac of timber houses in Kent Gardens (named after the Duchess of Kent) (**fig 41**). The plain granite houses in Marconi Road (Marconi had established communication between Cornwall and the experimental station here in 1904) and in Walker Crescent were both built (presumably by special licence for armaments workers) in 1940,[424] by which date some 1000 new houses had been added to the town since 1918.[425]

The factories gave Fraserburgh a strategic importance in the British war effort and ensured that the town became a target for bombing raids by German aircraft based in Norway. Defences constructed during this period survive within the burgh, particularly in the vicinity of the cemetery. A Type 24 pillbox is situated in the field to the north of the cemetery and a second is in the dunes at the east end of Fraserburgh Bay. A radio station recorded from aerial photographs to the immediate south of the cemetery had two masts and four wooden huts, and a possible Type 27 pillbox.[426]

FIGURE 41
Timber housing, Kent Gardens (Paula Martin)

There were, in total, seventeen raids on Fraserburgh between July 1940 and April 1943, killing 53 people, injuring over 300 more, and inflicting heavy damage on properties throughout the town. The first, a daylight attack, occurred on 16 July 1940. Four bombs struck the town along a diagonal line between the bottom of Station Brae (between the railway station and Dalrymple Hall) and the rear of the Alexandra Hotel at the western end of the High Street. The most severe damage occurred at No 20 Frithside Street, where a tenement block was almost completely demolished and major structural damage was done to the rear of the Royal Bank.[427] The second raid came in the early morning eleven days later, with the Consolidated Pneumatic Tool Company plant clearly the target.[428] Two more raids followed in August and October, and then on 5 November came one of the most destructive when planes, drawn by the flames of an accidental fire in Mid Street, dropped

95

their bombs over the town centre. One hit the Commercial Bar at the top of Kirk Brae, killing 34 people and injuring 52.[429] In early 1941, the main target appears to have been the Maconochie plant at the north end of the town, which was producing rations for the armed forces and whose chimney was a prominent feature of the townscape. One attack on the factory in April 1941 killed six and injured a further 126.[430] By the time the air raids ended in April 1943, extensive damage had been inflicted over a wide area of the town centre and suburbs, with landmark buildings, such as the Union Bank at the corner of Seaforth Street and Commerce Street, almost destroyed.[431]

While the risk of air raids had quickly become apparent in 1940, there was at first little official response to the threat of a German landing occurring anywhere in eastern Scotland, as the chief danger seemed to be that Hitler would follow up his conquest of the Netherlands, Belgium and France with a direct assault across the English Channel. Some general precautions had been set in place immediately upon the outbreak of war in September 1939: black-out was imposed on street lighting, houses, and work and business premises, while factories and other important facilities had their roofs painted in camouflage colours and their distinctive plans and profiles broken up with netting. After the fall of Norway, however, the risk was reappraised and plans set in train to defend the stretches of coast most vulnerable to landings. Around Fraserburgh, this included mining parts of the beach and placing massive concrete-block 'tank traps' along the shoreline at the bents. Concrete pillboxes were placed at strategic points around the town, such as major crossroads and junctions, important facilities (such as the Consolidated Pneumatic Tool Company), on Kinnaird Head (now demolished) and on the Links. There was also a fear of airborne assault by troops carried in gliders from Norway, which led to the erection of timber posts in open areas, such as the town's playing fields, to prevent glider landings.[432]

1945 to the present

As had happened in 1918–19, it was expected that the end of the Second World War would bring a speedy return to peace-time levels and areas of commerce and industry. In common with many other parts of Britain, the post-war dream of peace and prosperity, with a booming economy and a new social order provided by the Welfare State, only briefly seemed likely to materialise. The long-term reality for Fraserburgh has been painful and protracted economic decline, largely a product of the progressive contraction of the white fish industry, and a decisive shift in the regional economic focus towards Aberdeen at the expense of its smaller competitors in the north-east.

Immediately post-war, there were initiatives to stimulate the local economy and fill niches in the national sector. In 1945, for example, under the auspices of the Herring Industry Board, a fish-meal factory was established, as well as a herring-freezing factory which soon moved to freezing white fish too. The Board encouraged such developments, and guaranteed minimum prices.[433] There was, however, no significant development of a light industrial base, such as government initiatives were encouraging in central Scotland. Such industries as existed still revolved largely around the harbour. In the 1950s the leading industries were Park & Company, a barrel and timber business; Samuel Robb, a smaller coopering business; and the British Oil and Guano Company Limited, a manure works at West Shore, providing good jobs despite the smell. There were also two engineering shops and seven boatbuilding yards, seven firms of marine engineers, two fish-selling companies, and two firms of boat painters.[434] A post-war boom in the domestic fish trade had encouraged a continued focus on support for this sector, and, although not reaching the same scale as the pre-1914 herring industry, Fraserburgh's fish trade remained dominant in the local economy and represented a substantial segment of the national trade. In the 1950s there were 'trains being run in season direct to Billingsgate Market in London'.[435] The pelagic fishing industry, which grew after 1945, was carried on in larger and larger boats, and increasingly far offshore, using diesel engines, and new technology such as echo sounders.[436] With fishing thriving, there was no need to diversify or encourage inward investment in new industries.

The growth of pelagic fishing lasted into the 1980s, but has been in steady decline since then, and has recently been hit yet again by reduced quotas and foreign competition. Recognition of the threat faced by the local fleet saw various initiatives designed to encourage diversification. These attempted to break down the traditional exclusivity of fishing communities, but have singularly not provided viable – and lasting –

FRASERBURGH
GLORIOUS SANDS · BATHING · GOLF · TENNIS
BOOKLET FROM TOWN CLERK (DEPT P) OR ANY
L·N·E·R INQUIRY OFFICE

alternatives. Despite the vast sums of money spent on the harbour and its associated infrastructure, Fraserburgh has once again found itself suffering from over-dependence on the fishing industry.

Although Fraserburgh's first attempt at promoting itself as a tourist destination in the first decade of the nineteenth century had failed, after the Second World War its bracing air and sandy beach once again attracted visitors: 'A considerable number of holidaymakers come to the town every summer and many homes are opened to receive paying guests' (**fig 42**).[437] This was typical of the north and east coasts of Scotland, but the railway which transported these visitors closed to passengers in 1960 and to freight in 1979.[438] Tourist traffic in the late twentieth century was increasingly dependent on road transport, but the loss of the rail link removed an important means of access from the main regional centre, Aberdeen.

Suburban expansion continued and eventually accelerated. Despite the economic upheavals after 1945, the later twentieth century saw the footprint of Fraserburgh increase dramatically, though its population less so. The boundary had been extended by 65 acres to 5645 acres in 1948. By the early 1950s there were 2712 inhabited houses, but despite the building of 1000 houses since 1914, 19% of the population still lived in overcrowded conditions.[439] West Road was laid out in 1947, Gallowhill Terrace in 1949, Thompson Terrace in 1950, and Mormond Avenue in 1952.[440] The town laid out more streets and roads during the later post-war period than during any previous period in its history. While only three streets were constructed in the 1960s, 38 were laid out during the following decade, and a further 11 in the 1980s. To keep things simple, each of the 12 new streets laid out in 1970 began with the letter 'A', and the five streets laid out in 1973 began with 'B'.[441]

Changes in the fishing industry and in fishing practice gave Fraserburgh a taste of post-industrial dereliction and demolition at the north end of the town, and only sporadic replacement by new activity. The twentieth century saw a few new public buildings. Such new construction as has been undertaken has been driven largely by changing social and educational needs. For example, as the post-1945 'baby boom' generation passed through the education system, existing facilities proved inadequate in terms of both space and expanded curriculum requirements. The new Fraserburgh Academy was built in 1962, and has been further extended since.

Proposals for a restructuring of Scottish local government had been on the political agenda since the 1960s, and were implemented in 1974 with the most radical changes since the sixteenth century. Town councils and burgh status were abolished and replaced with a two-tier system of District and Regional Councils. From 1975 Fraserburgh was administered as part of Banff and Buchan District, with the administrative headquarters located in Banff. Local offices were maintained in major population centres within the new district, including Fraserburgh, but the main administrative apparatus had been removed. Strategic decision-making had also been handed to a new higher authority, Grampian Regional Council, with its administrative headquarters in Aberdeen. This hierarchy lasted barely two decades before a sweeping reorganisation in 1995–96 introduced unitary authorities. Grampian Region and Banff and Buchan District ceased to exist, and in their place emerged Aberdeenshire Council, with administrative headquarters at Inverurie.

Since the 1980s there have been a number of initiatives founded on Fraserburgh's rich heritage to reinforce local identity and to attract a larger share of Scotland's tourist market to the town. In 1988, the Cross, the symbolic heart of the old burgh community, was restored and 'tinctured' (painted and gilded) as a centrepiece of Saltoun Square. This was the first stage in a programme of 'environmental improvements', the partial pedestrianisation of the square and the provision of visitor information panels and signposts. More recently the lighthouse on Kinnaird Head, automated in 1991, has become the prestigious Museum of Scottish Lighthouses. This was selected in preference to all the others around Scotland that might have been chosen because it was one of the first four lighthouses to be built by the Northern Lighthouse Board; its urban location also brought economic benefits. Its key location means it still serves as an aid to navigation. An adjacent building, once a cooperage and later the foundry of the Consolidated Pneumatic Tool Company, has been converted into a heritage centre by the Fraserburgh Heritage Society and interprets a fascinating and tempestuous local history.

Notes

1   G Warren, Towards a social archaeology of the Mesolithic in eastern Scotland: landscapes, contexts and experience (unpublished PhD thesis, University of Edinburgh, 2001).

2   Warren, *The Mesolithic in eastern Scotland*, fig 26.

3   Eg NMRS NJ96SE 14, a beaker and a late Bronze Age sword were found under a tumulus at Memsie before 1849.

4   Eg NMRS NK06SW 1, a large cairn containing burnt bone and ashes, removed during land improvement at Tershinity in 1834.

5   Eg NMRS NJ96SE 12, a short cist, containing some beaker sherds and no surviving bones discovered at Upper Cairns; NJ96 SE2, a stone cist containing an inhumation discovered at Wester Cardno in 1848.

6   Eg NMRS NJ96SW 8, five Bronze Age short cists, all with inhumations and some containing beakers, found at Upper Boyndlie since 1908.

7   Eg NMRS NJ96NE 3, flint arrowheads found at Percyhorner in 1853; NJ96SW 5, flint arrowheads found at Upper Cairnmurnan in the mid-nineteenthth century.

8   NMRS NK06SW 22, flint chisel found in a field at Home Farm, Philorth in 1961.

9   NMRS NJ96NW 11, two axes, of micaceous claystone found in Pitsligo, donated to the National Museum of Scotland in 1895.

10 NMRS NK06SW 44, a Neolithic carved stone ball with six knobs was found in Lonmay in 1974.

11 Eg NMRS NK06SW 42, a circular enclosure at Hillhead House recorded in 1977; NJ96SW 23, an oval enclosure at Mains of Bodychell recorded in 1992; NJ96SW 24, faint traces of a circular enclosure at Lochhills recorded in 1992.

12 Eg NMRS NK06SW 25, faint traces of a ring-ditch at Lochhills recorded in 1992; NJ96SW 41, possible ring-ditch at Woodhead recorded in 1976.

13 NMRS NJ96SE 41, pits and other possible features at Fordafour recorded in 1976; NJ96NE 42, two pits and other features at Glenbuchty Cottage recorded at an unknown date.

14 Cranna, *Fraserburgh*, 4.

15 Cranna, *Fraserburgh*, 5.

16 B Jones and D Mattingly, *An Atlas of Roman Britain* (Oxford, 1990), 19 (map 2:4), 21 (map 2:6), 82 (map 4:18); C Martin, 'Water Transport and the Roman Occupations of North Britain' in T C Smout (ed), *Scotland and the Sea* (Edinburgh, 1992), 6–7; A L F Rivet and C Smith, *The Place-Names of Roman Britain* (Cambridge, 1979), 464, who suggest the remote possibility that the name should be applied to Rattray Head instead.

17 NMRS NJ45SE 2.

18 NMRS NJ63NE 2.

19 A S Robertson, 'Roman coins found in Scotland, 1971–1982', *Proceedings of the Society of Antiquaries of Scotland* 113 (1984), 405. Unassociated Roman coins are found widely in Scotland, and are not necessarily significant.

20 I Ralston, 'The Green Castle and the Promontory Forts of North-East Scotland' in *Settlement in Scotland 1000 BC–AD 1000*, Scottish Archaeological Forum, **10** (1980), 27–40.

21 RCAHMS, *Pictish Symbol Stones: a handlist 1994* (Edinburgh, 1994), 8. See also I A Shepherd, 'Pictish Settlement Problems in N E Scotland', in J C Chapman and H C Mytum (eds), *Settlement in North Britain 1000 BC–1000 AD*, BAR British Series **118** (1983), 327–37.

22 Shepherd, 'Pictish Settlement Problems', 328–9.

23 For Aberdour, see A O Anderson, *Early Sources of Scottish History AD 500–1286* (Edinburgh, 1922), ii, 174–5; for Deer, see *ibid* and R Fawcett, *Scottish Abbeys and Priories* (London, 1994), 135; D E Easson and I B Cowan, *Medieval Religious Houses: Scotland* (London, 1976).

24 Murison and Noble, *Names and Places*, iv. For Modan see D Farmer, *Oxford Dictionary of Saints*, new edn (Oxford, 1997), 351.

25 A Smith, *A New History of Aberdeenshire* (Aberdeen, 1875), 612–13; Murison, *Broch*, 7; Cranna, *Fraserburgh*, 18; Murison and Noble, *Names and Places*, iv.

26 Anderson, *Early Sources*, i, 468–70.

27 A Woolf, *From Pictland to Alba 789–1070* (Edinburgh, 2008), 93–102.

28   D Broun, The Origin of Scottish Identity , in C Bjørn, A Grant and K
      J Stringer (eds), *Nations, Nationalism and Patriotism in the European Past*
      (Copenhagen, 1993), 35–55.

29   A Young, 'The earls and earldom of Buchan in the Thirteenth Century', in A
      Grant and K J Stringer (eds), *Medieval Scotland: Crown, Lordship and Community*
      (Edinburgh, 1993), 174–202.

30   For Gartnait earl of Buchan (c1131–32) see A C Lawrie, *Early Scottish Charters
      prior to AD 1153* (Glasgow, 1905), no 97; Colban, mormaer of Buchan, see
      Anderson, *Early Sources*, ii, 180. It is possibly the same Colban, described
      as 'earl' of Buchan, who is recorded by the English poet-chronicler Jordan
      Fantosme, fighting in King William the Lion's army in northern England in
      1174, R C Johnston (ed), *Jordan Fantosme's Chronicle* (Oxford, 1981), 36–7.

31   A Young, *Robert the Bruce's Rivals: The Comyns, 1212–1314* (East Linton, 1997),
      22–3.

32   Young, *The Comyns*, 203–4.

33   Young, 'Earls and earldom of Buchan', 174–202.

34   *Illustrations of the Topography and Antiquities of the Shires of Aberdeen and Banff*,
      4 vols (Spalding Club, 1847–69), iv, 87–9; A Fraser, *The Frasers of Philorth*, 3
      vols (Edinburgh, 1879), ii, 209–11.

35   KC MS 2004, vol 412, 1, box 1, bundle 1, no 4, for sale dated 18 August 1381;
      Antiquities of Aberdeen and Banff, iv, 84–85, for confirmation dated 14 February
      1381/82.

36   KC MS 3004, vol 412, 5, box 1, bundle 2, no 28; *Antiquities of Aberdeen and
      Banff*, iv, 124; *Frasers of Philorth*, ii, 240.

37   *Antiquities of Aberdeen and Banff*, iv, 95–6, 122–3, gives the date as 1418.
      However, this is queried in *Frasers of Philorth*, i, 142–3, which states that in
      1418 neither Lawrence Mercer, nor Alexander Fraser existed.

38   KC MS 3004, vol 412, 2, box 1, bundle 1, no 9.

39   KC MS 3004, vol 412, 2, box 1, bundle 1, no 12; *Antiquities of Aberdeen and
      Banff*, iv, 124–5; *Frasers of Philorth*, ii, 225.

40   *Antiquities of Aberdeen and Banff*, iv, 86; *Frasers of Philorth*, ii, 226–8, gives the
      date as 1445/46 although the charter clearly shows it as 1455.

41   *Frasers of Philorth*, ii, 233–5.

42   KC MS 3004, bundle 532, and vol 412, box 1, bundle 2, no 30; *Antiquities of
      Aberdeen and Banff*, iv, 98–100 (Amiens, in France). *Frasers of Philorth*, i, 153,
      he stayed abroad for several years, but there is no evidence where else he
      travelled to, or how.

43   *NSA*, 254–5; J F Tocher, *The Book of Buchan* (Peterhead, 1910), 319; Murison,
      Broch, 8. It is almost certain that any harbour construction took the form of
      a breakwater to provide a sheltered haven, rather than piers or quays against
      which vessels could moor.

44   *Frasers of Philorth*, ii, 240–43.

45   Cranna, *Fraserburgh*, 18.

46   *RMS*, iii, no 2849; *Antiquities of Aberdeen and Banff*, iv, 645; *Frasers of Philorth*, i,
      149.

47 *Frasers of Philorth*, i, 149.

48 *RMS*, iv, 5; *Antiquities of Aberdeen and Banff*, iv, 645–6.

49 These were held regularly until *c* 1865, Cranna, *Fraserburgh*, 24–5, 'the opening up of the country by railways completely swept away the small provincial fairs'.

50 *SP*, vii, 438–9, gives Alexander 8th's date of birth as *c* 1537; *Antiquities of Aberdeen and Banff*, iv, 101–4, 649. Some later sources give the March 1570 date as either Alexander's coming-of-age or the date at which he laid the foundation stone of the castle on Kinnaird Head. No evidence has so far been found to support either of these statements.

51 *Frasers of Philorth*, i, 152.

52 Gordon of Straloch, quoted in Sir A Mitchell (ed), *Geographical Collections Relating to Scotland made by Walter Macfarlane*, 3 vols (SHS, 1906–08), ii, 278.

53 *RMS*, v, no 1524, precept of sasine from George Gordon, portioner of Kindrocht.

54 *RPC*, vi, 653–4.

55 *Frasers of Philorth*, i, 152.

56 J Wormald, *Lords and Men in Scotland: bonds of manrent 1442–1603* (Edinburgh, 1985), 408, no 24.

57 KC MS 3004, bundle 534.

58 *SP*, vii, 437–9, Alexander was born *c* 1537; Cranna, *Fraserburgh*, 16.

59 R Oram, 'Community of the Realm: The Middle Ages', in M Glendinning (ed) *The Architecture of Scottish Government: From Kingship to Parliamentary Democracy* (Dundee, 2004), 69–72.

60 According to *Frasers of Philorth*, i, 152. Local tradition through the nineteenth century consistently refers to the castle on the headland as 'Fraserburgh Castle'.

61 Cranna, *Fraserburgh*, 17.

62 See C McKean, *The Scottish Chateau* (Stroud, 2001), 145–8.

63 The raggle (groove cut into stone to receive flashings) of a roof and a tall blocked aperture like a door appeared when the harling was removed. The second Daniell engraving of Fraserburgh shows two buildings in the vicinity, R Ayton and W Daniell, *A Voyage Round Great Britain ...* 2 vols, facsimile edn (London, 1978), ii, 4.

64 I D Bryce has suggested that the carved bosses form part of the Counter Reformation iconography so common in north-east Scotland, and that the Wine Tower was a place for covert worship. The former is certainly true, but the latter is questionable given the fact that the Wine Tower was not only prominent, but the first structure met with in the approach to the castle. Hardly furtive.

65 Cranna, *Fraserburgh*, 18, 90, work is said to have started in 1571 and the congregation moved from the old kirk in 1574.

66 A I Dunlop (ed), 'Bagimond's Roll', *SHS Miscellany* vi [1939], 18, 43; Murison, *Broch*, 6.

67   Murison and Noble, *Names and Places*, iv; Pratt, *Buchan*, 153; Cranna,
      Fraserburgh, 18, the old church was 'close to, if not adjoining, the west end of
      the churchyard of Kirkton', 90.

68   Cranna, *Fraserburgh*, 5, 88, it stood on the line of the west wall of the old
      graveyard. *Christian Watt Papers*, 181, 'He (Wulla Fraser) roofed over the old
      Kirk at Kirktoun and made it into the Burial Vault of Fraser of Park'. This
      vault, however, is built entirely of brick and is unlikely to incorporate part of
      the medieval church.

69   *OSA*, 173; Cranna, *Fraserburgh*, 119. Roy does not show the church as
      cruciform on his map *c* 1750, though he does show a small extension on the
      south side.

70   *OSA*, 176.

71   Cranna, *Fraserburgh*, 27.

72   For the tenor of the bond, see Wormald, *Lords and Men*, 409, no 29, where
      the burgh of Aberdeen's bond is cited.

73   This period saw the Kirk and Presbyterian nobles oblige the young James VI
      and his favourites to issue the so-called 'Negative Confession' (1581) which
      denounced all forms of 'papistry'; the 'Ruthven Raid' (1582), in which an
      ultra-Presbyterian noble faction seized control of the king and, consequently,
      political power; while in 1584, James issued the so-called 'Black Acts',
      which reaffirmed Episcopal government in the Kirk and re-established the
      supremacy of King, Parliament and Council over the estates, both spiritual
      and temporal.

74   *Macfarlane*, i, 40–41; Cranna, *Fraserburgh*, 36, 389, described it as having been a
      'very humble and small erection'.

75   RCAHMS, 33205 (DC8803), *c* 1809; NAS RHP 45434, 1818.

76   *OSA*, 176.

77   Cranna, *Fraserburgh*, 381, on the north-eastern corner of Saltoun Square Lane.

78   Murison, *Broch*, 15, according to the 1613 charter, both High Street and Cross
      Street were 40ft wide, the width of Broad Street is not mentioned, Mid Street
      and what is probably to be identified with Manse Street were both 24ft wide,
      and Braehead 8ft.

79   J A Henderson, *Aberdeenshire Epitaphs and Inscriptions* ... (Aberdeen, 1907),
      250, Faithlie's burghal status and privileges drew settlers from across the
      north-east of Scotland and farther afield.

80   Cranna, *Fraserburgh*, 316, and others, identify the traditional site of the very
      first harbour as the cove under Kinnaird Head.

81   *Frasers of Philorth*, i, 152–3, quoting G Crawford, *Lives and Characters of
      the Officers of the Crown and of the State* (Edinburgh, 1726), 283; Gordon of
      Straloch (1662) in *Macfarlane*, 3ii, 278; *NSA*, 254–5. It is possible that the inner
      portion of the present north pier encases portions of earlier structures.

82   *Macfarlane*, iii, 143.

83   *Antiquities of Aberdeen and Banff*, iv, 649, the land to be held from the king.

84   KC MS 3004, bundle 534.

85   KC MS 3004, vol 412, 13–15, box 4, bundle 9, no 2; *RMS*, v, no 1526;
      Antiquities of Aberdeen and Banff, iv, 649–53.

86   KC MS 3004, vol 412, 15, box 4, bundle 9, no 5.

87   *RMS*, v, no 2117; *Antiquities of Aberdeen and Banff*, iv, 649–651.

88   See T C Smout (ed), *Scotland and Europe: 1200–1850* (Edinburgh, 1986).

89   There is no evidence for the origin of this unusual plan. *Frasers of Philorth*,
i, 152, suggests that Alexander 9th got off to such a quick start with his
improvements that he may have been jointly planning them with his
grandfather. It was his grandfather who had travelled in Europe for several
years, though there is no evidence he travelled to the Iberian peninsula, where
the closest parallels are perhaps to be found. For example, D Stanislawski,
'Early Spanish Town Planning in the New World', *Geographical Review* **37.1**
(1947), 104, Philip II's detailed instructions issued in 1573 said that 'if the
town is a port, the main plaza should be at the harbour. It should be in the
middle of the town in inland places'.

90   KC MS 3004, vol 412, 15–16, box 4, bundle 9, no 6; *RMS*, v, no 2117;
Antiquities of Aberdeen and Banff, iv, 649–51.

91   KC MS 3004, vol 412, p 17, box 4, bundle 9, no 10; T Thomson and C Innes
(eds), *Acts of the Parliaments of Scotland* (Edinburgh, 1814–75), iv, 147–8 (52);
Antiquities of Aberdeen and Banff, iv, 653–4; *Frasers of Philorth*, ii, 263–5.

92   *Wodrow*, 272.

93   *Wodrow*, lxxvii–lxxviii; *Tocher, Buchan*, 327–329.

94   *Wodrow*, 270, 'This holy and learned man was one of the most burning
and shining lights in his time ... he was the head and only teacher of [the]
little, learned Colledge, or Schola Illustris, in one of the remotest corners in
Scotland. He was the first teacher of Philosophy and Divinity at Fraserburgh'.

95   *Fasti Academiae*, i, 78–9.

96   *Fasti Academiae*, i, 79.

97   *Wodrow*, lxxviii; Cranna, *Fraserburgh*, 207–8, however, suggests that quarrying
for the buildings only began in the eighteenth century. Certainly, substantial
portions of the building, including the college tower, were still upstanding
in the later 1780s, and Christian Watt states that substantial portions of the
buildings survived into the mid-nineteenth century and stones from them had
been used in the building of the new Free Kirk in 1844 (*Christian Watt Papers*,
90). Smith, *Aberdeenshire*, 601, mentions the 'remains of an old quandrangular
tower' as still visible.

98   *NSA*, 272.

99   For more about the university see I Malley, *The University of Fraserburgh*
(Shepshed, Leicestershire, 1988).

100 Cranna, *Fraserburgh*, 202–7; Murison, *Broch*, 13.

101 Murison and Noble, *Names and Places*, 20, the name was borrowed from
Aberdeen to commemorate the university, but does not reflect the exact
location of the university or its bounds.

102 *OSA*, 174. It is now inside the South Church.

103 *Extracts from the Council Register of the Burgh of Aberdeen, i, 1398–1570*
(Aberdeen, 1844), 356–7.

104 *Extracts from the Council Register of the Burgh of Aberdeen, ii, 1570–1625*
(Aberdeen, 1848), 10–11.

105 *RMS*, vi, no 1167.

106 *Aberdeen Council Register*, ii, 279–80, 284; *Records of the Convention of the
Royal Burghs of Scotland* ..., vol ii, 1597–1614 (Edinburgh, 1870), 204, in 1605
Aberdeen expressed concern that Philorth might have ambitions for his burgh
to become a royal burgh.

107 *Aberdeen Council Register*, ii, 336–7; Tocher, *Buchan*, 325.

108 *SP*, vii, 439.

109 *SP*, vii, 437.

110 *OSA*, 174.

111 Cranna, *Fraserburgh*, 25; Murison, *Broch*, 21, the merchant guild seems to
have been established in 1671; *OSA*, 178, burgess and guild exclusivity was no
longer enforced by 1791.

112 Cranna, *Fraserburgh*, 25.

113 'Report by Thomas Tucker upon the Settlement of the Revenues of Excise
and Customs in Scotland. AD MDCLVI', in *Miscellany of the Scottish Burgh
Records Society* (Edinburgh, 1881), 34; a folk memory may survive in the
statement, *OSA* 167, that soon after its foundation Fraserburgh 'became a
place of considerable trade'.

114 Cranna, *Fraserburgh*, 29; L Diack, *The People of Fraserburgh and Pitsligo, 1696*
(Aberdeen, 1992), also 29 tradesmen (including 9 tailors, 4 weavers, 4 wrights
and a glazier, 3 shoemakers, 2 coopers). There were 20 households in
Broadsea, presumably each headed by a fisherman.

115 Cranna, *Fraserburgh*, 381, 'The first hotel in Fraserburgh about the close of
the seventeenth century was situated on the Braeheads, at the east end of
Saltoun Square Lane, north corner'.

116 Henderson, *Aberdeenshire Epitaphs*, 257, John Gordon of Kinellar, longtime
factor to the Saltoun family, died in 1764 at the age of 80. He bought the
small estate of Park, which through one of his daughters became the home
of the Frasers of Park. Alternatively, a leading name in the Poll Tax list of
1696 was Alexander Gordon, notary public (Cranna, *Fraserburgh*, 29).

117 Cranna, *Fraserburgh*, 381; G E Dey, *Fraserburgh, Now and Then* (Fraserburgh,
1987), 13, the house was replaced by shops and stables, 23–9 High Street.

118 The armorial stone was, in 1907, built into the house of Auchinroath, by
Rothes. See Henderson, *Aberdeenshire Epitaphs*, 256; D MacGibbon and T
Ross, *The Castellated and Domestic Architecture of Scotland*, 5 vols (Edinburgh,
1887–92), v, 83.

119 Cranna, *Fraserburgh*, 381.

120 Cranna, *Fraserburgh*, 389; D S Rennie, *A Walk down Cross Sreett and High Sreett*
(Fraserburgh, 2000), 100, the old coach-house, No 80 High Street, built by Dr
Leslie in 1761, also known as Haunted House, was demolished in the 1950s.

121 *SP*, vii, 440–1; Cranna, *Fraserburgh*, 32–3.

122 *Frasers of Philorth*, i, 162, the trustees were Simon Fraser, Lord Lovat, George
Ogilvy of Carnoustie, and William Forbes of Tolquhoun (future father-in-law
of the 10th laird); *SP*, vii, 439.

123 The lands sold were: Inverallochy, bought by Simon Fraser of Lovat (one of the trustees appointed by Sir Alexander); Kindrocht, Denend, a third part of Faithlie and Easter Tyrie to Thomas Fraser of Strichen (which his descendants still held in the eighteenth century); and Cairnbulg and Invernorth to Alexander Fraser of Durris and his son, Robert, to whom they had already been pledged as security on a loan in 1613. The sale of estates to relatives was a standard way to protect them in the hope of redemption in better times.

124 *SP*, vii, 413, 441.

125 *Frasers of Philorth*, i, 170.

126 J Spalding, *History of the Troubles and Memorable Transactions in Scotland and England ...*, 2 vols (Bannatyne Club, 1828), i, 193, 196.

127 F D Dow, *Cromwellian Scotland* (Edinburgh, 1979), 226.

128 Dow, *Cromwellian Scotland*, 101, the resistance was not entirely Royalist, but included some former Protesters, extreme Covenanters who had opposed what they had considered to be the backsliding policies of the 1650 and 1651 General Assemblies.

129 Dow, *Cromwellian Scotland*, 85, 239.

130 Dow, *Cromwellian Scotland*, 273.

131 See, for example, *Christian Watt Papers*, 8, 10, 21–2, 176.

132 *SP*, vii, 442, in 1610 John, 8th Lord Saltoun, had begun to sell off the family's main northern properties, centred on Rothiemay in Banffshire, and in 1643 his son Alexander, 9th Lord Saltoun, disposed of the East Lothian properties from which their title derived to Sir Andrew Fletcher, with the result that despite the new title the focus of Fraser power and influence would remain firmly in northern Buchan.

133 *SP*, vii, 442, Balvenie passed to Arthur Forbes of Echt, the legal costs were borne by the Philorth estate and eventually the lands of Pittulie and Pittendrum were sold to cover Alexander's mounting debts.

134 *Christian Watt Papers*, 178, this town-house stood on the site on The Green now occupied by the Saltoun Arms Hotel. He was buried in the Fraser Aisle at the parish kirk.

135 *SP*, vii, 444.

136 Inverallochy, with 'a number of his friends and tenants sojourned to Fraserburgh, and there at the town's Cross in right royal style proclaimed James II King of Great Britain', Cranna, *Fraserburgh*, 30; J Taylor, *The Great Historic Families of Scotland*, 2 vols (London, 1887), ii, 291.

137 *SP*, vii, 444.

138 B Lenman, *The Jacobite Risings in Britain, 1689–1746* (Aberdeen, 1980), 130.

139 *SP*, vii, 444.

140 J H Burton (ed), *The Darien Papers* (Bannatyne Club, Edinburgh, 1849), 375, he subscribed £500, while John Hay, merchant in Fraserburgh, subscribed £100.

141 *SP*, vii, 444, Anti-Union sentiment remained strong in Fraserburgh throughout the eighteenth century. Helen Noble stated that her father remained anti-Union until his death in 1785 (*Christian Watt Papers*, 171).

142 See for example P G B McNeill and H L MacQueen (eds), *Atlas of Scottish History to 1707* (Edinburgh, 1996), 262, 272–4, 276.

143 T C Smout, *Scottish Trade on the Eve of Union* (Edinburgh and London, 1963), 295, William Coutts of Montrose, writing from Bergen, June 1698, 'I wrote to you on the 8th instant, but iff it bee come to your hands I know nott, for it was with a Frazerburgh ship att the woods'; ibid, 143, about half the outgoing ships from the north-east were carrying cloth, provisions and corn to Holland, while one-fifth were taking corn to Norway.

144 *Records of the Convention of the Royal Burghs of Scotland ..., vol iv, 1677–1711* (Edinburgh, 1880), 381, the others were Doune, Kilmarnock, Coldstream, Falkirk, Kelso, Dalkeith, Old Meldrum and Bo'ness, all 'not to be disturbed in the enjoyment of their trade in time coming'.

145 Cranna, *Fraserburgh*, 93–119; Lenman, *Jacobite Risings*, 130.

146 Cranna, *Fraserburgh*, 36–7.

147 Lenman, *Jacobite Risings*, 137.

148 *Christian Watt Papers*, 10.

149 *Christian Watt Papers*, 8–10.

150 *Christian Watt Papers*, 12. The school is said to have been founded in 1656.

151 *Christian Watt Papers*, 178. Helen Noble, Christian Watt's 'Granny Lascelles', noted that her father, who died in 1785, 'did not live to see the military leave'.

152 *Christian Watt Papers*, 172, 177. The building was described as having a 'high watch toor to set all over the country'. After the withdrawal of the garrison, it was bought by the Corinthian Church and used as a meeting hall. Murison and Noble, *Names and Places*, 6.

153 *Christian Watt Papers*,178, this transaction was regularised under the 1787 agreement between Saltoun and the town. *OSA*, 178, By a late transaction between Lord Saltoun and the town, the feuars, in lieu of some privileges and claims over commonable lands, which they gave up, obtained, in property, lands which rent at £23. Of this the feuars, at large, have the sole disposal'. The 1787 agreement may have been prompted by the need to sort out land rights after the withdrawal of the garrison.

154 *Christian Watt Papers*, 10.

155 *Christian Watt Papers*, 177.

156 B G Seton and J G Arnot (eds), *The Prisoners of the '45*, 3 vols (SHS, 1928–29), i, 221.

157 'Non-jurors' or 'non-jurant' clergy were those Episcopalian clerics who refused to take any of the required oaths of allegiance to the post-1688 monarchs.

158 Cranna, *Fraserburgh*, 146–8; *Christian Watt Papers*, 10. They later worshipped in a building in Mid Street before the construction of a new Episcopalian church in 1788 (Cranna, *Fraserburgh*, 151).

159 A H Miller (ed), *A Selection of Scottish Forfeited Estate Papers 1715; 1745* (SHS, 1909), 179–80, 380.

160 A Livingstone, C W H Aikman and B S Hart (eds), *No Quarter Given. The Muster Roll of Prince Charles Edward Stuart's Army, 1745–46* (Glasgow, 2001), 61.

161 *Prisoners of the '45*, i, 71.

162 *A List of Persons Concerned in the Rebellion 1745–46* (SHS, 1890), 302–3. Those accused were John Cruikshank (surgeon), William Christie (ship-master), William Chalmers (baxter), George Chain (sailor) and James Ferrier (sailor).

163 *Christian Watt Papers*, 7–8, 171.

164 E J Graham, *A Maritime History of Scotland 1650–1790* (East Linton, 2002), 195–6.

165 Cranna, *Fraserburgh*, 426–30. The incident cited, however, occurred in 1758.

166 The 1613 contract between Fraser of Philorth and the burgh was replaced in 1787 by a new contract, concerned primarily with exchanges of small parcels of land and clarifying certain rights that had been left open to question in terms of the Entail Act, which also involved portions of property in the areas used by the military. It is likely that the new agreements immediately followed the withdrawal of the garrison.

167 Cranna, *Fraserburgh*, 62, 64–5, in 1798 there was a shortage of stables in the town for quartering cavalry horses.

168 Cranna, *Fraserburgh*, 69–70.

169 Cranna, *Fraserburgh*, 441.

170 K J Logue, *Popular Disturbances in Scotland 1780–1813* (Edinburgh, 1979), 28, 31–2, 35, 42.

171 D Defoe, *A Tour through the whole island of Great Britain*, 2 vols (London, 1962), 404.

172 Defoe, *Tour*, 403.

173 W Mackay (ed), *The Letter-Book of Bailie John Steuart of Inverness 1715–1752* (SHS, 1915), 72.

174 Mackay, *Letter-Book of Bailie John Steuart*, 195.

175 Mackay, *Letter-Book of Bailie John Steuart*, 320, the cargo was destined for the Sound of Mull. On 20 May he wrote to John McLeod of Glenelg, commenting that the ship had sailed on 6 May, had probably put in to Stornoway and Loch Bracadale in Skye, but was expected also to call at Glenelg before heading for Mull (*ibid*, 324).

176 D Defoe, *A Tour through the Island of Great Britain*, 8th edn, with additions by various authors, 4 vols (London, 1778), iv, 188, 'The Lord Saltoun built (in the year 1738) at Fraserburgh, an excellent new pier and bulwark, all of free-stone; which render that harbour as safe and commodious as any on the east coast'.

177 *OSA*, 177–8; *Frasers of Philorth*, i, 149; Cranna, *Fraserburgh*, 182, the earliest reference he found to a distinct community at Broadsea was in the Kirk Session records in 1612; *ibid*, 56, gives a figure of 42 fishermen in Broadsea in 1789, with seven boats each crewed by six men (from KC MS 3004, bundle 338). This figure is confirmed in 1791 (*OSA*, 179).

178 *OSA*, 169, 177–8.

179 Cranna, *Fraserburgh*, 236–65; *NSA*, 255, it was in 1815 that the commercial success of the herring fishing was finally secured.

180 *Christian Watt Papers*, 70–1.

181 *OSA*, 177.

182 Cranna, *Fraserburgh*, 440–1.

183   *OSA*, 179.

184   Cranna, *Fraserburgh*, 316–21, Stewart left in 1811 'to fill an important appointment at Plymouth'; Wood, *Shaping of 19th Century Aberdeenshire*, 210, Stewart had been recommended by Rennie.

185   *NSA*, 254–5; Cranna, *Fraserburgh*, 316–24.

186   Cranna, *Fraserburgh*, 321–2, 327.

187   Cranna, *Fraserburgh*, 72; J Morris, *An Illustrated Guide to our Lifeboat Stations, Part 7, Scotland* (Coventry, 1992), 33.

188   NAS, RHP 45434, Fraserburgh Harbour Plan, Robert Stevenson, 1818, shows the lifeboat house just north of the Middle Pier.

189   The castle had been lived in until the 1780s by the family of John Gordon of Kinellar, husband of Henrietta, daughter of the 11th Lord Saltoun (*Christian Watt Papers*, 6, 172–3; *SP*, vii, 445).

190   R W Munro, *Scottish Lighthouses* (Stornoway, 1979), 52, 54–7, 85, 87, 94. The first lighthouses in Scotland, established by private or municipal enterprise, had been the Isle of May, 1636, followed by Buddon Ness, at the mouth of the Tay, 1687, Southerness, near Dumfries, 1748, and Little Cumbrae, 1757. Kinnaird Head was quickly followed by the Mull of Kintyre in 1788 and North Ronaldsay and Eilan Glas in 1789.

191   *OSA*, 177.

192   Cranna, *Fraserburgh*, 346.

193   Cranna, *Fraserburgh*, 67–8, blames both the decline of sailing ships and the arrival of the railway. The rope-work is shown on the Admiralty Charts of Fraserburgh surveyed in 1834 (1438, Slater) (**map 6**) and 1858 (1439, Bedford) (**map 7**), but has gone by the time of the 1st edition OS 6 inch and 25 inch maps of 1869.

194   *OSA*, 168, 170, 174–5. D Loch, in 1778 (*Tour of Scotland*), quoted in Murison, *Broch*, 28, said that 'spinning and other branches of industry begin to go on here, as the inhabitants have in a great measure given over smuggling'.

195   M Lynch, *Scotland: a New History* (London, 1991), 363.

196   *OSA*, 175 'the only manufacture is linen yarn'.

197   R Heron, *Scotland Described …* (Edinburgh, 1797), 241, 'the quantity of yarn and linen cloth manufactured in this part of the country affords an unequivocal proof of the industry of the inhabitants'.

198   *Christian Watt Papers*, 5. The looms found in many households into the first half of the nineteenth century were primarily for homespun woollens rather than cottage-industry production for linen merchants.

199   *Christian Watt Papers*, 181–2. Noble owned Denduff House, had the fermtoun at Upper Wachtouhill, and a croft known as Betty's Yard, occupied by a shepherd who looked after Noble's sheep flock.

200   Murison, *Broch*, 22; Cranna, *Fraserburgh*, 400; *ibid*, 35, identified as being near to where the mid-nineteenth-century Royal Hotel stood, at the junction of Broad Street and Frithside Street.

201 Cranna, *Fraserburgh*, 50, 331, 455; Murison, *Broch*, 29, 56, the building but was also later used for both Baron Court (from 1796) and Harbour Commissioners' meetings. The Commissioners later built their own hall in Frithside Street 'lately known as Batchan's Hall' (after the shop on the ground floor). This may be the building used as a temporary Town-house in 1852 (*Slater's Directory, 1852*, 'Town-house, Frithside Street').

202 Cranna, *Fraserburgh*, 50.

203 C W Munn, *The Scottish Provincial Banking Companies 1747–1864* (Edinburgh, 1981), 173–4; Cranna, *Fraserburgh*, 44–5, 446, in a rented room above what later became the Oak Tree Inn.

204 Murison and Noble, *Names and Places*, 80, the original purpose of this building is not clear. It was an inn (The Whitehall) at some time during the nineteenth century, but the place name 'Whitehall' pre-dates the 1791 building.

205 A town-house of the Gordons of Glenbuchat from 1735 until forfeited in 1746. The given date of 1767 is a guess, as the house was not likely to have been built or significantly altered between its forfeiture after 1746 and its sale in 1767, though its use to house the governor of the garrison has not previously been considered by historians. Its setting was almost terminally damaged by the arrival of the railway outside its front door in 1865.

206 *OSA*, 170. The mineral well was located at the bottom of Station Brae on the site now occupied by the Job Centre.

207 T Newte, *A Tour in England and Scotland* (London, 1791), 168–70.

208 *Aberdeen Journal* 26 August 1807, quoted in Cranna, *Fraserburgh*, 436.

209 *Aberdeen Journal*, 29 June 1808, quoted in Cranna, *Fraserburgh*, 435–7. Murison, *Broch*, 56, Kelman was baron bailie between 1796 and 1811.

210 *SP*, vii, 448.

211 *Aberdeen Journal*, 29 June 1808, quoted in Cranna, *Fraserburgh*, 435–7.

212 Rev W M Wade, *Watering and Sea-Bathing Places of Scotland …* (Paisley, 1822), 242, and in a view by Daniell, between the harbour and Kinnaird Head. Although far from the well, the headland was presumably chosen for its views, and for rocks to cut pools in. The buildings are shown on Admiralty charts of 1834 and 1858 (1438 and 1439) and the OS map of 1869.

213 Cranna, *Fraserburgh*, 437, the buildings became 'in turn a blacksmith's shop, a curer's store, and an epidemic hospital'.

214 Logue, *Popular Disturbances*, 31, the riots in 1813 related to the export of grain and potatoes.

215 Cranna, *Fraserburgh*, 453–5.

216 *Sasine Abridgements, Aberdeenshire, 1781–1820*, nos 212, 367, the property in question appears to be that occupied by the Registrar's Office at Nos 14–16 Saltoun Square; Cranna, *Fraserburgh*, 454.

217 Cranna, *Fraserburgh*, 72, 455–9.

218 Murison, *Broch*, 33; NLS Acc.4796/Box 124, minute book.

219 *OSA*, 173; Cranna, *Fraserburgh*, 151–3, Jolly was appointed to the charge of Fraserburgh in 1788 and was elected Bishop of Moray in 1796, though he continued to live in Fraserburgh.

220 Murison and Noble, *Names and Places*, 28, 77–8.

221 Murison, *Broch*, 31–2, lists the Garvage Well, which served the developing fishing community at the northern end of Shore Street, Lind's Well on Braeheads, a well near the High Street end of Barrasgate Road, and Gaw's Well in Gaw Street, Broadsea.

222 Cranna, *Fraserburgh*, 448–50. The scheme had been under consideration for some time, being mentioned in the *OSA*, 178.

223 McNeill and MacQueen, *Atlas of Scottish History*, 437–9, list of documented Lowland schools before 1633; I J Simpson, *Education in Aberdeenshire before 1872* (London, 1947), 12, it was one of only three schools in Deer Presbytery at this date, the others being Peterhead and Crimond.

224 Murison and Noble, *Names and Places*, 35, 67.

225 Cranna, *Fraserburgh*, 223, 378–9; *OSA* 174; Simpson, *Education in Aberdeesnhire*, 141, it cost £122 5sh 2d. Early maps show the 1787 building as being located well away from the southern edge of the town. The Moses stone was incorporated into the building, with the date 1787 added to it.

226 *OSA*, 176.

227 Cranna, *Fraserburgh*, 72.

228 J G Kyd (ed), *Scottish Population Statistics* (Edinburgh, 1975), 52; R Forsyth, *Beauties of Scotland* (Edinburgh, 1805–08), iv, 423, 441. The increase for Aberdeenshire as a whole over this period was only 6.5%, but towns with a linen industry showed much higher percentage increases; Cupar (Fife) increased by 103%, for example, and Forfar (Angus) by 111%.

229 NLS MS.5850.59, Stevenson manuscript plan of Fraserburgh harbour, the southern end of Castle Street is labelled Kelman Street after the Saltoun's factor, Broad Street is renamed Philorth Street, and the north end of Shore becomes St Kinnaird Street. The first evidence for these new streets being laid out is RCAHMS, 33205 (DC8803), plan of Fraserburgh produced for the Northern Lighthouse Board, signed AGH, which is undated but on internal evidence cannot be earlier than *c* 1809.

230 Murison and Noble, *Names and Places*, 25–6.

231 *Aberdeen Journal* 26 August 1807, quoted in Cranna, *Fraserburgh*, 436. This view is reinforced by the fact that 33% of those on the roll of the Fraserburgh Regiment of Local Militia, 25 September 1808, were from the building trades (NAS CS96/217).

232 NAS RHP 45434, *Plan of Harbour of Fraserburgh*, Robert Stevenson, 1818, shows Castle Street with only one building on it beyond the junction with North Street and Duke Street, and Bath Street (not named) at right angles at the end, leading to the Baths, but with no other buildings along it. But this area seems to have changed later, as the western part of Bath Street has disappeared by the 1858 Admiralty Chart (1439), only to re-emerge on a slightly different alignment on the 1901 OS 25 inch map. A few plots in Bath Street were feued by Lord Saltoun in 1833–34 (*Sasine Abridgements, Aberdeenshire, 1831–40*), but as they are described as on the east and west sides, they may be on what is now the north end of Shore Street, *NSA*, 254; *Christian Watt Papers*, 83, 'stances were still available in North Street' *c* 1860.

233 If Saltoun Square had not been so named when the inn was built in 1801, it too probably dates to this period, but is the only name change which endured.

234 Murison and Noble, *Names and Places*, 16, 46, but as a path rather than a built-up street. It is not shown on the Roy map of *c* 1750.

235 Murison and Noble, *Names and Places*, 20. Their dates of *c* 1810–20 can be narrowed by the non-appearance of Commerce Street on Robert Stevenson's plan of the harbour, dated 1818 (NAS, RHP 45434).

236 *Christian Watt Papers*, 40, 181; *SP*, vii, 446. Originally occupied by an unmarried daughter of the 12th Lord Saltoun, it became overspill accommodation for Philorth House in the early 1800s. The house was partly demolished when the street was extended through its former gardens in 1873 and the rest was demolished in 1934 (Cranna, *Fraserburgh*, 389; Melville, *Walks*, 16).

237 Cranna, *Fraserburgh*, 53; Murison and Noble, *Names and Places*, 35, tradition records that its name was changed from Puddle Street in the 1780s.

238 NAS RHP 45434, Stevenson Harbour Plan of 1818.

239 The evidence of this northern extension lies in the breach of the urban wall (the large gap) between the Saltoun Arms, and the 1801 building to the north facing into The Green.

240 Cranna, *Fraserburgh*, 458.

241 *Sasine Abridgements, Aberdeenshire, 1781–1820*, nos 212, 367; Cranna, *Fraserburgh*, 446.

242 *OSA*, 173. It was demolished in 1969 to make way for a bus station (Murison, *Broch*, 32).

243 Other examples include Forres (1775), Banff (1778), Strichen (1799), Peterhead (1804–06), Huntly (1805), Nairn (1811), Keith (1816), and Elgin (1827).

244 NLS, MS.5850.59, *Plan of Fraserburgh Harbour, with inset Sketch Plan of the New South Pier ...*, Robert Stevenson, 1818; and plan of Fraserburgh, detail from Admiralty chart 1438, surveyed 1834, published 1842.

245 Cranna, *Fraserburgh*, 68–9, 120; *NSA* 256 'a plain good structure, and capable of containing 1000 sittings'.

246 *NSA*, 256; Cranna, *Fraserburgh*, 125, 379; C McKean, *Banff and Buchan: an illustrated architectural guide* (RIAS, Edinburgh, 1990), 133, the building is almost certainly to be identified as Craigielea, No 7 Saltoun Place. The datestone from the previous manse of 1758 was built into the new church.

247 *SP*, vii, 448–50.

248 Murison, *Broch*, 56, Chalmers was baron baillie for 37 years from 1811 (followed by his son for a further 16 years). *Pigot and Co's New Commercial Directory of Scotland for 1825–26* (London and Manchester) lists Chalmers as bailie, factor to Lord Saltoun, agent for the Hercules Insurance Company, Admiral Substitute, a writer (solicitor) and a shipowner. He was also one of the first Harbour Commissioners (Cranna, *Fraserburgh*, 322).

249 Cranna, *Fraserburgh*, 228, 378–9.

250 *Pigot and Co's Directory for 1825–26*.

251   *NSA*, 256; McKean, *Banff and Buchan*, 133, in the building now Britannic
      Insurance at No 83 Broad Street.

252   C A Malcolm, *The Bank of Scotland 1695–1945* (Edinburgh, 1945), 178. This
      may well have been the same building on the corner of Frithside Street
      and Broad Street which was also referred to as 'bailie Chalmers house' (as
      for example Smith, *Aberdeenshire*, 601). This property was purchased by the
      Bank in 1865, and remained in use as a bank until 1959 (information kindly
      provided by Sian Yates, Assistant Archivist, HBOS Group Archives, Edinburgh,
      11 July 2002).

253   A Keith, *The North of Scotland Bank Limited 1836–1936* (Aberdeen, 1936), 46;
      S G Checkland, *Scottish Banking: a history, 1695–1973* (Glasgow and London,
      1975), 347, 'By the end of 1837 the Aberdeen region had an extraordinary
      provision of bank offices and sub-offices: the Town and County with 13, the
      North of Scotland with 32, and the Aberdeen Banking with 15, giving a total
      of 60. In addition, there were the branches of non-Aberdonian banks'. Cranna,
      Fraserburgh, 446; McKean, *Banff and Buchan*, 129–33; Smith, *Aberdeenshire*, 601.

254   See, for example, the Square in Cullen.

255   *Sasine Abridgments, Aberdeenshire, 1821–30*. There is a lack of evidence for
      feuing in the town at this period, which might suggest that the landower was
      developing the new streets himself and letting the new buildings. Further
      research in the Barony Council and Court books might help to clarify how
      and when the southern new town was developed.

256   *Sasine Abridgments, Aberdeenshire, 1821–30*. Further research is needed in
      Barony Council and Court books to clarify the timing and extent of changes.

257   R and W Chambers, *Gazetteer of Scotland* (Edinburgh, 1832).

258   *Christian Watt Papers*, 32–3.

259   *NSA*, 254.

260   *NSA*, 250.

261   Murison and Noble, *Names and Places*, 75, only the Strichen Road tollhouse
      survives, in a much-altered state; Dey, *Fraserburgh, Now and Then*, 9, the High
      Street tollhouse stood at the junction with Denmark Street.

262   Analysis of data from *Pigot's Directory, 1837*, see Appendix 4.

263   *Pigot's Directory, 1825*.

264   Chambers, *Gazetteer*.

265   *NSA*, 255; Cranna, *Fraserburgh*, 324–6.

266   *OSA*, 179.

267   *Pigot's Directory, 1825*. Checks of surviving Customs Establishment Books
      (NAS CE3/17-21, up to 1822), show no evidence of any presence in
      Fraserburgh. It is possible that the Customs House listed in 1825 was purely
      local, or that it had been established between 1822 and 1825. It is not
      clear where it was based, though there is a local tradition that the Bank of
      Scotland building on the corner of Frithside Street and Broad Street was
      once a Customs House. If this was the case, it is likely to have been at this
      early period (probably another business for which Lewis Chalmers was the
      agent). In 1837 the Customs Office was in Frithside Street, in 1852 in Saltoun
      Place, and in 1867 in Commerce Street (the site is undeveloped on the 1858

Admiralty Chart, 1439, but a building marked on the 1869 OS 6 inch map), in 1882 in Dalrymple Street, and in 1903 at Quay Side.

268 *Pigot's Directory, 1825.*

269 *NSA*, 255–6.

270 *Christian Watt Papers*, 20–21, he was conveyed in a decorated boat-carriage, drawn by 60 Broadsea fishermen, with himself seated at the tiller, and escorted by crowds several thousand strong.

271 *Christian Watt Papers*, 24, 'the braes [were] black with people'; Smith, *Aberdeenshire*, 608.

272 Cranna, *Fraserburgh*, 165, 409–10; F H Groome, *Ordnance Gazetteer of Scotland*, 6 vols (London, 1894), iii, 60. The church was demolished after a fire in 2000.

273 Cranna, *Fraserburgh*, 165, 167–8; *Ordnance Gazetteer*, iii, 60.

274 Cranna, *Fraserburgh*, 125.

275 Cranna, *Fraserburgh*, 443–4

276 Cranna, *Fraserburgh*, 82–6, 449.

277 Murison, *Broch*, 58; Cranna, *Fraserburgh*, 389, the old tolbooth was 'very dilapidated and disreputable'.

278 McKean, *Banff and Buchan*, 130. RCAHMS, 33205 (DC8803), *c* 1809; NAS RHP 45434, Stevenson Harbour Plan, 1818, it is possible that the new building was further south, or had a larger footprint, thus narrowing the space between it and the church.

279 Cranna, *Fraserburgh*, 77–80, 389. The covered market was not a success, and the area was soon converted into a store. The fact that Fraserburgh's tolbooth had not been replaced earlier may be explained by Lord Saltoun's absence on military service.

280 *Ordnance Gazetteer*, iii, 60, set on a smaller base.

281 NLS, Admiralty Chart 1438 (1834), shows the northern half of Castle Street beyond the junction with Duke Street to be largely unbuilt. Wood, *Shaping of 19th Century Aberdeenshire*, 202; Murison and Noble, *Names and Places*, 55, North Street was laid out in 1845. By 1858 (NLS, Admiralty Chart 1439), most of the east side of Castle Street had been built on, and half of the west side beyond the junction with North Street.

282 Murison and Noble, *Names and Places*, 55; *Christian Watt Papers*, 83, 'it was a bonnie [street] and near the Broch harbour'.

283 Murison and Noble, *Names and Places*, 14; *Christian Watt Papers*, 89–90, the breaking up of the remainder of the Castle Parks for commercial and housing use followed the death in 1851 of Margaret, dowager Lady Saltoun, widow of the 15th Lord Saltoun, whose jointure property it had been.

284 NLS, Admiralty Chart 1439 (1858).

285 Murison and Noble, *Names and Places*, 6, 16; Bath Street is shown laid out on the 1818 harbour plan, the western portion has disappeared by the Admiralty chart of 1858, is still absent on the 1st edn OS 6 inch map of 1869, but has reappeared by the revised 25 inch OS map of 1901. Denmark Street was laid out in 1875 (Wood, *Shaping of 19th century Aberdeenshire*, 202, and plan 208, from Police Commissioners Minutes). The Broadsea Tollhouse was demolished for the opening up of Denmark Street (*Christian Watt Papers*, 90).

286 It is listed in *Slater's Directory, 1852*, and shown on the 1858 Admiraly chart (NLS, 1439). Pratt, *Buchan*, 162, notes that in 1858 the prison stood 'at the entrance of the castle park', and was described as 'small, but secure'.

287 *Christian Watt Papers*, 90, 'Barrasgate was opened up and all those other Sts and yards and huts and smokehouses in such ugly array covered the whole of McCallum's farm [not Mains of Broadsea but South Broadsea Farm – which actually lay east of Broadsea] and came right to Broadsea. The Rumbling, quite a beauty spot (deadly to young loons) was completely ruined [The Rumbling – or Rummlin' Goit – was a deep and narrow natural gully cut through the rocks on the east side of Broadsea Bay, named after the thundering noise of the water in it during storms, Cranna, *Fraserburgh*, 388]. All the smoke houses spewing out reek and on a wet day the black stuff from them fell from the sky – my granny used to speak of the Braun Seere [Brahan Seer, a seventeenth-century 'prophet' from Easter Ross] who foretold when we saw the black rain to watch out for this was undoubtedly a sign of the times. Mister's Annie, who lived at 1 Broadsea, said "To be born amid beauty and to die with such ugliness around you!" When Ptolemy, the great Roman map maker, sailed round Kinnaird he called it the majestic headland, "Taixalon Akron". If he saw it today, with open sluices for herring guts and the local rubbish dump ...'. The reference to Ptolemy is an example of the good education Christian Watt received in the local schools.

288 Cranna, *Fraserburgh*, 233–4; Smith, *Aberdeenshire*, 610; *Ordnance Gazetteer*, iii, 60; Anon, *Fraserburgh 400, 1592–1992* (Fraserburgh, 1990), 24. Its reused buildings survive on the corner of Barrasgate Road and High Street.

289 Smith, *Aberdeenshire*, 601.

290 Murison and Noble, *Names and Places*, 20, 65, 68, 76.

291 Cranna, *Fraserburgh*, 378–89.

292 Plans for the establishment of the gas company had required the adoption of extended powers under the Police Act in 1840. It flourished despite initial local suspicion, and was finally taken over by the town council in 1911 (Cranna, *Fraserburgh*, 450–2).

293 The site is undeveloped on the 1858 Admiralty chart (1439); see note 268 for the various locations of Customs offices.

294 Smith, *Aberdeenshire*, 601; Checkland, *Scottish Banking*, 340, 349.

295 Smith, *Aberdeenshire*, 601; *Slater's Directory, 1867*.

296 Analysis of data from *Pigot's Directories, 1825, 1837,* and *Slater's Directories, 1852, 1860, 1867*, see Appendix 4.

297 J P S Ferguson, *Directory of Scottish Newspapers* (National Library of Scotland, Edinburgh, 1984), 142; Rennie, *Cross Street*, 11, it was based at No 26 High Street, and survived until 1941.

298 Cranna, *Fraserburgh*, 455, 155, developing leisure activities are also symbolised by the establishment of the Fraserburgh Musical Society in 1869.

299 *Pigot's Directory, 1837*; *NSA*, 253, a 'new market' had recently been opened up in local cattle being exported to London; Cranna, *Fraserburgh*, 366–7, 'the ships that ran on the passage in the 'forties and 'fifties were not so much general cargo vessels as cattle ships ... From its geographical situation,

Fraserburgh was in these days the chief mainland port for Orkney and Iceland in the trade. Vessels proceeding to these islands loaded cargoes of cattle, which they brought across and landed at Fraserburgh. The animals were sometimes not in the best of condition when taken on board, and the voyage across, often unduly protracted owing to headwinds, did not improve their appearance. The beasts were therefore distributed all over the district, and allowed to graze on the fine rich grass for which Buchan is famous, until they were in prime condition for the London market. When they reached that stage, they were once more put on board the London traders and carried to the Thames'.

300   Cranna, *Fraserburgh*, 448; Murison and Noble, *Names and Places*, 28.

301   *NSA*, 256; Smith, *Aberdeenshire*, 604.

302   Smith, *Aberdeenshire*, 604; 1st edn OS map, 1869, it sits on top of what was once the western part of Bath Street.

303   Murison and Noble, *Names and Places*, 78.

304   Cranna, *Fraserburgh*, 345–53.

305   Cranna, *Fraserburgh*, 325–8.

306   *Third Statistical Account of Scotland, County of Aberdeen*, 'The Burgh and Parish of Fraserburgh', J Noble, Town Chamberlain, 1952, 326; Morris, *Guide to Lifeboat Stations*, 33. NLS, Admiralty Chart, 1439 (1858).

307   Smith, *Aberdeenshire*, 604.

308   Cranna, *Fraserburgh*, 366, the decline is difficult to quantify, for although there were fewer ships, they were larger. Coastal shipping continued to carry heavy goods such as coal well into the twentieth century, though the railway took away the passengers and perishable goods. See K L Moore, 'The Northeast of Scotland's Coastal Trading Links Towards the End of the Nineteenth Century', *Scottish Economic and Social History* **21**, 2 (2001), 95–120.

309   Cranna, *Fraserburgh*, 354–9; the Fraserburgh Seal and Whale Fishing Co, run by a Mr Wallace, started with one sealer in 1852, and two more in 1853. In 1856 there were two more, and another in 1859. Six was the highest number of ships involved, and only for one year. There were few good years, and the last ship was sold in 1868. The boilyards stood to the south-east of the town, on a site later used for the railway station; G Jackson, *The British Whaling Trade* (London, 1978), 145–6, of the six Scottish ports, Fraserburgh was second in seal catches, fifth in tuns of oil, sixth in whale and whalebone. Its whaling activity was dwarfed by that of Peterhead.

310   B Macdonald, *Boats and Builders: the history of boatbuilding around Fraserburgh* (Fraserburgh, 1993), 4. This move followed soon after another boost to the fishing industry, the abolition of fish teinds (tithe payable to the minister of the parish) in 1828 (*Christian Watt Papers*, 15). For problems caused in some fishing ports by the refusal to abolish teinds, see P Aitchison, *Children of the Sea: the story of the Eyemouth disaster* (East Linton, 2001).

311   *Christian Watt Papers*, 90.

312   Cranna, *Fraserburgh*, 262–82.

313 Not just bulk fish, but the women who sold fish could cover a wider area than they had previously done on foot, *Christian Watt Papers*, 88 'The railway was a blessing for the fishwife, I could go to Strichen and New Deer in a day'.

314 *Christian Watt Papers*, 71.

315 Cranna, *Fraserburgh*, passim; for more on the herring industry see M Gray, *The Fishing Industries of Scotland, 1790–1914: a study in regional adaptation* (Oxford, 1978).

316 See for example, *Christian Watt Papers*, 71–2.

317 *Christian Watt Papers*, 71, Bruce's built a gutting station in Commerce Street.

318 J Thomas and D Turnock, *The North of Scotland: a Regional History of the Railways of Great Britain*, vol xv (Nairn, 1989), 18, railway transport halved the cost of getting fish to distant urban centres such as Manchester. 'The fish traffic was certainly very profitable for the railway companies, although it could be very variable'.

319 Thomas and Turnock, *North of Scotland*, 12–13, 'considerable investment was stimulated in new farm buildings and land improvements, and in harbours and fishing boats'.

320 Thomas and Turnock, *North of Scotland*, 183.

321 *Christian Watt Papers*, 109.

322 *Slater's Royal National Commercial Directory of Scotland ...*, 1867.

323 T C Smout, *A Century of the Scottish People 1830–1950* (London, 1986), 41; Cranna, *Fraserburgh*, 443–4.

324 Smith, *Aberdeenshire*, 604, bounded on the east and north by the sea, then from shore just west of Broadsea south and east to the mouth of the Kethock burn, then back (on the line of the windmill) but excluding the lands of Derbyhall.

325 Cranna, *Fraserburgh*, 444; *Third Statistical Account*, 326.

326 *Fraserburgh 400*, 7; *Slater's Directory, 1886*, he was described as 'late Lord Provost of Aberdeen'; Cranna, *Fraserburgh*, 329, 'his brilliant and unequalled services to the town will be remembered "as long as grass grows and water runs"'.

327 It was Anderson who arranged and inspired the pageant and ceremony that surrounded the laying of the foundation stone of the Balaclava Breakwater in 1875, *Christian Watt Papers*, 109.

328 Wood, *Shaping of 19th Century Aberdeenshire*, 229, 231; *Ordnance Gazetteer* iii, 60, a few years earlier its lack had been deplored by Smith, *Aberdeenshire*, 603.

329 Cranna, *Fraserburgh*, 449–50; *Third Statistical Account*, 330–1.

330 *Christian Watt Papers*, 88.

331 *Christian Watt Papers*, 88, 'a new race had arisen up, the fishcurer'.

332 *Christian Watt Papers*, 95; Murison and Noble, *Names and Places*, 33.

333 Fraserburgh Police Commissioner's Minutes, 1891, quoted in T C Smout and S Wood, *Scottish Voices 1745–1960* (London, 1991), 22–3; the following year the Police Commissioners listed 41 piggeries within the town, housing 105 pigs (Wood, *Shaping of 19th Century Aberdeenshire*, 224).

334 *Christian Watt Papers*, 97.

335 *Christian Watt Papers*, 94.

336 Cranna, *Fraserburgh*, 469–73.

337 Cranna, *Fraserburgh*, 378.

338 Wood, *Shaping of 19th Century Aberdeenshire*, 202, 223. The status of Broadsea seems to have unusual, in that it had its own office of 'constable' (which disappeared after 1746). *Christian Watt Papers*, viii, 8–10, 166–82, 'Granny Lascelle's account' said that William Lascelles was the last constable.

339 Cranna, *Fraserburgh*, 386–7, old housing survived longest in parts of Shore Street and in Broadsea.

340 *Ordnance Gazetteer*, iii, 59.

341 B Macdonald, *Fraserburgh Harbour – the Boom Years* (Fraserburgh, 1995), 26.

342 Cranna, *Fraserburgh*, 469, only five miles long, it cost £15,000.

343 D S Rennie, *A Walk down Broad Street* (Fraserburgh, 1997), 15; Rennie, *Cross Street*, 11; J Leatham, *Faithlie-by-the Sea: an account of the rising town of Fraserburgh* (Fraserburgh, 1904), advertisements at beginning and end, 12 'in this the third week of August the hotel and boarding houses are crowded with fish buyers, curers, salesmen, commission agents, and commercial travellers'.

344 Rev J M Wilson (ed), *The Imperial Gazetteer of Scotland, Topographical, Statistical and Historical*, 2 vols (London, *c* 1870); Smith, *Aberdeenshire*, 604.

345 *Slater's Directory, 1911.*

346 Cranna, *Fraserburgh*, 383–4, 'drastic changes have taken place on the ground at the head of the North Pier, in front of the Oak Tree Inn, within the last forty years. The vacant area was then occupied by Mr John Webster, shipbuilder, as a storage place for logs of wood used in his business. The place was a well-known rendezvous for sailors home on leave, shore labourers and loafers etc. Itinerant preachers, travelling quacks, packmen and other nondescript visitors found a refuge, in the fishing season, at this spot … The logs formed convenient seats … Boys played hide-and-seek among the timber, and altogether, for many years, "The Logs" remained a well-known public institution in the town'.

347 *Ordnance Gazetteer*, iii, 60.

348 *Slater's Directory, 1886.* By 1911 they were only representing Denmark, Sweden and the German Empire.

349 *Slater's Directory, 1911*, 128.

350 Cranna, *Fraserburgh*, 473.

351 Cranna, *Fraserburgh*, 328–44.

352 *Ordnance Gazetteer*, iii, 60.

353 *Third Statistical Account*, 72.

354 *Third Statistical Account*, 327.

355 Cranna, *Fraserburgh*, 335–44.

356 Leatham, *Faithlie-by-the-Sea*, 7, 12.

357 McKean, *Banff and Buchan*, 130.

358 Ferguson, *Directory of Scottish Newspapers*, 142; Rennie, *Cross Street*, 11, based in Cross Street, in 1896 moved to Shore Street, it survives, now based at No 60 High Street.

359 *Slater's Directory, 1886.*

360   Smith, *Aberdeenshire*, 608; Cranna, *Fraserburgh*, 129; *Third Statistical Account*, 327; *Ordnance Gazetteer*, iii, 60.

361   Cranna, *Fraserburgh*, 129, 410–14; *Third Statistical Account*, 327; Anon, *Famous Brochers* (Fraserburgh, 1992), 7–9, born 1845, at age 12 he was apprenticed in the North of Scotland Bank, Saltoun Square, and gained rapid promotion until by 1889 he was manager of the head office in Aberdeen. In 1898 he was appointed Treasurer of the Bank of Scotland, a post he held with great success for 15 years. He was an active member of the Free Church. In 1905 he was knighted, the first Brocher and the first Scottish banker to be so honoured.

362   Cranna, *Fraserburgh*, 161–3, the congregation was established in 1863, started raising funds in 1871, and the church opened in 1875. After the union of the UP and Free Churches in 1900 it became the United Free Church. The building was sold in 1922 to the Fraserburgh ex-servicemen for use as a club.

363   Cranna, *Fraserburgh*, 142–3.

364   Cranna, *Fraserburgh*, 169–70; *Ordnance Gazetteer*, iii, 60.

365   Cranna, *Fraserburgh*, 158–9; McKean, *Banff & Buchan*, 133–4. From the union of the UF and the Church of Scotland in 1929 it was known as the South Church.

366   *Third Statistical Account*, 327.

367   Cranna, *Fraserburgh*, 156–7; McKean, *Banff and Buchan*, 135.

368   Cranna, *Fraserburgh*, 160–1.

369   Cranna, *Fraserburgh*, 171–2; Melville, *Walks*, 17, the architects were Ellis and Wilson of Aberdeen.

370   Cranna, *Fraserburgh*, 234–5; McKean, *Banff and Buchan*, 135.

371   Cranna, *Fraserburgh*, 232–3; Smith, *Aberdeenshire*, 609; *Third Statistical Account*, 326, 330; the old building was endowed by Thomas Macaulay for use as a church hall, called the Macaulay Hall.

372   T M Devine, *The Scottish Nation 1700–2000* (London, 1999), 392–6.

373   Cranna, *Fraserburgh*, 231.

374   Cranna, *Fraserburgh*, 234.

375   Cranna, *Fraserburgh*, 233; *Slater's Directory, 1911*.

376   Melville, *Walks*, 25, gives the date of 1894 for its opening. However, according to *Slater's Directory, 1889*, Broadsea Fishermen's Hall was built by public subscription in 1887.

377   G E Dey, *Old Fraserburgh* (Fraserburgh, 1987), 15, they were built in 1883.

378   Cranna, *Fraserburgh*, 378.

379   Murison and Noble, *Names and Places*, 20.

380   Cranna, *Fraserburgh*, 386.

381   Named after Charlotte Evans, wife of the 17th Lord Saltoun; Cranna, *Fraserburgh*, 380; Murison and Noble, *Names and Places*, 17.

382   Named after Provost Finlayson. Murison and Noble, *Names and Places*, 23, 27, from 1896.

383   Murison and Noble, *Names and Places*, 31, 55.

384   *Slater's Directory, 1911*.

385 Murison and Noble, *Names and Places*, 3, 65 (Alexandra Terrace was not named and adopted until 1909).

386 Analysis of data from *Slater's Directories, 1867, 1886, 1911* (see Appendix 4).

387 Murison and Noble, *Names and Places*, 33; analysis of data from Directories (see Appendix 4).

388 Murison and Noble, *Names and Places*, 46, 61, 68.

389 *Worrall's Directory of Aberdeenshire, 1877*, 'Note – The name of Back-St is now changed to High-St'; analysis of data from *Slater's Directories, 1867, 1886, 1911* (Appendix 4).

390 *Slater's Directory, 1911*; Murison, *Broch*, 60, the hospital site had been gifted by Lord Saltoun and the buildings erected at a cost of £3,000, but the 25-bed establishment was maintained by voluntary contributions and the profits of a £1,000 endowment from the Helen Watson Memorial Fund rather than from public monies. Opened in 1877, it closed in 1968.

391 McKean, *Banff and Buchan*, 135; *Slater's Directory, 1903, 1911*; Melville, *Walks*, 5. it was built on a site donated by Lord Saltoun and with a contribution of £3630 from Andrew Carnegie towards the £4000 building cost. There was a competition for its design, and the winner was Mr W S F Wilson of Frithside Street.

392 *Ordnance Gazetteer*, iii, 60; *Slater's Directory, 1882*; McKean, *Banff and Buchan*, 129. *Fraserburgh 400*, 29.

393 Melville, *Walks*, 18; Dey, *Old Fraserburgh*, 26; *Fraserburgh 400*, 44.

394 Melville, *Walks*, 13.

395 Cranna, *Fraserburgh*, 455.

396 *Ordnance Gazetteer*, iii, 60.

397 *Third Statistical Account*, 329; H Hamilton, 'Industries and Commerce', in *The North-East of Scotland* (British Association for the Advancement of Science, Aberdeen, 1963), 182.

398 Cranna, *Fraserburgh*, 353; for more detail see Macdonald, *Boats and Builders*. Many Fraserburgh-built boats were as big as or bigger than the earlier ships, the distinction being between foreign-going boats and inshore ones, retained despite the large size now reached by fishing boats.

399 Cranna, *Fraserburgh*, 480; Leatham, *Faithlie-by-the-Sea*, 8, suggested that 'in all respects save rapid building, Fraserburgh suggests an American town'.

400 *Third Statistical Account*, 330; Hamilton, 'Industries and Commerce', 171–2.

401 Macdonald, *Fraserburgh Harbour*, 67.

402 G E Dey, *Fraserburgh at 'War' and the 'Coronation'* (Aberdeen, nd), 11.

403 Macdonald, *Fraserburgh Harbour*, 67.

404 Macdonald, *Fraserburgh Harbour*, 67.

405 Macdonald, *Fraserburgh Harbour*, 68.

406 Macdonald, *Fraserburgh Harbour*, 70.

407 Macdonald, *Fraserburgh Harbour*, 73, 76.

408 Smout, *A Century of the Scottish People*, 77–8.

409 Macdonald, *Fraserburgh Harbour*, 84.

410 Macdonald, *Fraserburgh Harbour*, 77.

411 Macdonald, *Fraserburgh Harbour*, 87.

412   Macdonald, *Fraserburgh Harbour*, 89.

413   *Third Statistical Account*, 327.

414   A Walker, *The Fleet: a guide to the historic vessels at the Scottish Fisheries Museum* (Anstruther, 2002), the Fifie *Reaper*, now based at the Scottish Fisheries Museum in Anstruther, was built by J & G Forbes, Sandhaven, in 1901. Another boat in the Museum, *Swallow*, was built by Mr Barclay of Broadsea *c* 1900.

415   Macdonald, *Fraserburgh Harbour*, 89.

416   Melville, *Walks*, 4, 11–12, 16, 26.

417   Rennie, *Cross Sreett*, 54; *Third Statistical Account*, 331, the following year saw the conversion of all the street lighting from gas to electricity.

418   Dey, *War and Coronation*, 14–15.

419   Hamilton, 'Industries and Commerce', 171–2.

420   T Begg, *Housing Policy in Scotland* (Edinburgh, 1996), chapters 1 and 2, the 1919 Act proved too expensive, and subsequent legislation reduced the subsidies paid by central government. It was only in 1938 that the subisdy was related to the size of house.

421   G W Clark, *The Housing of the Working Classes of Scotland* (Glasgow, 1930), Table XX, in 1921 Fraserburgh was more overcrowded than Aberdeen or Peterhead, in fact more overcrowded than anywhere else north of Falkirk.

422   KC MS 3004/209.

423   KC MS 3004/249, 250.

424   Murison and Noble, *Names and Places*, 33, 34, 39, 40, 47, 61, 76, 77.

425   *Third Statistical Account*, 327–8, an increase of some 50% in the town's housing provision.

426   Scheduled Type 24 pillbox (NMRS NK06NW 5) is in the field to the north of the cemetery. A second Type 24 pillbox (NK06NW 6) is sited in the dunes at the east end of Fraserburgh Bay. A radio station (at NJ96NE 29), and a possible Type 27 pillbox, are seen on aerial photographs.

427   Dey, *War and Coronation*, 21.

428   Dey, *War and Coronation*, 24.

429   Dey, *War and Coronation*, 24–5.

430   Dey, *War and Coronation*, 26.

431   Dey, *War and Coronation*, 32–3, 35.

432   Dey, *War and Coronation*, 19.

433   *Third Statistical Account*, 73, 329.

434   *Third Statistical Account*, 329.

435   *Third Statistical Account*, 331.

436   *Third Statistical Account*, 73, the same boats now worked in the herring fishery (with drift nets) and the white fishery (with seine nets).

437   *Third Statistical Account*, 330.

438   Murison, *Broch*, 62.

439   *Third Statistical Account*, 324, 327–8.

440   Murison and Noble, *Names and Places*, 30, 52, 73, 79.

441   Murison and Noble, *Names and Places*, 83–4, 1970.

5 The potential of Fraserburgh

Archaeology

While there have been few, if any, archaeological remains identified in the burgh itself, the area around Fraserburgh is rich in recorded remains of all periods from prehistory onwards. It has to be suspected that the dearth of archaeological finds within the town reflects a low level of recording during the main episodes of building rather than a lack of use of this area in earlier periods. In terms of the archaeological potential of pre-burghal Fraserburgh, this absence of previous work means that any observations are general and based on extrapolation from the archaeology of the wider region. These limitations should be a central consideration in the devising of any future development strategy; current absence of evidence should not be regarded as evidence of absence of human activity on this site from the earlier prehistoric through to the late medieval period.

A human presence in parts of Scotland can now be traced with confidence back to c 6000 BC, and possibly earlier still. These first settlers were hunter-gatherers of the northern European Mesolithic, seasonal migrants or semi-nomads who exploited the rich natural resources of post-glacial Scotland. Seasonal encampments of these people have been identified on a number of sites along the east coast of Scotland, and demonstrate exploitation of both maritime resources and of those of the interior. Until the 1990s few Mesolithic sites in eastern Scotland had been the subject of large-scale excavation or had yielded firm dating evidence, but understanding has expanded considerably in recent years through focused research and publication (footnotes in Section 4 carry detailed references to these). This work, reinforced by identification of a range of stray Mesolithic finds from throughout modern Aberdeenshire, has overturned long-established traditional assumptions that human colonisation of what became Buchan was very late.

While no such finds have been identified within modern Fraserburgh, it can be suggested by analogy from known Mesolithic sites that the raised beach on which much of the town stands is a likely repository of such remains. The dearth of finds from this period is most probably a consequence of the lack of archaeological survey or excavation undertaken along the former shoreline occupied by Fraserburgh. For example, the mid-twentieth-century housing redevelopments along the line of the raised beach between Castle Street and Shore Street were not accompanied by archaeological investigation, and the same is true of the late twentieth-century redevelopments on the east side of Shore Street. To the south of the town, around the site of the medieval parish church and in the dunes to its east, shell middens and hearth sites were uncovered in the mid-nineteenth century during grave-digging operations but no diagnostic artefactual remains were either recorded or preserved. These middens may have been deposited in later periods, but their location points towards the early exploitation of the maritime resources of Fraserburgh Bay.

A more settled society based on agricultural exploitation began to replace the semi-nomadic hunting and gathering Mesolithic culture by c 4000 BC. Neolithic society produced the first substantial monuments in the Scottish landscape, burial and ritual monuments as well as settlements. Many Neolithic and subsequent Bronze Age sites have been recorded in the surrounding area. Most were identified and explored in the nineteenth century, and few were recorded to modern archaeological standards. Most are funerary monuments and include cairn-covered interments and cremations, unmarked cists containing inhumation burials and cemeteries of both urn-accompanied inhumations and cremations contained within urns, all evidently of Bronze Age date. No firmly identified prehistoric settlement sites have been found, although programmes of aerial photographic reconnaissance from the 1980s onwards have revealed a number of potential sites as cropmarks. Sites identified in this manner include enclosures, ring-ditches, and clusters of pits. Only limited reconnaissance excavations have been undertaken on such sites in northern Scotland, and none near Fraserburgh, but work undertaken further west in Moray has indicated that the majority are likely to be of prehistoric date. In addition to the structural remains, a range of unprovenanced stone artefacts has also been recorded which together point to a rich succession of prehistoric cultures. Again, there is a dearth of any such remains within the core of Fraserburgh and the 'halo' of findspots within the later twentieth-century extensions to the west and south of the town simply represents modern statutory recording processes rather than any actual physical distribution.[1]

The blank in the archaeological record continues into later prehistory. Unlike the other major headlands along the southern coast of the Moray Firth from Burghead to Dundarg, there is no evidence that a promontory fort was ever built on Kinnaird Head in the later first millennium BC. Given General Roy's antiquarian predilections, had significant remains of such a structure existed it can probably be assumed that he would have recorded them in his plan of Fraserburgh in the same manner as those at Burghead. Nevertheless, the absence of any obvious late prehistoric power-centre in the vicinity of Fraserburgh, coupled with the apparent richness of the earlier prehistoric archaeological landscape, begs the question of where the high-status settlements of later Bronze Age and earlier Iron Age date are located. A number are probably represented by the cropmark sites identified in aerial surveys. Again, the lack of nineteenth- and twentieth-century archaeological survey within the town prevents any absolute statements being made.

Roman military or commercial activity in the vicinity of Fraserburgh has also failed to leave any impression in the archaeological record. The first written reference to the area is the map of Britain by the second-century AD Alexandrian geographer Ptolemy. It is generally accepted that Kinnaird Head is to be identified with Ptolemy's *Taixalon Akron* (Latin: *Taezalorum Promontorium*, the 'headland of the Taezali', the Iron Age tribe of the region). Ptolemy's data were most probably gathered by a Roman coasting voyage, possibly during Agricola's governorship in the late 70s or early 80s AD, rather than from a land-based expedition. Several Roman marching camps have been identified through aerial survey in the area to the south-west of Fraserburgh (see Section 4), but no Roman site has been identified in the Buchan coastal zone. Nor are any of the Roman sites so far identified in the region securely dated.

The blank in the archaeological record continues through the early historic period, but here the surviving place-names suggest that the absence of physical evidence is a consequence of the absence of survey and excavation in the nineteenth and twentieth centuries. The 'pit'-names dispersed to the south and west of Fraserburgh, for example, indicate that the local landscape was organised into a series of economic units during the Pictish period from the sixth to ninth centuries AD and on through subsequent periods. It is likely that Pictish farm or estate centres, such as Pitblae, have been lost beneath the spreading burgh.

What can be reconstructed of the twelfth- to early sixteenth-century settlement history of the Fraserburgh district indicates that there was probably a series of small agricultural or agricultural and fishing communities dispersed around the medieval parish. The place of Philorth/Fraserburgh within the estates of the medieval earls of Buchan and the properties of their various successors down to the foundation of the burgh is fairly well understood, and analogies can be offered for the economic structures within which they operated. Rather than a single nucleus for population around either the lordship centre (Philorth/Cairnbulg) to which most of the medieval parish was tied, or the parish church, there were clearly several such foci. The two most important were probably Kirkton and Faithlie, while a third may have evolved into Broadsea. With the exception of the scant physical remnants of a portion of post-Reformation burial vault attached to the site of the medieval parish church, no certain archaeological evidence has been found of any medieval settlement at Kirkton. However, it should be noted that the middens and hearths identified here in the nineteenth century could be medieval rather than prehistoric. Any development undertaken in the vicinity of the current cemetery around the medieval parish church site, or any proposed extension to the cemetery, should be accompanied by survey, geophysical evaluation and sample excavation.

Clear evidence for the medieval phase of Faithlie is similarly lacking, although it is likely that the layout seen in the earliest plans of Fraserburgh (**maps 4, 5 & 6**) preserves some indication of its nature. The line of Shore Street probably follows the curve of the medieval settlement ranged along the Shore between the steep brae of the raised beach and the foreshore, protected from north and west winds in the lee of the scarp. This area is one of the most consistently redeveloped within the modern burgh, with one side of the street having been swept away in the mid-nineteenth-century harbour expansion programme, but it is possible that medieval remains lie sealed either on the seaward side of Shore Street or beneath the late eighteenth-, nineteenth- and twentieth-century structures on the west side. Shore Street therefore constitutes one of the most archaeologically sensitive sectors of the burgh and any redevelopment in this area should take due cognisance of that fact.

Not only does the Fraserburgh district seem to have lacked serious antiquaries in the nineteenth and earlier twentieth centuries, but also, until relatively recently, a late sixteenth-century new town would not have been regarded as of much archaeological significance. The archaeological potential of the burgh constitutes a great unknown, given the absence of any watching brief or excavation work during the various phases of redevelopment undertaken in central Fraserburgh since 1945. This situation arose largely as a consequence of a disciplinary trend within Scottish archaeology which did not recognise the significance of post-medieval urban archaeology. Indeed, given the limited development of urban archaeology in Scotland in the 1970s and early 1980s, it is unsurprising that a small provincial burgh of apparently late sixteenth-century date failed to attract archaeological interest when limited resources were being directed towards the 'historic' royal burghs in which significant twelfth- to sixteenth-century remains were preserved.

The apparently unique development of Fraserburgh in the late sixteenth century, however, where a pre-burgh community formed a core onto which was grafted a substantial planned town of a form without clear parallel in the British Isles, argues strongly for a re-evaluation of development strategies within the town. Recognition of the significance in international terms of the late sixteenth-century town plan makes it important to take seriously the archaeological potential of current vacant town-centre sites and to ensure that archaeological investigation forms part of any future development plans within at least the historic core of the burgh. Investigation of these may be the last chance to find out about the archaeology of this prominent coastal site.

FRASERBURGH

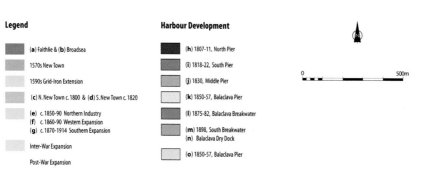

MAP 9
Fraserburgh development
map (above)
MAP 10
Fraserburgh character map
(facing page)

Legend

(**a**) Faithlie & (**b**) Broadsea

1570s New Town

1590s Grid-Iron Extension

(**c**) N. New Town c. 1800 & (**d**) S. New Town c. 1820

(**e**) c. 1850-90 Northern Industry
(**f**) c. 1860-90 Western Expansion
(**g**) c. 1870-1914 Southern Expansion

Inter-War Expansion

Post-War Expansion

Harbour Development

(**h**) 1807-11, North Pier

(**i**) 1818-22, South Pier

(**j**) 1830, Middle Pier

(**k**) 1850-57, Balaclava Pier

(**l**) 1875-82, Balaclava Breakwater

(**m**) 1898, South Breakwater
(**n**) Balaclava Dry Dock

(**o**) 1850-57, Balaclava Pier

0   500m

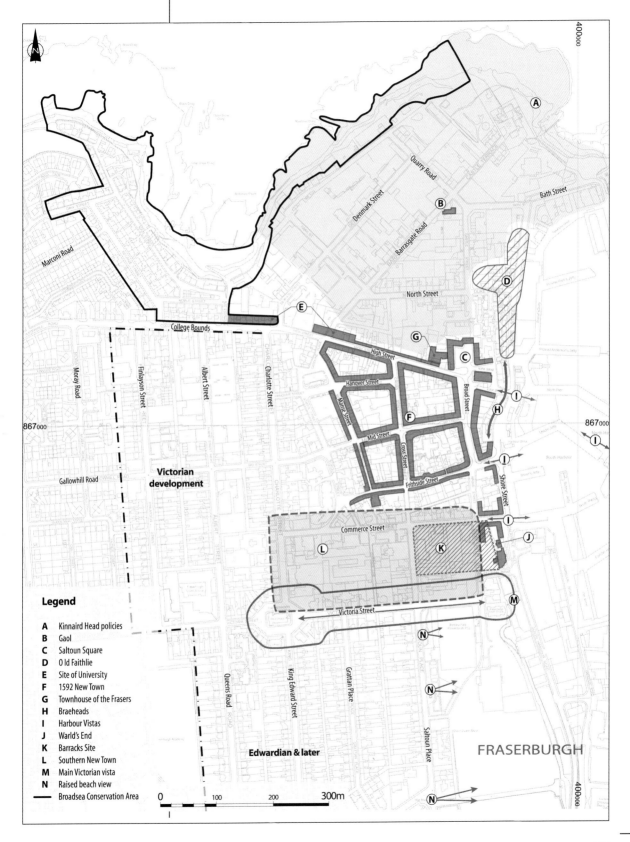

Legend

A Kinnaird Head policies
B Gaol
C Saltoun Square
D Old Faithlie
E Site of University
F 1592 New Town
G Townhouse of the Frasers
H Braeheads
I Harbour Vistas
J World's End
K Barracks Site
L Southern New Town
M Main Victorian vista
N Raised beach view
━━ Broadsea Conservation Area

Victorian development

Edwardian & later

FRASERBURGH

0   100   200   300m

Townscape: area-by-area assessment (maps 9 & 10)

Shore Street and Braeheads

This area possibly formed part of the pre-burghal core from which Alexander Fraser began development of his burgh in the mid-sixteenth century, and evidence for late medieval, sixteenth-, seventeenth- and eighteenth-century Faithlie might survive in places beneath the dramatic changes wrought in the nineteenth century. Harbour plans and navigational charts between 1818 and 1858 (**maps 6 & 7**) clearly document the former buildings on the east side of Shore Street from the Mid Pier northwards. In view of the nineteenth- and early twentieth-century tradition of constructing harbours by building out from the existing shoreline and levelling up behind the quay

FIGURE 43
Old building on the corner of Kirk Brae and Shore Street (Paula Martin)

FIGURE 44
Examples of decorative ironwork from around the burgh
(Charles McKean and Paula Martin)

and pier retaining walls, it is possible that substantial remains of these older buildings, which stood in the way of harbour improvements from the 1850s, survive sealed under the modern ranges of sheds and harbour buildings. Much of the twentieth-century development between Shore Street and the quayside of the Balaclava and North harbours consists of large shed buildings erected on concrete rafts.

The upper limit of old Faithlie was probably Braeheads. The inland side, between Shore Street and Braeheads/Castle Lane, still clings into the slope, recalling the contours and curves of the old village. Its fine urban grain represents a so far unexploited opportunity for enhancement and visitor potential. Several buildings along the Shore, from Frithside Street northwards up to and beyond Duke Street, retain considerable character and quality (**fig 43**). Significant buildings include the one at the foot of Kirk Brae, the 1885 Kirk Green tenements behind it, the Mariners Bar, and the substantial warehouses of R D Downie. The scrolled downpipes of Michael Watt/Denholm Fish provide an indication of quality (**fig 44**). Perhaps the most crucial section lies around the Stinking Stairs (this name first occurs in the Town Council Minutes for 12 November 1782; it probably relates to the consequences of fish-processing carried on in the vicinity). This is an area worthy of further study and investigation if the opportunity arises.

The sixteenth-century planned town

The central block of the town bounded by the High Street and Saltoun Square to the north, Frithside Street to the south, Broad Street to the east and Manse Street to the west constitutes an area of significant archaeological potential and sensitivity, albeit one which has suffered from considerable erosion through later nineteenth- and twentieth-century development of both street frontages and back properties. There are no clearly recognisable upstanding structures within this area to which a sixteenth- or seventeenth-century date can be assigned with confidence, and only isolated eighteenth-century buildings and architectural fragments survive.

Most of the street frontages appear to have been redeveloped in two phases, c 1825–50 and post-1875, and it is impossible to determine the extent to which such redevelopment represented complete rebuilds on cleared sites as opposed to the refacing of earlier structures without detailed building survey on a property-by-property basis. On the north side of High Street towards its eastern end, the tenement block that runs parallel with the former stable yard of the Saltoun Arms Hotel has incorporated the original outer wall of the stables and entrance pend in its ground-floor rear wall. There may be other such fossilised survivals in the rear walls of the buildings further to the west. It is probable that several of the property boundaries in the backlands of the block bounded by Broad Street, High Street, Cross Street and Mid Street stand on late sixteenth- and seventeenth-century alignments, and may contain portions of early fabric.

There is much to be found out or understood about the late sixteenth-century new town itself. The street plan and its boundaries are not clearly defined on paper, and the first map, Roy's military survey of *c* 1750 (**map 5**), is not always easy to reconcile with what is now on the ground, or with other documentary records. Much of the character of the town centre derives from its layout, with its square plots rather than the traditional long narrow rigs. Some of the early streets were also ambitiously wide.

FIGURE 45
No 66 Frithside Street
(Paula Martin)

FIGURE 46
Long staircase window in the rear of a house on the north side of Frithside Street
(Paula Martin)

FIGURE 47
Mid-eighteenth-century
house, Mid Street
(Paula Martin)

The original townscape of a two-street by four-street rectangular grid, probably later expanded to four by four, is just perceptible today, and may best be seen in the relatively narrow Frithside Street and Love Lane (a later addition to the original plan), which travel westwards from the uphill plateau, where they kink. The evidence from surviving buildings implies that these streets switched from residential to fishing activity in the nineteenth century. At the uphill end of Love Lane there is a fine, disused, cantilevered timber shed in the backlands; and on the south downhill side of Frithside Street there is an equally atmospheric yard. Much of the north-east side of Love Lane comprises small cottages and buildings relating to fish processing – some derelict. The most imposing building in the street, the RAFA Clubhouse, is a substantial three-bay, three-storeyed granite building/warehouse with great potential. Buildings become larger as Frithside Street moves uphill, the most imposing being the later eighteenth-century white-harled house at No 66 (**fig 45**), although both Nos 55 (roof apart) and 59 (with its fine rear stair window) (**fig 46**) are equally valuable. The later dormered cottages of pedestrianised Manse Street provide a pleasing contrast in scale.

The first new town's character has been serially eroded in the other streets. Cross Street was realigned with Saltoun Place with the arrival of the turnpike road in 1810, and the scale of Hanover Street was blown apart when redeveloped for council houses between the wars. Much (eg Mid Street) has been damaged by insensitive development throughout the twentieth century. One can still find traces of early Fraserburgh, however: No 30 Cross Street, for example, is a fine three-bay two-storey house of whinstone with granite dressings that might predate the street's widening and reorientation; and the building adjacent to Traill's, Mid Street, likewise appears to be eighteenth-century (**fig 47**). Yet poorly designed car parking and redevelopment have exploded the contained quality of most of the original backlands. This makes the principal survivor, a backland of immense potential bounded by Broad, High, Mid and Cross Streets, all the more significant and precious.

High Street and northwards

The area extending north from the High Street to the rear boundary of the properties on the south side of North Street consists at present of a series of yards, cleared sites and blocks of waste ground intersected by boundary walls of several dates. These together form an area of archaeological potential, as between Barrasgate Road and Saltoun Square the north side of High Street seems originally to have been the favoured location of some of the more substantial properties of the sixteenth- to eighteenth-century burgh. Here rear gardens could be obtained and extended, in contrast to the limited scope offered in the gridded streets to the south.

These High Street properties included at least one large courtyard house recorded in the late nineteenth century (see **fig 2**). While most of the properties appear to have been built on the line of the present street frontage by at least the mid-eighteenth century, as attested by the one surviving *in situ* skewput dated 1761 embedded in the gable angle of No 78 High Street, the southern wall of the Saltoun Arms courtyard indicates that there was a significant section of set-back properties towards its east end (**map 8**). There appears also to have been one large later eighteenth- or early nineteenth-century house set back from the north side of High Street with its rear wall on the line of what became the boundary between the High Street and North Street properties (**map 8**), of which only the wall, formerly with railings, and gateway to High Street and the truncated stump of its northern façade survive. At the western end of High Street to the east of its junction with Barrasgate Road is the probable site of the university. Local tradition speaks of a well, and infilled street-front cellars, at this location. While early frontages may have been obliterated by later nineteenth-century redevelopment, it is possible that the rear portions of earlier courtyard buildings and backland structures might survive.

The former quality of the High Street is indicated, *inter alia*, by the solitary *in situ* sandstone skewput attached to No 78, mentioned above. The

FIGURE 48
Part of the range of old
buildings surviving in the
courtyard behind the Saltoun
Arms Hotel. Four lighter-
coloured sandstone panels
with concentric circular
carving are set along the
wall-head (Richard Oram)

house it graced once had 'several steps and iron hand-railings leading from
the pavement up to the door'. So, although the evidence is slight, there is
sufficient to conclude that Fraser's Broch had evolved into a substantial, well-
built town of good quality and some distinction. During the boom years of
the later nineteenth century, however, High Street overtook Broad Street as
the commercial centre of the town; much was rebuilt with the characteristic
mansard roofs of that period. Tenements replaced most of the seventeenth-
and eighteenth-century buildings lining the north side, and the set-back
section at the east end of the street was filled to conceal the earlier building
behind. These earlier buildings may comprise elements of the former stable
courtyard of the Kinnaird Castle estate and Saltoun town-house, later the
Saltoun Arms. Largely eighteenth-century in appearance, this high-quality
courtyard has sandstone dressings (**fig 48**). Curiously, the new High Street
tenements cannibalised their south wall, as indicated by blocked windows
with wide internal splays surviving on the stable-yard side.

North Street to Kinnaird Head

This northern extension to the sixteenth-century burgh covers what appears to
have once been a series of fields, yards and gardens associated with the castle on
Kinnaird Head. There seem to have been no substantial structures within this area
away from the main castle complex at its northern end and the possible Fraser

FIGURE 49
Broadsea Conservation Area,
2007 (Crown Copyright:
Historic Scotland)

town-house and attendant stable block on the Saltoun Arms site at its southern extremity. The archaeological potential of this area comprises the surviving portions of the castle, Wine Tower, lighthouse, the Saltoun Arms, and sites of the baths, prison and bone mill. But there has been some recent clearance.

An interesting aspect of industrial archaeology is represented by the herring barrel store in Quarry Road, later the foundry of the Consolidated Pneumatic Tool Company Ltd and now Fraserburgh Heritage Centre. Another is the Museum of Scottish Lighthouses.

Broadsea

This is a classic North-East fisher town community of single-storey terraces beside a sheltered bay into which small fishing boats were formerly hauled. A large model of Broadsea in Fraserburgh Heritage Centre was built by Fraserburgh Academy and Fraserburgh North School pupils from 1989 to 1992 as part of a project and shows the village as it was in 1861, drawn from the First edition OS map. At the north end is the original scatter of buildings before the terraced form was adopted, shown as 'Seatown' on Roy's map (**map 5**). A similar nineteenth-century transition from chaos to order can be found in other Moray Firth and North Sea fishing communities from Avoch through Cullen to Johnshaven. Here is the greatest concentration of listed buildings and the only conservation area in Fraserburgh (**fig 49** and see **fig 31**).

South of the town centre

World's End (see **figs 15 & 16**) survives as Fraserburgh's finest house, though now spoiled both by its surroundings at the front, and the high wall close behind it, supporting a terrace above. This made-up ground immediately behind World's End and extending westward as far as Seaforth Street, retained by a substantial stone wall, may represent a parade-ground associated with the eighteenth-century barracks. It is possible that the levelling operation has sealed remains of the offices, court, outbuildings and part of the garden area

FIGURE 50
John Noble, netmaker,
Barrack Lane (Paula Martin)

of this substantial early eighteenth-century (or earlier?) property. This terrace is used at present as a car park.

While the exact extent of the barrack grounds is not clear, there is a possibility of surviving military buildings at its westwards edge, along Barrack Lane. There is little identifiable on the barrack site itself save clearly disturbed and built-up ground, and a fine wall from No 32 Barrack Lane up to the turnpike. However, a large, plain-harled building, whose former quality is indicated by quoin stones, a battered wall, and an impression of strength – despite its later cut-down roof – may be a relic of the soldiers' quarters that popular tradition identified as built in Barrack Lane. Its current harling conceals its history. The premises of John Noble, netmaker, closes Barrack Lane in style, with quoin stones and a ball finial (**fig 50**).

Victorian suburbs

The vast expanse of suburban development, on greenfield sites, is described in Section 4. Most of it is still standing and in use, and any archaeological potential will be for prehistoric settlement, as discussed earlier in this section.

Twentieth-century expansion

The population of the centre of the town has been declining ever since the First World War, the residents moving out to spacious housing schemes to the west and south-west. Some of these, described in Section 4, are notable for the quality of their architecture, but their unity can easily be undermined by the individual aesthetic ideas of private owners.

Genius loci and conclusion

A sense of place depends on a sympathetic appreciation of the range of building materials, the range of architectural styles available in the nineteenth and twentieth centuries, and their place within the wider townscape. A good example of this is the red sandstone local-authority housing at Gallowhill Terrace, built with traditional materials, and designed to form a western entrance to the town. Also needed is an awareness of the possibility that nineteenth- and twentieth-century street frontages may only be façades to earlier buildings preserved behind. The car showroom at the corner of

FIGURE 51
Car showroom, on the corner of Saltoun Place and Victoria Street, a modern façade imposed on an earlier house (Paula Martin)

Saltoun Place and Victoria Street, for example (**fig 51**), is a façade imposed on most but not all of an early nineteenth-century building, the combination being striking.

The backs of many buildings are worthy of record, as for example one in Frithside Street with massive granite lintels over its small windows, and a long narrow stair window, possibly of eighteenth-century date (see **fig 46**).

Sense of place also depends on an appreciation of the intrinsic value of the community and the buildings which give it substance. Fraserburgh's particular patterns of economic and social development through the nineteenth and twentieth centuries have served to create a palpable disjunction between the modern community and its past. This break has weakened recognition of the distinctive physical character of the town which provided it with its individuality and identity. The first new town may be unique in Scotland at that period. Subsequent new towns followed in the eighteenth and nineteenth centuries, to the north, the south, and the south-west, and the twentieth century saw the building of major areas of public-sector housing on the west and south-west. Post-1945 expansion cemented the segregation of private and public sectors that had emerged between the wars. Initial private-sector house building infilled in Strichen Road and then continued on West Road and Queen's Road with substantial bungalows, some with stained glass, facing wide streets. The expansion to the south-west of this district now governs the first image of Fraserburgh on arrival from Strichen. This belies the particular individuality of Fraserburgh itself. Suburbs have eaten up the town's peripheral land, softened its edge and thereby perhaps damaged what gives Fraserburgh its identity. By comparison with the tight first new town of the 1590s, land-use has been generous, but this has its drawbacks; the Buchan winds can blow uninterrupted through the wide new streets and along their broad pavements. Construction of these successive arcs of housing along the landward margins of the town is an important reason why so much property within the urban core has fallen into disfavour with residential and commercial owners and tenants. The impact of the closure of wartime industries, and of changes in fishing practice compounded the effects of this trend and is particularly noticeable at the north end of the town. Sporadic replacement within the former Castle Parks meant a landscape of marooned walls, cottages and vacancy.

A trend for further development on the western and southern peripheries of the modern town rather than the reuse of vacant ground within its earlier northern and eastern core continued into the 1990s. As a consequence, like in many old urban communities, there was a protracted decline in the level of population in the town centre, and an associated proliferation of vacant or low-occupancy properties in some areas has resulted in some problems of building maintenance. Similarly, the common British trend for relocation of commercial activity to town-edge locations and changes in consumer shopping behaviour has resulted in a contraction in the number of occupied units in the town centre streets. Two centuries of suburban development and the southward and westward drift of population shifted the focus of the town centre and affected the viability of the High Street in particular. Visible dilapidation is widespread, particularly evinced by blocked gutters with vegetation growing from them. Through redevelopment, many of the streets of the first new town have lost, or come perilously close to losing, their innate character, and the priorities of road transport has put further pressure on the townscape through road widening and car parking. More recently, however, a reversal of these processes has begun, with derelict industrial areas in Castle Parks district and on High Street being redeveloped as residential zones and the associated return of population is helping to stimulate a revival in town-centre commercial activity. Broadsea, however, has the only conservation area in Fraserburgh, designated in 1975, and there is none in the centre of the town that might serve as a means to coordinate maintenance and enhancement of character in partnership with public- and private-sector developers.

The special character of the heart of the town – of Fraser's Broch – has been generally overlooked, to its great but not irretrievable damage. Yet this heart has a scale and character that might be the envy of the citizens of a more economically favoured location. Fraser's Broch could yet, with vision and sympathetic development, recover adequate attractiveness for town-centre living in the twenty-first century, and developments with that aim have already commenced. It is a matter of understanding its importance, and taking the necessary creative steps to build upon, rather than neglecting or rejecting, the legacy of the past.

Notes

1   Details of the recorded sites in the vicinity of Fraserburgh can be found on Pastmap and in the Royal Commission on the Ancient and Historical Monuments of Scotland map sheets NJ96NE, NW, SE and SW, and NK06NW and SW.

Appendix 1: Update of the original Survey

It can be useful to note change from a baseline assessment over a five-year period. In March 2007, the team revisited the town to assess changes to the urban landscape since the completion of the original survey in 2003. The changes and developments that were noted were discussed with the Aberdeenshire Archaeology Service (AAS) in January 2008. All comments about archaeological works are based upon that discussion, and run from north to south.

North of High Street

1. At the west side of the former Castle Parks area towards the Denmark Street end of Park Street, there has been a major programme of demolition and clearance of disused warehouses and industrial units. This area is scheduled for private housing development in the course of 2007–08, mainly of detached or semi-detached homes; this represents a major reorientation of the residential zoning in Fraserburgh. This area of the outer yards and parks associated with the castle on Kinnaird Head had been incorporated into the town in the mid-nineteenth century, almost wholly for industrial or commercial purposes. In January 2008 AAS stated that they expected to request a programme of archaeological work in advance of development.
2. On the north side of High Street there has been a major insertion of private housing. This sensitive development has infilled the former cinema and 'town-house' site, preserving the street line and building frontage while extending northwards over the backlands of the two burgages involved. An evaluation of the site was requested by AAS in advance of development.
3. On the north side of College Bounds, the fire-damaged Alexandra Hotel has been completely demolished and the site is currently vacant. A condition of the permission to demolish was for the recovery of the sculptured stonework reported in Pratt *Buchan* and Henderson *Aberdeenshire Inscriptions*, but nothing was found which matched the descriptions. It was suggested by AAS that the inscribed plaques described there were perhaps of more recent origin, but nothing was found when the internal plaster was removed in the relevant area. The inscriptions were said to have come from the University buildings and were believed to constitute one of the few physical survivals of that short-lived institution. It appears that no detailed survey of the hotel was undertaken prior to demolition to determine if any portions of earlier structures were incorporated into its fabric.

Western district

1. The grain mill and commercial brewery buildings at Watermill on the Banff road, partly ruinous by 2003, have been completely demolished. The site is currently vacant. This had been the location of a mill since at least the later-sixteenth century; one at the outlet burn from the Loch of Fingask was noted on Timothy Pont's map of the district (**map 4**). A desk-based evaluation, map regression exercise and site visit of the surrounding land was carried out prior to demolition but revealed nothing. The mill building was not included within the evaluation. A planning application for development of a supermarket on the site has been received by Aberdeenshire Council. It is anticipated that a programme of evaluation trenching and building recording will take place in advance of any construction work on the site.
2. The northern sector of 1930s and 1940s council housing centred on Marconi Drive was, in March 2007, mainly boarded up and apparently scheduled for demolition.

Saltoun Square/Church Street

Saltoun Square remains the focus of the community but there has been a marked decline in its physical state and in commercial activity since 2002. A number of retail units were vacant in 2007.

1. The Saltoun Arms Hotel, the dominant building in the Square, was shut. The rear court of the hotel, possibly containing components of eighteenth-century or earlier buildings associated with the former town-house of the Frasers of Philorth, was inaccessible. The ornamental cast-iron brattishing around the turret and along the main roof ridge is missing, giving the building a truncated appearance. AAS has been assured that the brattishing is to be replaced.
2. The condition of Kirk Brae has deteriorated significantly since 2002. The Market Hall, empty in 2003, remains boarded up, its rainwater goods grass-filled and in places fallen away. A fire occurred in the upper storeys of the tenement to the north-east of the parish church. AAS is aware of the likely archaeological sensitivity of the site.

Central grid

1. Changes in occupancy in some buildings in the closes running north from Mid Street may have reduced maintenance of roofs, gutters and drainpipes. This is evident in Gordon's Court off Mid Street, the location of one of the few surviving seventeenth-century inscribed panels in the town. The close is an example of the good but unrealised amenity potential of the mixed residential/commercial elements in the historic core of the burgh.

2. Mid Street, United Reformed Church. The early nineteenth-century church building was destroyed by fire in May 2000. Its replacement was rededicated in October 2003. The new building, designed by Law and Dunbar Naismith, is a 'modern-gothic' structure entirely in sympathy with the adjoining architecture in terms of materials and scale. It contains some fine modern stained glass by the Jennifer-Jane studio.

Faithlie/Harbour

1. There has been recent investment in buildings in the central part of old Faithlie along the Shore. The George 'n' Dragon public house, one of the principal historic buildings in this sector of the town, has been repainted and externally improved.

2. Braeheads. Some partial demolition of buildings has occurred on the east side of the lane running parallel with Broad Street. Pantiled roofs to the rear of buildings fronting the Shore have been removed.

Kirkton

1. A significant development with potential consequences for the old commercial centre of the town in the High Street/Saltoun Square area is the building of a superstore complex at the south-eastern edge of Fraserburgh. Adjacent to the medieval church and cemetery site at Kirkton, this development may in part overlie the site of one of the pre-burghal settlements which were consolidated into the new burgh in the sixteenth century. AAS requested that a programme of archaeological work be undertaken on this site. AAS is considering the extension of archaeological work into the brownfield parts of the site.

Appendix 2: Lists of previous archaeological work, chance finds and Scheduled/Listed Historic Buildings

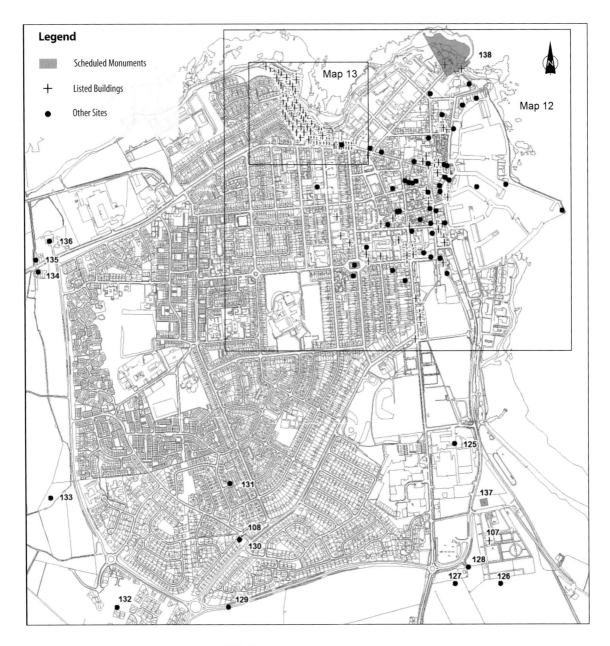

MAP II

Location of Scheduled Ancient Monuments, Listed Buildings and other sites
(outer area)

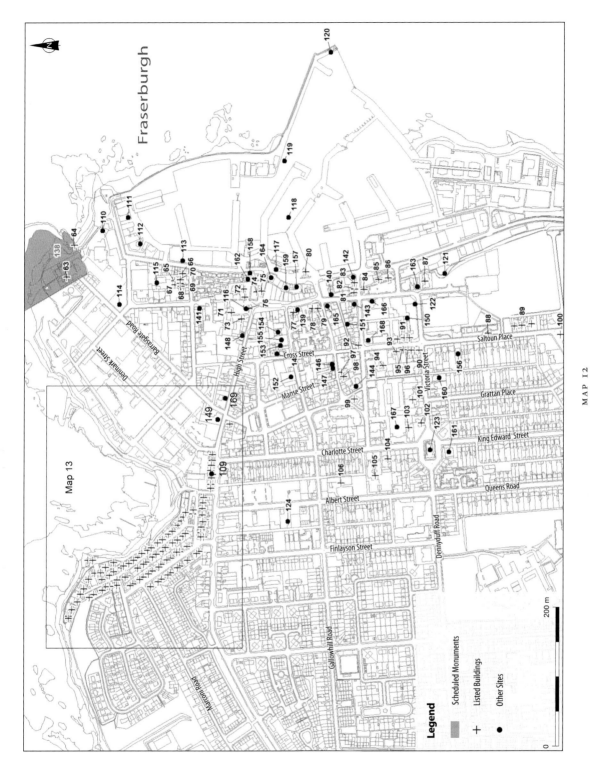

Fraserburgh

Map 13

Denmark Street

Barrasgate Road

Marconi Road

Gallowhill Road

High Street

Cross Street

Manse Street

Charlotte Street

Albert Street

Finlayson Street

Dennyduff Road

Victoria Street

Saltoun Place

Grattan Place

King Edward Street

Queens Road

200 m

Legend

Scheduled Monuments

Listed Buildings

Other Sites

MAP 12

Location of Scheduled Ancient Monuments, Listed Buildings and other sites (wider area)

143

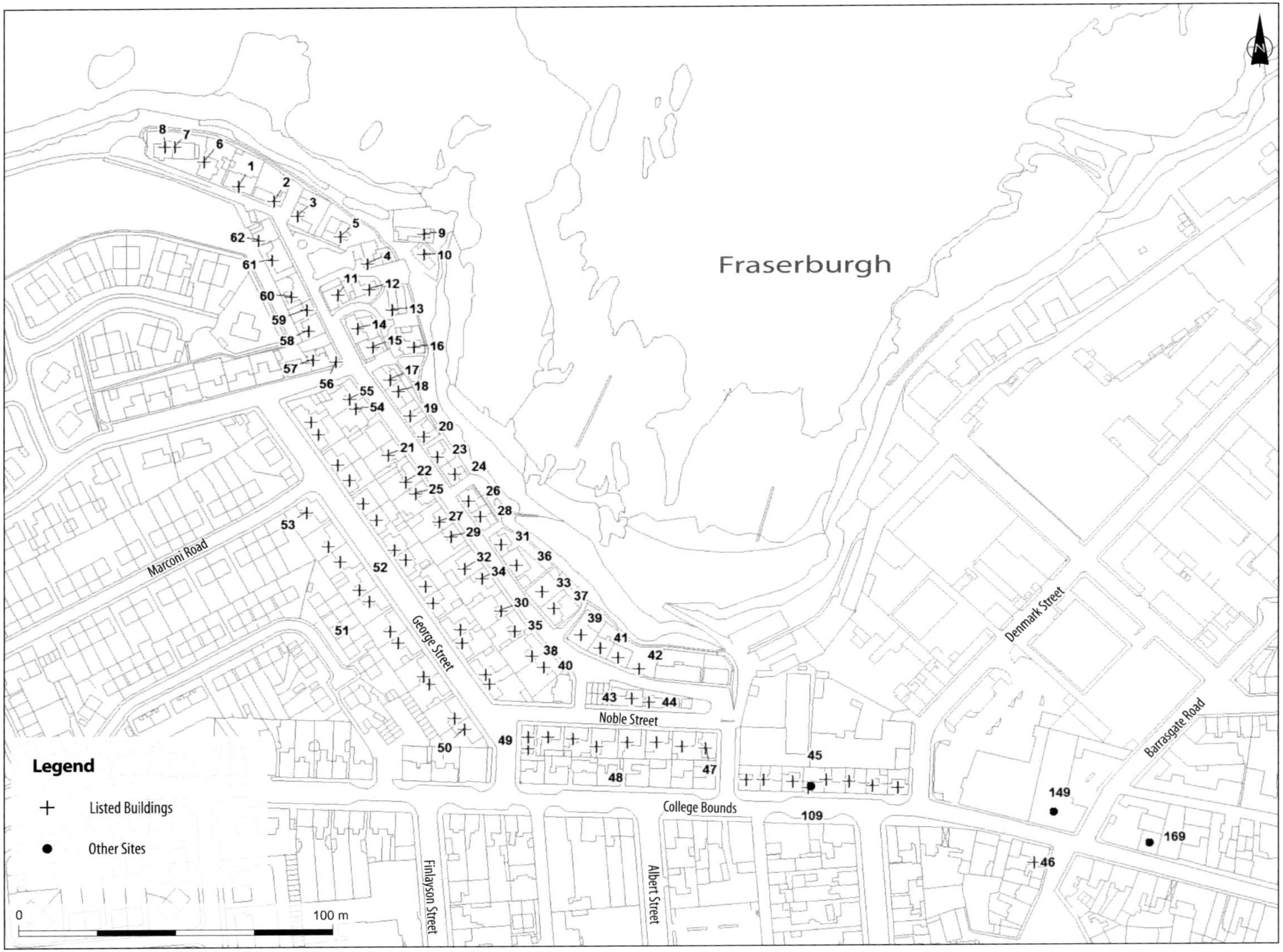

Fraserburgh

MAP 13

Location of Scheduled Ancient Monuments, Listed Buildings and other sites (inner area)

Legend

+ Listed Buildings

● Other Sites

No	Name	NGR	RCAHMS No	Status	Historic Scotland Ref
1	78 Main Street	NJ 9911 6750	NJ96NE 146	C(S)	31956
2	73 Main Street	NJ 9913 6749	NJ96NE 153	C(S)	31955
3	Shalom, 72 Main Street	NJ 9914 6748	NJ96NE 161	C(S)	31954
4	64 Main Street	NJ 9918 6745	NJ96NE 122	C(S)	31952
5	69 Main Street	NJ 9916 6747	NJ96NE 151	C(S)	31953
6	80 Main Street	NJ 9909 6751	NJ96NE 155	C(S)	31957
7	82 Main Street	NJ 9908 6752	NJ96NE 156	C(S)	31958
8	84 Main Street	NJ 9907 6752	NJ96NE 157	C(S)	31959
9	54 Main Street	NJ 9921 6747	NJ96NE 149	C(S)	31949
10	52 Main Street	NJ 9921 6746	NJ96NE 159	C(S)	31948
11	60 Main Street	NJ 9916 67442	NJ96NE 150	C(S)	31951
12	56 Main Street	NJ 9918 6744	NJ96NE 158	B	31950
13	46 Main Street	NJ 9919 6743	NJ96NE 101	C(S)	31947
14	44 Main Street	NJ 9917 6742	NJ96NE 100	C(S)	31946
15	42 Main Street	NJ 9918 6741	NJ96NE 99	C(S)	31945
16	40 Main Street	NJ 9920 6741	NJ96NE 142	C(S)	31944
17	38 Main Street	NJ 9919 6739	NJ96NE 147	C(S)	31943
18	36 Main Street	NJ 9919 8673	NJ96NE 163	C(S)	31942
19	34 Main Street	NJ9920 6737	NJ96NE 144	C(S)	31941
20	32 Main Street	NJ 9921 6736	NJ96NE 165	C(S)	31940
21	35 Main Street	NJ 9919 6735	NJ96NE 94	C(S)	31920
22	33 Main Street	NJ 9920 6734	NJ96NE 98	C(S)	31919
23	30 Main Street	NJ 9921 6735	NJ96NE 166	C(S)	31939
24	28 Main Street	NJ 9922 6734	NJ96NE 93	C(S)	31938
25	31 Main Street	NJ 9920 6733	NJ96NE 135	C(S)	31918
26	26 Main Street	NJ 9923 6733	NJ96NE 160	C(S)	31937
27	29 Main Street	NJ 9921 6732	NJ96NE 136	C(S)	31917
28	24 Main Street	NJ 9924 6732	NJ96NE 148	C(S)	31936
29	27 Main Street	NJ 9922 6731	NJ96NE 137	C(S)	31916
30	19 Main Street	NJ 9925 6727	NJ96NE 140	C(S)	31913
31	22 Main Street	NJ 9925 6730	NJ96NE 164	C(S)	31935
32	25 Main Street	NJ 9923 6729	NJ96NE 138	C(S)	31915
33	16 Main Street	NJ 9927 6728	NJ96NE 96	C(S)	31933
34	23 Main Street	NJ 9924 6729	NJ96NE 139	C(S)	31914
35	17 Main Street	NJ 9925 6726	NJ96NE 145	C(S)	31912
36	20 Main Street	NJ 9925 6729	NJ96NE 97	C(S)	31934
37	14 Main Street	NJ 9927 6727	NJ96NE 162	C(S)	31932
38	15 Main Street	NJ 9926 6725	NJ96NE 141	C(S)	31911
39	Former Church Hall, Main Street	NJ 9929 6726	NJ96NE 107	C(S)	31931
40	13 Main Street	NJ 9927 6724	NJ96NE 134	C(S)	31910
41	8, 10 Main Street	NJ 9930 6725	NJ96NE 92	C(S)	31930
		NJ 9931 6724	NJ96NE 91		
42	6 Main Street	NJ 9932 6724	NJ96NE 208	C(S)	31929
43	5 Noble Street	NJ 9931 6722	NJ96NE 236	C(S)	31967
44	3 Noble Street	NJ 9932 6722	NJ96NE 83	C(S)	31966

No	Name	NGR	RCAHMS No	Status	Historic Scotland Ref
45	2–16 College Bounds	NJ 9945 6718	NJ96NE 126	B	31909
		NJ 9944 6718	NJ96NE 127		
		NJ 9943 6718	NJ96NE 128		
		NJ 9941 6718	NJ96NE 129		
		NJ 9940 6718	NJ96NE 130		
		NJ 9940 6718	NJ96NE 131		
		NJ 9938 6718	NJ96NE 132		
		NJ 9937 6718	NJ96NE 133		
46	1, 3 Caroline Place & 89 High Street	NJ 9952 6714	NJ96NE 76	C(S)	31890
47	3, 5 Broadsea Road	NJ 9935 6720	NJ96NE 84	C(S)	31969
48	2–28 Noble Street	NJ 9935 6720	NJ96NE 236	C(S)	31968
		NJ 9932 6722	NJ96NE 83		
		NJ 9931 6722	NJ96NE 236		
		NJ 9934 6720	NJ96NE 237		
		NJ 9933 6720	NJ96NE 238		
		NJ 9931 6720	NJ96NE 239		
		NJ 9930 6720	NJ96NE 240		
		NJ 9928 6720	NJ96NE 241		
		NJ 9927 6720	NJ96NE 242		
49	4, 4½ George Street & 32 Noble Street	NJ 9926 6720	NJ96NE 210	C(S)	31964
		NJ 9926 6720	NJ96NE 211		
50	3, 5 George Street	NJ 9923 6721	NJ96NE 80	C(S)	31961
51	7–37 George Street	NJ 9922 6721	NJ96NE 212	C(S)	31962
		NJ 9921 6723	NJ96NE 213		
		NJ 9921 6723	NJ96NE 214		
		NJ 9919 6725	NJ96NE 215		
		NJ 9919 6726	NJ96NE 216		
		NJ 9918 6727	NJ96NE 217		
		NJ 9917 6728	NJ96NE 218		
		NJ 9916 6730	NJ96NE 219		
		NJ 9916 6730	NJ96NE 220		
52	6–46 George Street	NJ 9924 6723	NJ96NE 222	C(S)	31965
		NJ 9924 6724	NJ96NE 223		
		NJ 9923 6725	NJ96NE 224		
		NJ 9923 6726	NJ96NE 225		
		NJ 9921 6727	NJ96NE 226		
		NJ 9921 6728	NJ96NE 227		
		NJ 9920 6730	NJ96NE 228		
		NJ 9919 6730	NJ96NE 229		
		NJ 9918 6732	NJ96NE 230		
		NJ 9918 6733	NJ96NE 231		
		NJ 9917 6734	NJ96NE 232		
		NJ 9916 6735	NJ96NE 233		
		NJ 9915 6736	NJ96NE 234		
		NJ 9915 6737	NJ96NE 233		
53	39 George Street	NJ 9915 6732	NJ96NE 221	C(S)	31963
54	39 Main Street	NJ 9917 6738	NJ96NE 121	C(S)	31921

No	Name	NGR	RCAHMS No	Status	Historic Scotland Ref
55	41 Main Street	NJ 9917 6738	NJ96NE 143	C(S)	31922
56	43 Main Street	NJ 9916 6740	NJ96NE 95	C(S)	31923
57	2 Gaw Street	NJ 9915 6740	NJ96NE 85	C(S)	31960
58	45 Main Street	NJ 9915 6742	NJ96NE 152	C(S)	31924
59	47 Main Street	NJ 9915 6743	NJ96NE 154	C(S)	31925
60	49 Main Street	NJ 9914 6744	NJ96NE 120	C(S)	31926
61	51 Main Street	NJ 9913 6746	NJ96NE 119	C(S)	31927
62	53 Main Street	NJ 9912 6747	NJ96NE 115	C(S)	31928
63	Kinnaird's Head Castle Lighthouse	NJ 9986 6752	NJ96NE 7	A; SM	31888 / 90344
64	Wine Tower	NJ 9993 6751	NJ96NE 9	A	31889
65	7 Duke Lane	NJ 9985 6727	NJ96NE 104	C(S)	31885
66	2 Duke Lane	NJ 9987 6725	NJ96NE 102	C(S)	31887
67	9 Duke Lane	NJ 9984 6726	NJ96NE 103	C(S)	31886
68	5 Duke Lane	NJ 9984 6725	NJ96NE 105	C(S)	31884
69	3½ Duke Lane	NJ 9984 6725	NJ96NE 106	C(S)	31883
70	3 Duke Lane	NJ9985 6725	NJ96NE 108	C(S)	31882
71	Registrar's Office, 14, 16 Saltoun Square	NJ 9978 6713	NJ96NE 123	B	31869
72	Town-house and Police Office 3 Saltoun Square & 1–5 Kirk Brae	NJ9981 6710 NJ 9983 6710	NJ96NE 47 NJ96NE 245	B	31868
73	Saltoun Arms, Saltoun Square	NJ9976 6711	NJ96NE 57	B	31870
74	Old Parish Church, Saltoun Square	NJ 9982 6707	NJ96NE 10.00	B	31865
75	Saltoun Mausoleum east of Old Parish Church	NJ 9983 6706	NJ96NE 10.01	B	31866
76	Market Cross, Saltoun Square	NJ 9979 6709	NJ96NE 8	A	31867
77	Clydesdale Bank, Broad Street & 1 Mid Street	NJ 9978 6699	NJ96NE 58	B	31871
78	50–54 Broad Street	NJ 9979 6694	NJ96NE 75	B	31872
79	Customs House (formerly occupied by Bank of Scotland) Broad Street & Frithside Street	NJ 9979 6693	NJ96NE 44	A	31873
80	Harbour Works Office at Middle Jetty	NJ 9987 6693	NJ96NE 88	C(S)	31879
81	Britannic Assurance Company Building, Broad Street & Commerce Street	NJ 9982 6684	NJ96NE 81	B	31874
82	7, 9 Commerce Street	NJ 9983 6684	NJ96NE 77	B	31875
83	5 Commerce Street	NJ 9985 6684	NJ96NE 209	B	31876
84	10 Commerce Street	NJ 9983 6682	NJ96NE 78	B	31877
85	The Warld's End, 11 Dalrymple Street	NJ 9985 6678	NJ96NE 54	B	31880
86	Dalrymple Hall & Café, Dalrymple Street	NJ 9986 6676	NJ96NE 53	C(S)	31881
87	Fraserburgh South Church of Scotland	NJ 9985 6667	NJ96NE 50	B	31878
88	Saltoun Place, fountain	NJ9973 6652	NJ96NE 19	B	31970
89	Coastguard Station Houses, 60–70 Saltoun Place	NJ 9975 6646 NJ 9975 6644 NJ 9975 6642	NJ96NE 52 NJ96NE 243 NJ96NE 244	B	31901
90	31, 33, 35 Saltoun Place	NJ 9969 6670 NJ 9969 6669	NJ96NE 167 NJ96NE 168	C(S)	31900

No	Name	NGR	RCAHMS No	Status	Historic Scotland Ref
91	24–32 Saltoun Place	NJ 9972 6674	NJ96NE 114	B	31896
		NJ 9972 6672	NJ96NE 113		
		NJ 9972 6671	NJ96NE 116		
			NJ96NE 117		
92	41 Commerce Street & 66, 68 Cross Street	NJ9970 6683	NJ96NE 79	C(S)	31893
93	21, 23 Saltoun Place	NJ 9969 6674	NJ96NE 118	C(S)	31897
94	Craiglea (Old Manse), 7 Saltoun Place	NJ 9965 6677	NJ96NE 51	C(S)	31895
95	25 Saltoun Place	NJ9969 6673	NJ96NE 113	C(S)	31898
96	27, 29 Saltoun Place	NJ 9969 6671	NJ96NE 124	C(S)	31899
		NJ 9969 6671	NJ96NE 125		
97	62 Frithside Street	NJ 9964 6687	NJ96NE 82	C(S)	31892
98	64, 68 Frithside Street (Salvation Army)	NJ 9963 6687	NJ96NE 111	B	31891
99	1, 3 Lodge Walk	NJ 9958 6684	NJ96NE 86	C(S)	31894
100	War Memorial, Saltoun Place & St. Modan's Gate	NJ 9973 6635	NJ96NE 56	B	31902
101	St Peter's School, Victoria Street	NJ 9958 6670	NJ96NE 59	B	31903
102	St Peter's Rectory, Victoria Street	NJ 9952 6668	NJ96NE 60	B	31904
103	St Peter's Episcopal Church, Charlotte Street	NJ 9951 6671	NJ96NE 49	B	31905
104	113 Charlotte Street	NJ 9944 6676	NJ96NE 109	C(S)	31907
105	Central School, Charlotte Street	NJ 9940 6679	NJ96NE 66	B	31906
106	Windmill Tower within Gray's Timber Yard, Albert Street, Mid Street & Charlotte Street	NJ 9938 6687	NJ96NE 14	B	31908
107	Philorth Churchyard within Fraserburgh Cemetery	NK 0005 6548	NK06NW 1	B	9588
108	South Middleburgh Tollhouse	NJ 3990 8655	NJ96NE 35	B	9593
109	College Bounds	NJ 9941 6718	NJ96NE 6		
110	Dovecot	NJ 9997 6744	NJ96NE 12		
111	Balaclava Quay, James Noble Ltd Boatbuilding Yard	NK 0000 6738	NK06NW 3.01		
112	Harbour, Balaclava Quay, J & G Forbes & Co. Boatbuilders	NJ 9994 6735	NJ96NE 38		
113	Bisset's Quay, Ice-Factory	NJ 9990 6725	NJ96NE 34		
114	Kinnaird Head Fish-Canning Works	NJ 998 674	NJ96NE 16		
115	Shore Street, Fish-smoking House	NJ 9985 6731	NJ96NE 17		
116	Saltoun Square, Market Cross	NJ 9979 6710	NJ96NE 8		
117	Shore Street, Fish Market	NJ 9988 6703	NJ96NE 45		
118	Harbour, Boatyards	NK 00 67	NK06NW 3.02		
119	Harbour	NK 0013 6701	NK06NW 3		
120	Harbour, Lighthouse	NK 0038 6690	NK06NW 3.03		
121	Fraserburgh Station	NJ 9987 6663	NJ96NE 30		
122	Victoria Street, Scottish Tractors (Abd) Ltd. Garage	NJ 9980 6670	NJ96NE 67		
123	The Hexagon, West Parish Church	NJ 9946 6664	NJ96NE 62		
124	Fish-Smoking House	NJ 993 670	NJ96NE 18		
125	Maconochie Road, Consolidated Pneumatic Works	NJ 9990 6590	NJ96NE 32		
126	Cemetery	NK 001 653	NK06NW 2		
127	Radio Station	NJ 999 653	NJ96NE 29.00		
128	Pillbox	NJ 9996 6537	NJ96NE 29.01		
129	Cairn Hill	NJ 989 652	NJ96NE 23		
130	South Middleburgh, Tollbar	NJ 9895 6549	NJ96NE 35		

No	Name	NGR	RCAHMS No	Status	Historic Scotland Ref
131	Broomhill, L-shaped building (site of)	NJ 9891 6573	NJ96NE 41		
132	North Pitblae, 'The Mote'	NJ 984 652	NJ96NE 22		
133	Greenbank farmstead (site of)	NJ 9811 6567	NJ96NE 39		
134	Fraserburgh, Watermill Road, Mill	NJ 9806 6664	NJ96NE 26		
135	Watermill Cottages	NJ 9805 6669	NJ96NE 33.01		
136	Watermill	NJ 9811 6677	NJ96NE 33.00		
137	Fraserburgh Cemetery, pillbox 280m east-north-east of Kirkton Cottages	NK 000 656	NK06NW 5	SM	8220
138	Kinnaird Head Castle and Lighthouse	NJ 999 675	NJ96NE 7	SM	90344
139	36–38 Broad Street	NJ 9979 6698			
140	73 Broad Street	NJ 9982 6690			
141	19–21Castle Street	NJ 9979 6721			
142	1–3 Commerce Street	NJ 9986 6685			
143	Beside Glover and Co. Fresh Fish Shop, 15 Commerce Street	NJ 9980 6684			
144	Roman Catholic Church, Commerce Street & School Street	NJ 9961 6684			
145	Coffee Shop, 30 Cross Street	NJ 9969 6703			
146	55 Frithside Street	NJ 9966 6690			
147	59 Frithside Street	NJ 9965 6689			
148	42 High Street	NJ 9923 6711			
149	Strachan's Female Industrial School, High Street & Barrasgate Road	NJ 9955 6716			
150	Barrack Lane, John Noble, netmaker	NJ 9977 6672			
151	RAFA clubhouse, Love Lane	NJ 9975 6686			
152	Congregational Church, Manse Street	NJ 9963 6699			
153	Gordon's Court, 32 Mid Street	NJ 9971 6702			
154	Macaulay Hall, Mid Street	NJ 9974 6702			
155	Picture House, Mid Street	NJ 9972 6702			
156	UP Church, Saltoun Place	NJ 9969 6660			
157	George & Dragon, Shore Street	NJ 9984 6698			
158	Oak Tree Buildings, Shore Street	NJ 9987 6709			
159	Shore House, Shore Street	NJ 9984 6701			
160	Baptist Church, Victoria Street	NJ 9963 6664			
161	Public Library, Victoria Street & King Edward Street	NJ 9946 6662			
162	Tenements, Kirk Brae	NJ 9986 6710			
163	Saltoun Estate Office, Seaforth Street	NJ 9984 6669			
164	Crown Inn, Stinking Steps	NJ 9986 6704			
165	Frithside Street	NJ 9980 6691			
166	Seaforth Street	NJ 9981 6680			
167	Thomas Walker Hospital, Charlotte Street	NJ 9951 6674			
168	Former Post Office, Commerce Street	NJ 9972 6681			
169	Annabell's, 78–80 High Street	NJ 9958 6715			

Appendix 3: Significant buildings identified during this Survey

Street/Area	No	Name	Built as	Date
Barrack Lane		Store		eighteenth century
Barrack Lane		John Noble, netmaker		nineteenth century
Broad Street and Mid Street	34	Clydesdale Bank	Commercial	1874
Broad Street	36–38		Commercial	1930s
Broad Street	73		Residential	1894
Broad Street		Property Showroom	Commercial	c 1835
Broad Street and Commerce Street	83	Britannic Assurance	Commercial	c 1830
Charlotte Street		Central School	School	1882
Charlotte Street		St Peter's Church	Public	1891
Charlotte Street		Thomas Walker Hospital	Public	1877
Charlotte Street		Windmill	Industrial	eighteenth century
Commerce Street		Former Post Office	Commercial	1907
Commerce Street	1–3		Residential	
Commerce Street	10		Residential	
Commerce Street and School Street		Roman Catholic church	Public	1895–96
Cross Street	30	Coffee Shop	Residential	eighteenth century
Dalrymple Street		Dalrymple Hall	Public	1881
Dalrymple Street	11	Warld's End	Residential	1767?
Frithside Street	55		Residential	eighteenth century
Frithside Street	57		Residential	c 1810 ?
Frithside Street	59		Residential	eighteenth century?
Frithside Street	66	Salvation Army	Residential	eighteenth century
Hexagon		West Church	Public	1876–77
High Street	42		Residential	late eighteenth century
High Street	78–80	Sugar & Spice	Residential	eighteenth century
High Street	89		Residential	
High Street and Barrasgate Road		Strachan's Female Industrial School	Public	1863
Kinnaird Head		Kinnaird Head Castle	Tower	1570?
Kinnaird Head		Kinnaird Head Lighthouse	Lighthouse	1787; 1830
Kinnaird Head		Wine Tower	Tower	late sixteenth century?
Kirk Green		Tenements	Residential	1885
Kirkton		Graveyard		
Kirkton		Pillbox		
Lodge Walk	1–3	Derelict house	Residential	eighteenth century
Love Lane		RAFA clubhouse	Commercial?	eighteenth century

Builder/Owner	Architect	Grid Ref	Listed	Comments
				Quoins? Part of original barracks
				Quoins, ball finial etc
	J Russell		y	High Victorian
				Rather good 1930s
Lewis Chalmers ?	Archibald Simpson ?		y	Classy. Often referred to as 'Customs House', but no evidence found
	James Matthews		y	
Episcopal Church	John Kinross	NJ 9950 6671	y	
		NJ 9939 6888	y	
				Curved corner
				Set-back villa with Doric pilastered doorway
Roman Catholic church	Ellis & Wilson, Aberdeen			
				Handsome plain house
	Jenkins & Marr		y	Baronial
Gordons of Glenbuchat			y	Flamboyant Dutch gable
				Poor roof
				Fine rear stair window
				Fine harled house
	MacGibbon & Ross			
				Fanlight
				1761 skewput
				Pedimented entrance
Alexander Fraser 8th		NJ 9986 6752	y	
	Thomas Smith; Robert Stevenson	NJ 9986 6752	y	
		NJ 9993 6751	y	
		NK 0009 6549	y	Site of medieval church
		NK 0003 6565	s	Scheduled
				Three bay, three storey, warehouse?

Street/Area	No	Name	Built as	Date
Manse Street		Congregational Church	Church	1854
Mid Street	32	Gordon's Court	Residential	nineteenth century
Mid Street		Macaulay Hall	Public	1870
Mid Street		Picture House	Commercial	1921
Saltoun Place	24–32		Residential	early nineteenth century
Saltoun Place		Coastguard Station and houses		
Saltoun Place	7	Craigielea	Residential	1818
Saltoun Place		Fountain	Public	1904
Saltoun Place		UP Church	Public	1875
Saltoun Place		War memorial	Public	1923
Saltoun Square		Mercat Cross		
Saltoun Square		Old Parish Church	Public	1803
Saltoun Square	14–16	Registrar's Office		*c* 1800
Saltoun Square		Town House	Public	1853–55
Saltoun Square		Saltoun Arms	Commercial	1801
Seaforth Street		Saltoun Estate Office	Commercial	
Seaforth Street		South Church	Public	1878–80
Seaforth Street	7		Residential	1810?
Shore Street		George & Dragon		eighteenth century ?
Shore Street		Harbour Office	Residential	1791
Shore Street		Oak Tree Buildings	Residential	
Shore Street		Shore House	Commercial	1766–67
Stinking Steps		Crown Inn	Commercial	
Victoria Street		Baptist Church		1877–80
Victoria Street and King Edward Street		Public Library	Public	1905
Victoria Street		St Peter's Rectory	Residential	
Victoria Street		St Peter's School	Public	1859

Builder/Owner	Architect	Grid Ref	Listed	Comments
				Now Bethesda Church
				Nice court and garden, 1687 datestone
			y	
			y	Manse?, offices behind
		NJ 9973 6652	y	Saracen Iron Works. Moved when War Memorial built
		NJ 9973 6635	y	
	Alexander Morrice	NJ 9982 6707	y	
	Thomas Mackenzie	NJ 9982 6711	y	
Gardener's Society	Alexander Morrice		y	Victorian upper floors and roof
Free Church	J B Pirie	NJ 9985 6667	y	
				Very pleasant classical villa
				Wallhead gable
				Warehouse with assembly rooms above
				Important building with old cottage behind
	Mr Wilson, Frithside Street			
		NJ 9953 6669	y	
Episcopal Church		NJ 9958 6670	y	

Appendix 4: Street-by-street profile of commercial use/occupation (from Trades Directories)

Street	Gentry, professionals				Banks, offices, ship owners			
	1837	1867	1886	1911	1837	1867	1886	1911
Albert Street				1				
Back Street/ High Street	2	1	5	2	1	1	1	1
Barrack Lane				1				
Barrasgate Lane/Street								
Braeheads						2		
Broad Street	2	2	6	7		17	16	4
Castle Street	1	1	1			6	2	1
Charlotte Street			3	9			5	
College Bounds							1	
Commerce Street	1	3	6	9	1	7	7	4
Cross Street	4	1	2	3		2	7	1
Dalrymple Street			2			1	4	1
Denmark Street								
Duke Street								
Frithside Street	4		4	10	3	6	3	4
Gratton Place				21				
Hanover Street								
King Edward Street				9				1
Kirk Brae								
Links								
Manse Street	1			1			1	
Mid Street	2	2	2	4		3	3	4
North Street								
Park Street								
Saltoun Place			18	24		3	2	1
Saltoun Square			2	2		3	1	4
School Street			1					
Seaforth Street			1	1		3	3	2
Shore Street	1			1	5	2	11	6
Strichen Road				14				
Victoria Street			5	19			1	1
Broadsea								
Other	8	5	9	5		1		

Retail, merchants, vintners				Trades and manufactures				Fish curers and coopers			
1837	1867	1886	1911	1837	1867	1886	1911	1837	1867	1886	1911
							2				4
5	15	39	45	6	3	5	3	3	1	3	
			1		2				1	1	2
		1								8	7
			1								
17	45	69	40	7	1	4	4	3		1	1
1	2	9	9	3	3	5	3	9	5	7	9
		6	4			2	2			3	
		8	5			7	2				1
4	6	11	5	2	1		4		2	5	1
15	14	25	19	13	5	4	2	2	1	3	1
	1	3			1	2	1			1	
										10	8
		1	2						2		3
6	3	13	11	4	1	7	4	4	4	1	1
1		2	4	1						2	1
							1				
1	1	2	5	2	1				2	1	
	1	1			2	2			4	3	
	1	3	3	1	1	4	1	1			
7	12	21	20	5	4	4	8		2	2	3
		2	2			1			2	2	3
											3
	1				1	3	1		2	1	1
	2	9	6								
		2	3	1		3	1				2
	1	4								5	
18	15	15	16	7	5	13	9	10	2	7	11
			1							1	
			2				1				2
3		1		2	2	4	2			1	1

155

Appendix 5: List of dated and/or carved stones noted in Fraserburgh

Date	Original site	Present site	Reference
c 1600? *Trust in God, for he is good.* *His mercy is for ever.* *Give him thanks for all you have.* *For He's the only giver.*	University? Later High Street, demolished 1898	In Alexandra Hotel, built 1899?	Pratt, *Buchan*; Henderson, *Aberdeenshire Inscriptions*, 251
1613 Moses Stone	Town Gate?	South Church	
1687		Gordon's Close, Mid Street	Seen (see fig 13)
Seventeenth-century dormer pediment		Beside church	Seen
Seventeenth-century dormer pediment		Beside church	Seen
Seventeenth-century, monogram and three lines of text, last line possibly *ever [will] the good pro[sper]*		Set in N wall of close, W side of Broad Street	Seen
1716 Wm Forbes & Eliz Keith	Near Saltoun Inn	Side wall behind Registry Office	Dey, *Fraserburgh Then and Now*, 11
1718 PD PR			MacGibbon & Ross, v, 82
1736 LAS	Shaft of Cross	Shaft of Cross	Murison, *Broch*, 14
1746 PG BS		Auchinroath, Rothes	MacGibbon & Ross, v, 82–3
1749			MacGibbon & Ross, v, 82–3
1754 IM MC	Frithside Street	Lost	Dey, *Fraserburgh Then and Now*, 11
1758	Manse, Manse Street	Parish church	
1761	N side High Street	N side High Street	Seen
1763	No 12 Hanover Street	Lost	Murison & Noble, *Names and Places*, 35
1787 Moses Stone	School on Links	South Church	

Glossary

bailiary	The territory under the jurisdiction of a *bailie*.
bailie	The top councillors (in a *burgh of barony* either appointed by the baron or 'elected' by the rest of the council) were provost, bailies (usually between two and four), treasurer and Dean of Guild. These 'magistrates' ran the town on a day-to-day basis, called council meetings etc.
baron bailie	The bailie nominated by the baron, and who represented him. In the case of Fraserburgh, the baron was the nominal provost, and nominated the baron bailie as his deputy and therefore the leading magistrate for most purposes.
barony	The land or lands controlled by a baron.
burgess	Member of the core of craftsmen and merchants within a burgh, who had exclusive privileges within the burgh. Membership could be inherited, acquired by marriage to a burgess's daughter, or purchased.
burgh of barony	A town founded and controlled by a baron, by means of a grant from the monarch.
burgh of regality	Similar to a burgh of barony, but with more royal powers delegated to the baron.
busses	Large-decked vessels from which open boats were sent to catch fish with drift nets, and aboard which the catches were cured (ie an early factory ship, on the Dutch model). The Scottish buss fishery lasted from 1750–*c* 1830.
cairn	Pile of stones, often covering a prehistoric burial.
caput	The chief place of a barony or lordship, usually where the lord had his main residence.
cess	Local tax, assessed on the value of property.
charter	Formal legal document, usually issued by the crown or a superior lord, detailing the properties, rights and obligations of the recipient.
cist	Prehistoric grave lined with stone slabs
clay bool	A method of construction involving usually rounded stones and rammed clay, occurring where these are the locally available vernacular material.

common good	The lands or other sources of income which were held and managed by a burgh on behalf of its inhabitants.
cran	37½ gallons of herring, measured by four baskets, each holding quarter of a cran. By the early twentieth century this had generally been converted to a cran equalling 3½ cwt, and today herring is measured in tonnes (1 tonne being roughly 5.6 crans).
demesne	The portion of the lands of a barony or lordship kept in the lord's hands for the direct support of his household (from the latin *mensa*, a table, ie the table lands).
doocot	Dovecote, usually freestanding, only usually allowed to be built by landowners.
feu	Grant of land rights. In exchange for a fixed sum and a continued fixed annual rent, a tenant bought the right to hold a property in perpetuity, and to bequeath or sell it.
feuar	An individual who holds land in *feu*.
feuferme	Arrangement whereby property could be conveyed in return for an annual payment fixed in perpetuity. It preserved the fiction of the land being held from a superior lord, but the occupant had almost complete security in the property.
guildbrethren	Members of the merchant guild.
guildry	Merchant guild, entered by family links or purchase, with exclusive rights to trade within the liberties of a burgh.
harling	The traditional coating for rubble stone walls in Scotland, whether high-status or vernacular, both as a protection from the weather and to create the impression of geometric mass. Formed from a mixture of usually local gravel bound with lime.
harling check	Where window and door surrounds, which were not harled, stand proud of the rest of the wall, to allow for the depth of harling.
infeft	Technical term for the process by which an individual is given possession of property or rights by a superior lord.
liberty (re Aberdeen)	The area within which a burgh had exclusive trading rights. As more burghs were created, they inevitable impinged on the liberties of earlier ones.

Mesolithic	Of the middle Stone Age, the earliest period of prehistoric settlement in Scotland. Mesolithic people were nomadic hunter-gatherers, using fine stone tools.
midden	Rubbish heap, whether domestic, agricultural or mixed.
patronage	The right of appointment. The right of landowners to appoint ministers of the Church of Scotland had long been contentious, and eventually led to the Disruption in 1843.
precept	Writ commanding an officer or deputy to take legal action, eg a precept of *sasine* instructed the recipient to give an individual possession of heritable property.
provost	The chief magistrate of a burgh, the equivalent of a mayor in England.
raggle	Groove cut into stone to receive a flashing, for example where a roof cuts into a masonry wall.
regality	Lands and associated rights of jurisdiction where the landlord exercised all rights and legal powers usually associated with the crown – except the right to try treason cases – and where authority of royal justiciars and sheriffs did not operate. Abolished in 1747.
sasine	The act of taking possession of a property, symbolised by the handing over of an object (eg a piece of turf from the land in question etc), and recorded in a document called a sasine.
seised	Granted a *sasine*.
superior (feu superior)	The landowner from whom *feuars* have acquired their property and to whom they pay feu duty.
tolbooth	The central administrative building of a burgh, usually combining council and court rooms, weigh house and prison.
whinstone	A name given to a variety of very hard, dark-coloured stones, including greenstone, basalt and quartzose sandstone.

Bibliography

Maps, plans and charts

NLS Map Library

Adv. MS.70.2.9 (10), Pont Map, Buchan, *c* 1590

MS.5850.59, Plan of Fraserburgh Harbour, with inset *Sketch Plan of the New South Pier ...*, Robert Stevenson, 1818

MS.5850.60, *Sketch Plan of the Harbour of Fraserburgh ...*, Robert Stevenson, 1818

Admiralty Chart 1438, *Fraserburgh, surveyed by Commander Slater*, 1834 (London, 1842)

MS.5850.67–8, Plans of Fraserburgh Harbour, James Walker, 1838

Admiralty Chart 1439, *Fraserburgh, surveyed by Commander E. J. Bedford*, 1858 (London, 1859)

Ordnance Survey, 1st edition 6 inch map, Aberdeenshire, III, Parish of Fraserburgh, surveyed 1869 (1870)

Ordnance Survey, 1st edition 25 inch map, Aberdeenshire, III.1, Parish of Fraserburgh, surveyed 1869 (1870)

Ordnance Survey, 2nd edition 25 inch map, Aberdeenshire, revised 1901 (1902)

NAS

RHP 14593, Chart, Aberdeenshire coast (Ainslie?) 1784–85

RHP 45434, Fraserburgh Harbour Plan, Robert Stevenson, 1818

RHP 45436, Fraserburgh Harbour Plan, James Walker, 1838

RHP 45441, Fraserburgh Harbour Plan, James Walker, 1856–57

RHP 454555, Harbour Plan, post-railway

RCAHMS

33205 (DC8803), plan produced for the Northern Lighthouse Board, signed AGH, undated but on internal evidence cannot be earlier than *c* 1809

British Library

Maps C.9.b, William Roy, Military Survey of Scotland, 1747–55, 1:36,000, sheet 31/1a

Primary

Anderson, A O, *Early Sources of Scottish History AD 500–1286* (Edinburgh, 1922)

Anderson, P J (ed), *Fasti Academiae Mariscallanae Aberdonensis* (Spalding Club, 1889)

Anon, *The Burgh of Fraserburgh* (Fraserburgh, 1880?)

Anon, *Gazetteer of Scotland* (Dundee, 1803)

Ayton, R and Daniell, W, *A Voyage Round Great Britain* ... 2 vols, facsimile edn (London, 1978)

Burton, J H (ed), *The Darien Papers* (Bannatyne Club 1849)

Burton, J H *et al* (eds), *Register of the Privy Council of Scotland*, 38 vols (Edinburgh, 1877–1970)

Chambers, R and chambers, W, *Gazetteer of Scotland* (Edinburgh, 1832)

Crawford, G, *Lives and Characters of the Officers of the Crown and of the State* ... (Edinburgh, 1726)

Defoe, D, *A Tour through the whole island of Great Britain*, 8th edn, with additions by various authors, 4 vols (London, 1778)

Defoe, D, *A Tour through the whole island of Great Britain*, G D H Cole and D C Browning (eds), 2 vols (London, 1962)

Dunlop, A I (ed), 'Bagimond's Roll: statement of the tenths of the kingdom of Scotland' in *SHS Miscellany*, VI (1939)

Extracts from the Council Register of the Burgh of Aberdeen, i, 1398–1570 (Aberdeen, 1844)

Extracts from the Council Register of the Burgh of Aberdeen, ii, 1570–1625 (Aberdeen, 1848)

Farmer, D, *Oxford Dictionary of Saints*, new edition (Oxford, 1997)

Ferguson, J P S, *Directory of Scottish Newspapers* (National Library of Scotland, Edinburgh, 1984)

Forsyth, R, *The Beauties of Scotland* ..., 5 vols (Edinburgh, 1805–08)

Fraser, A, *The Frasers of Philorth,* 3 vols (Edinburgh, 1879)

Fraser, Sir D, *The Christian Watt Papers* (Collieston, 1983)

Groome, F H, *Ordnance Gazetteer of Scotland*, 6 vols (London, 1894)

Hepburn, A, 'Description of Buchan, Aberdeenshire, 8 May 1721', in Sir A Mitchell (ed), *Geographical Collections Relating to Scotland made by Walter Macfarlane*, I (SHS, 1906)

Heron, R, *Scotland Described* ... (Edinburgh, 1797)

Heron, R, *Scotland Delineated* ..., facsimile of 2nd edn, Edinburgh and London, 1799 (Edinburgh, 1975)

Illustrations of the Topography and Antiquities of the Shires of Aberdeen and Banff, 4 vols (Spalding Club, 1847–69)

Johnston, R C (ed), *Jordan Fantosme's Chronicle* (Oxford, 1981)

Kyd, J G (ed), *Scottish Population Statistics* (Edinburgh, 1975)

Lawrie, A C, *Early Scottish Charters prior to AD 1153* (Glasgow, 1905)

Lippe, R (ed), *Selections from Wodrow's Biographical Collections* (Spalding Club, 1890)

A List of Persons Concerned in the Rebellion 1745–46 (SHS, 1890)

Livingstone, A, Aikman, C W H and Hart, B S (eds), *No Quarter Given. The Muster Roll of Prince Charles Edward Stuart's Army, 1745–46* (Glasgow, 2001)

Mackay, W (ed), *The Letter-Book of Bailie John Steuart of Inverness 1715–1752* (SHS, 1915)

Miller, A H (ed), *A Selection of Scottish Forfeited Estate Papers 1715; 1745* (SHS, 1909)

Mitchell, Sir A (ed), *Geographical Collections Relating to Scotland made by Walter Macfarlane*, 3 vols (SHS, 1906–08)

Newte, T, *A Tour in England and Scotland* (London, 1791)

Parliamentary Gazetteer of Scotland, 2 vols (Edinburgh, 1848–51)

Paul, Sir J B, *The Scots Peerage*, 9 vols (Edinburgh, 1904–14)

Pigot and Co's New Commercial Directory of Scotland for 1825–26 (London and Manchester)

Pigot and Co's New Commercial Directory of Scotland for 1837 (London and Manchester)

Sasine Abridgements, Aberdeenshire, 1781–1820

Sasine Abridgments, Aberdeenshire, 1821–30

Sasine Abridgments, Aberdeenshire, 1831–40

Seton, B G and Arnot, J G (eds), *The Prisoners of the '45*, 3 vols (SHS, 1928–29)

Slater's (late Pigot & Co) Royal National Commercial Directory ... of Scotland (Manchester and London, 1852)

Slater's (late Pigot & Co) Royal National Commercial Directory ... of Scotland (Manchester and London, 1860)

Slater's Royal National Commercial Directory of Scotland ... (Manchester and London, 1867, 1873, 1878, 1882, 1886, 1889, 1893, 1900, 1903, 1907, 1911, 1915)

The Statistical Account of Scotland 1791–99, vol XV, North and East Aberdeenshire, D J Withrington and I Grant (eds) (Wakefield, 1982)

The Statistical Account of Scotland, XII, Aberdeenshire (Edinburgh, 1845), 'Parish of Fraserburgh', Revd J Cumming (1840)

Taylor, J, *The Great Historic Families of Scotland*, 2 vols (London, 1887)

Third Statistical Account of Scotland, County of Aberdeen, 'The Burgh and Parish of Fraserburgh', J Noble, Town Chamberlain (1952), 324–35

Thomson, T and Innes, C (eds), *Acts of the Parliaments of Scotland* (Edinburgh, 1814–75)

Thomson, J M *et al* (eds), *Registrum Magni Sigilli Regum Scotorum*, 38 vols (Edinburgh, 1877–1970)

Topographical, Statistical and Historical Gazetteer of Scotland, 2 vols (Glasgow, 1842)

'Report by Thomas Tucker upon the Settlement of the Revenues of Excise and Customs in Scotland. AD MDCLVI', in *Miscellany of the Scottish Burgh Records Society* (Edinburgh, 1881), 1–48

Wade, Revd W M, *Watering and Sea-Bathing Places of Scotland ...* (Paisley, 1822)

Wilson, Revd J M (ed), *The Imperial Gazetteer of Scotland, Topographical, Statistical and Historical*, 2 vols (London, [c 1870])

Withrington, D J and Grant, I (eds), *The Statistical Account of Scotland 1791–99, vol XV, North and East Aberdeenshire* (Wakefield, 1982), Revd Mr A Simpson, 'Parish of Fraserburgh' (1791)

Worrall's Directory of Aberdeenshire, 1877 (Oldham, 1877)

Secondary

Aitchison, P, *Children of the Sea: the story of the Eyemouth disaster* (East Linton, 2001)

Alexander, W M, *The Place Names of Aberdeenshire* (Spalding Club, 1952)

Anderson, James, *General View of the Agriculture and Rural Economy of the County of Aberdeenshire ...* (Edinburgh, 1794)

Anon, *Famous Brochers* (Fraserburgh, 1992)

Anon, *Fraserburgh 400, 1592–1992* (Fraserburgh, 1990)

Bannerman, J, 'The Scottish takeover of Pictland and the relics of Columba', *Innes Review*, xlviii (1997), 27–44

Begg, T, Housing Policy in Scotland (Edinburgh, 1996)

Bjørn, C, Grant, A and Stringer, K J (eds), *Nations, Nationalism and Patriotism in the European Past* (Copenhagen, 1993)

Broun, D, 'The Origin of Scottish Identity', in Bjørn, Grant and Stringer (eds), 1993

Chapman, J C and Mytum, H C (eds), *Settlement in North Britain 1000 BC–1000 AD*, BAR British Series **118** (1983), 327–37

Checkland, S G, *Scottish Banking: a history, 1695–1973* (Glasgow and London, 1975)

Clark, G W, The Housing of the Working Classes of Scotland (Glasgow, 1930)

Cranna, J, *Fraserburgh: Past and Present* (Aberdeen, 1914)

Cunningham, I C (ed), *The Nation Survey'd* (East Linton, 2001)

Diack, L, *The People of Fraserburgh and Pitsligo, 1696* (Aberdeen, 1992)

Devine, T M, *The Scottish Nation 1700–2000* (London, 1999)

Dey, G E, *Fraserburgh, Now and Then* (Fraserburgh, 1987)

Dey, G E, *Old Fraserburgh* (Fraserburgh, 1987)

Dey, G E, *Fraserburgh at 'War' and the 'Coronation'* (Aberdeen, nd)

Dow, F D, *Cromwellian Scotland* (Edinburgh, 1979)

Easson, D E and Cowan, I B, *Medieval Religious Houses: Scotland* (London, 1976)

Fawcett, R, *Scottish Abbeys and Priories* (London, 1994)

Graham, E J, *A Maritime History of Scotland 1650–1790* (East Linton, 2002)

Grant, A and Stringer, K J (eds), *Medieval Scotland: Crown, Lordship and Community* (Edinburgh, 1993)

Gray, M, *The Fishing Industries of Scotland, 1790–1914: a study in regional adaptation* (Oxford, 1978)

Hamilton, H, 'Industries and Commerce', in *The North-East of Scotland* (British Association for the Advancement of Science, Aberdeen, 1963)

Henderson, J A, *Aberdeenshire Epitaphs and Inscriptions* ... (Aberdeen, 1907)

Jackson, G, *The British Whaling Trade* (London, 1978)

Jones, B & Mattingly, D, *An Atlas of Roman Britain* (Oxford, 1990)

Keith, A, *The North of Scotland Bank Limited 1836–1936* (Aberdeen, 1936)

Leatham, J, *Faithlie-by-the-Sea: an account of the rising town of Fraserburgh* (Fraserburgh, 1904)

Lenman, B, *The Jacobite Risings in Britain, 1689–1746* (Aberdeen, 1980)

Logue, K J, *Popular Disturbances in Scotland 1780–1815* (Edinburgh, 1979)

Lynch, M, *Scotland: a New History* (London, 1991)

Macdonald, B, *Boats and Builders: the history of boatbuilding around Fraserburgh* (Fraserburgh, [1993])

Macdonald, B, *Fraserburgh Harbour – The Boom Years* (Fraserburgh, [1995])

MacGibbon, D and Ross, T, *The Castellated and Domestic Architecture of Scotland*, 5 vols (Edinburgh, 1887–92)

McKean, C, *Banff and Buchan: an illustrated architectural guide* (RIAS, Edinburgh, 1990)

BIBLIOGRAPHY

McKean, C, *The Scottish Chateau* (Stroud, 2001)

McNeill, P G B and MacQueen, H L (eds), *Atlas of Scottish History to 1707* (Edinburgh, 1996)

Malcolm, C A, *The Bank of Scotland 1695–1945* (Edinburgh, 1945)

Malley, I, *The University of Fraserburgh* (Shepshed, Leicestershire, 1988)

Martin, C, 'Water Transport and the Roman Occupations of North Britain', in Smout (ed), 1992, 1–36

Mellor, R E H (ed), *The Railways of Scotland: Papers of Andrew C O'Dell* (Aberdeen, 1985)

Melville, M W, *Historical Walks around Fraserburgh* (Peterhead, nd)

Moore, K L, 'The Northeast of Scotland's Coastal Trading Links Towards the End of the Nineteenth Century', *Scottish Economic and Social History* 21, 2 (2001)

Morris, J, *An Illustrated Guide to our Lifeboat Stations, Part 7, Scotland* (Coventry, 1992)

Munn, C W, *The Scottish Provincial Banking Companies 1747–1864* (Edinburgh, 1981)

Munro, R W, *Scottish Lighthouses* (Stornoway, 1979)

Murison, D, *The Broch as it was* ([Scotland], 1990)

Murison, D and Noble, L, *Names and Places: a history of place and street names in and around Fraserburgh* (Fraserburgh, *c* 1995)

The North-East of Scotland (British Association for the Advancement of Science, Aberdeen, 1963)

Oram, R D, 'Parliament to 1603', in Glendinning, M (ed), *The Architecture of Scottish Government,* Royal Commission on the Archaeological and Historical Monuments of Scotland, (Dundee, 2004)

Pratt, J B, *Buchan* (Aberdeen, 1858)

Ralston, I, 'The Green Castle and the Promontory Forts of North-East Scotland' in *Settlement in Scotland 1000 BC–AD 1000, Scottish Archaeological Forum,* **10** (1980), 27–40

Rennie, D S, *A Walk down Broad Street* (Fraserburgh, 1997)

Rennie, D S, *A Walk down Cross Street and High Street* (Fraserburgh, 2000)

Rivet, A L F and Smith, C, *The Place Names of Roman Britain* (Cambridge, 1979)

Robertson, A S, 'Roman Coins Found in Scotland, 1971–1982, *Proceedings of the Society of Antiquaries of Scotland* **113** (1984), 405–48

Royal Commission on the Ancient and Historical Monuments of Scotland, *Pictish Symbol Stones: a handlist 1994* (Edinburgh, 1994)

Royal Commission on the Archaeological and Historical Monuments of Scotland, *Tolbooths and Townhouses, civic architecture in Scotland to 1833* (Edinburgh, 1996)

Shepherd, I A, 'Pictish Settlement Problems in N E Scotland', in Chapman and Mytum (eds), 1983

Simpson, I J, *Education in Aberdeenshire before 1872* (London, 1947)

Smith, A, *A New History of Aberdeenshire* (Aberdeen, 1875)

Smout, T C, *Scottish Trade on the Eve of Union 1660–1707* (Edinburgh and London, 1963)

Smout, T C, *A Century of the Scottish People 1830–1950* (London, 1986)

Smout, T C (ed), *Scotland and Europe: 1200–1850* (Edinburgh, 1986)

Smout, T C (ed), *Scotland and the Sea* (Edinburgh, 1992)

Smout, T C and Wood, S, *Scottish Voices 1745–1960* (London, 1991)

Spalding, J, *History of the Troubles and Memorable Transactions in Scotland and England ...*, 2 *vols* (Bannatyne Club, 1828)

Stanislawski, D, 'Early Spanish Town Planning in the New World', *Geographical Review* **37.1** (1947)

Stone, J, *The Pont Manuscript Maps of Scotland* (Tring, 1978)

Summers, D, *Fishing off the Knuckle: the fishing villages of Buchan* (Aberdeen, 1988)

Thomas, J and Turnock, D, *The North of Scotland: a Regional History of the Railways of Great Britain,* Volume XV (Nairn, 1989)

Tocher, J F, *The Book of Buchan: a scientific treatise ...* (Buchan Field Club, Peterhead, 1910)

Walker, A, *The Fleet: a guide to the historic vessels at the Scottish Fisheries Museum* (Anstruther, 2002)

Warren, G, Towards a social archaeology of the mesolithic in eastern Scotland: landscapes, contexts and experience (unpublished PhD thesis, University of Edinburgh 2001)

Wood, J L, *Building Railways* (Natonal Museums of Scotland, Edinburgh, 1996)

Wood, S, *The Shaping of 19th Century Aberdeenshire* (Stevenage, 1985)

Wormald, J, *Lords and Men in Scotland: bonds of manrent 1442–1603* (Edinburgh, 1985)

Young, A, 'The earls and earldom of Buchan in the Thirteenth Century', in Grant and Stringer (eds), 1993

Young, A, *Robert the Bruce's Rivals: The Comyns, 1212–1314* (East Linton, 1997)

Index

Numbers in **bold** refer to figures

burgh school 58
grammar school (17th century) 35, 58
parish school 63
Victorian era 84–5
see also names of specific schools
Scott and Yule, boatbuilders 88, 91
Sea Insurance Company of Scotland 63
Seaforth Street 59, 64, 69, 86
South Church 36, 58, 84, **84**
Station Hotel 14, 70
Seven Years War 47
sewage system 77
Sharpe, Margaret, wife of 11th Lord Saltoun 42
shell middens 123, 124
shipbuilding 52–3, 73, 81, 88
shipping 11, 36, 43, 66
18th-century conflicts 47
port of registry 81
see also trade, seaborne
The Shore 54–5, 66, 129, 141
Shore House 54, **54**
Shore Street 54, 66, 69, 79, 125, 128–9, **128**
Sibbald, Sir Robert 14
Simpson, John 24
slum housing 78–9, 80
smoke house **88**
social life, 18th century 56–7
Solomon Lodge 56–7
South Church 36, 58, 84, **84**
sports facilities 87
Station Harbour 82, 83
Station (previously Railway) Hotel 14, 70
steam drifters 82, 91
Stevenson, Robert, engineer 52
Stewart, James, earl of Buchan 23
Stewart, James, earl of Moray, regent 25, 26
Stewart, John, merchant 49
Stewart, William, engineer 52
Stinking Stairs 54, 129
stonework 14
carved 14, 139
Strachan Female Industrial School 69, 85
street names 16, 59
Strichen 53, 58
Strichen Road 65, 86, 87, 93, 137
Stuart, James Francis (Old Pretender) 43–4
suburbs 5, 6, 14, 67, 71, 80, 85, 86, 93–4, 136, 137, 138

tank traps 96
Technical School 85
Temperance (Grand) Hotel 80
tenements 65, 85, 129, 133, 140
Thomas Walker Hospital 87
Thompson Terrace 98
Tibertie 38
tide-mill 72
tile making 14
timber trade 42–3, 81
timber yards 72
tolbooth 30, 69
tollhouses 65
tourism 55–6, 80, 98, 99
Town Council 76, 98
Town-house 15

old 56, 61
Saltoun Square 68–9, **68**, 79, 87, 140
town-houses 36–7
trade
17th century 36, 42–3
agricultural products 43, 49, 56, 66, 72, 73, 81
effect of World War I 90
import/export 73, 81
seaborne 36, 42–3, 48–51, 66, 73
coastal 49, 73
import/export 66
tradesmen, 17th century 36
transport
rail 11, 67–8, 70, 72, 73, 75, 80, 97, 98
road 11, 56, 63, 65, 98, 138
seaborne 11, 36, 43, 48–51, 66, 73
18th-century conflicts 47
Tyrie, church 32, 33

unemployment 89, 91
Union Bank of Scotland 70, 96
Union Grove 94
Union of Parliaments 42
United Free Church 84
United Presbyterian church, Saltoun Place 84
United Reformed Church 141
university 6, 32–4, 35, 132
Utlaw 38

Victoria Street 64, 69, **70**, 84, 85, 86
Victorian period, early (*c* 1840–70) 67–75
Viewfield Road 94
Vikings 21

Walker and Duncan 94
Walker Crescent 94
War Memorial 92
warehouses 54, 65, 129, 131, 139
Warld's End 46, **46**, 55, 59, 70, 135
water supply 57–8, 67–8, 72, 77, 78
Watergait *see* Frithside Street
Watermill 72, **72**, 140
Watermill Road 94
weaving 53
Webster, John, shipbuilder 81
Webster's shipyard 73
wells
holy 21
mineral 55
West Church 84
West Parish Church 84
West Road 98, 137
whaling 73–4
whinstone 14, 15
William of Orange 41
Wilson Noble, boatbuilder 9
windmill 12, **13**, 72
Windmill Street *see* Albert Street
Wine Tower **26**, 27, **28**, 29, 30, 48, 134
World War I 89–91, 92
World War II 92–3, 95–6

Ythan Wells 19